WALK, DON'T RUN
One Woman's Battle with Quadriplegia

A Memoir of Hope and Healing

by

Pamela Henline

Trillian,
Thank you for being a
caring sensitive teacher and
for becoming even more or a
person I consider a friend and
fellow spirit in life -

Pam

Published in 2012

The author my be reached at phenline@comcast.net

Introduction and Thanks

I HAVE TRIED to keep some of the clutter of my life from distracting the reader away from the real story of trying to recover from a terrible accident. However, I also am a stickler about book titles and understanding their significance.

I haven't written much about the many hours I spent running and enjoying my body in motion. As I tomboy I was best at Dodge ball and Tag-You're It because of my speed and agility. In my 30's I started 'jogging.' I was never a really competitive runner but spent many satisfying hours on trails and streets. As part of a corporate team I ran on wooden tracks in the San Diego Sports Arena and Los Angeles Forum. I ran distances from 200 meters to 50 kilometers (about 31 miles).

One summer after sophomore year of college, I served as a life guard at a local outdoor pool, which was teeming with small children. Although I never needed to rescue anyone there, my mantra to young and old was 'walk, don't run' because of the wet slippery deck surface.

I still have day dreams and night dreams about running. But I appreciate that I now can walk and do so many things that are difficult to do from a wheelchair and with limited upper body use. So I know that "Walk, don't run" is OK, and I still hope that one day I might use the word RUN for myself.

I hope that my story can help and inspire others who read these pages.

SO MANY PEOPLE helped me get through the immediate time after the accident, and a bit later. I have listed just a few of the people who were so important to my mental state and physical recovery. I am truly sorry that everyone cannot be mentioned here. Most names have been changed in the book.

Physicians -Dr. Joe, Dr. Wickersham, Dr. Lopez, Dr. Sullivan, Dr. Gerhart.

Physical Therapists and Occupational Therapists - Loretta, Marilyn, Annie and Vivian

Caregiver - Wendy Seltzer

Caregiver, friend and almost-daughter - Scheri Wilson Chavez

Caregiver and friend - Audrey Brown.

Friends - Joe and Alice Montgomery, Judie Richardson and her whole family, Anne and Erich Hoffman, John Lohr, Amy Schmitt, Bernie Gish, Elizabeth Jones, Martin Brickson, Alan Lewis, Debbie Norum, Fred and Carolyn McClain and many more unnamed

Relatives - Linda Shaffer, Bonnie Peregoy, Joey Peregoy.

Horse people - Ilona Radelow, Jennifer Javors, Rachel Amado, Terry Berg, Lori Peterson, friend and horse trainer Karen Nord.

Lawyers - Brian Burchett, Craig McClellan, LaMar Brown.

Several people have helped me with writing and publishing - Joan Torres, Shelly Moore, Belinda Perry

Husband and often-time savior Daniel Drobnis

Chapter One

The Accident and Rehabilitation Begins

I WAS LYING on my side across the center console of my car with my right shoulder on the passenger seat, my seat belt still around me and the front bumper of my 1987 Honda Accord resting against a cement barrier. My car was blocking the fast lane of the San Diego Freeway not far from my home. The blare of automobile horns had stopped. I no longer heard squealing tires. After ten seconds of careening back and forth across four busy freeway lanes my car was immobile and a veil of silence descended around me.

I was stunned, not moving or thinking. Then my mind started to race. 'That wasn't too bad. Nobody hit me during all the sliding around and the bump as I stopped wasn't hard. I must be safe now. Maybe I can sit up and see how much damage was done.'

But when I tried to grasp the steering wheel and pull myself into a sitting position, my arms wouldn't move. None of me would move. That was when I became conscious of a red-hot pain in my neck. Then I smelled an odor of something burning. Suddenly I was very afraid. I couldn't move. And my car could start to burn, with me in it! I wanted to get up and get out of the car but I was helpless. My mind kept whirling around but my body stayed frozen in place. I had a frightful premonition: I could have a spinal cord injury. Even if I got out of the car alive, my life could be changed forever.

It was Monday July 8, 1996. I had left my house about 8:30 a.m. to ride my horse. Ameego had nickered as usual when he'd seen my car. He always anticipated the carrots and other goodies I brought for him. He made his typical funny faces when I brushed and curried him. Then I tacked him up to ride. Jordan, my golden retriever, stayed nearby. He didn't go often with me to the stable, but today he would be with me, enjoying the exercise and the pungent smells of horses, sheep and open fields. Ameego was obedient and light in my hands. By the end of my ride, he was moving forward freely, and performed some half steps for me, lowering his haunches and keeping up a steady beat with his hooves. My horse seemed happy with his exercise and I felt like the morning's workout had been productive, accomplishing some dressage maneuvers I had been working towards for several months.

I took my time cooling Ameego down and taking him back to his corral. Then I cleaned him off, gave him his barley-corn treat, carefully put my gear away and got ready to leave. Jordan was tired and jumped into the back seat of the car and quickly went to sleep.

I turned south off of Carmel Valley Road to merge onto Interstate 5 southbound just outside of San Diego. I was heading for PetsMart. It was 11:20 in the morning, the weather was clear and traffic was moderate. Normally I merged onto Interstate 5 and continued south in the right-most lane but I needed to move over to the left lane in order to get onto Interstate 805. The highway was undergoing major construction. All the driving lanes had been narrowed. There was no shoulder on either side of the road. Instead cement K-rail barriers lined the right and left lanes.

I thought about switching one lane to the left, but was blocked by traffic next to me. I had almost reached the 55-mph speed limit when I slowed a little to glance back at traffic behind me. As my eyes shifted back to the roadway ahead of me, I saw a large truck swinging into my lane. I didn't see any details but the size of the truck frightened me. I realized it was going to hit my left front fender. My adrenaline started to rush. There was too much traffic to swerve. I didn't have time to check or move into the adjacent lanes. Contact and a crash seemed milliseconds from occurring. My only option was to slam on my brakes.

My car skidded left. All my senses were in high gear now. I released the brake and tried to steer and regain control. I turned the steering wheel to the right. The car started moving right but was still out of control. I was seeing everything in exquisite detail, like a slow motion movie. I almost had the car straight when I hit the cement barrier on the right side of the road. The car bounced off the cement and headed left across four lanes of freeway traffic. It seemed forever since I had first applied the brakes. Although my senses were very sharp, and I was thinking quickly, I didn't feel any impact. I heard horns from other cars and the screech of tires. I realized other vehicles might strike me but then my car came to rest against the left lane K-rail. It felt like only a moderate thump.

Many people saw the accident. Some stopped to help. Later, one person reported seeing me dangling lifelessly over the steering wheel. Several witnesses said my car crossed the freeway a total of four times – right, left, right, left - bouncing off the K-rails each time. The car must have looked like the steel ball in a pinball machine. I have no memory of it. Nor do I remember being knocked from sitting to lying across the console and passenger seat.

After a few moments - maybe seconds or minutes, since my sense of timing had no relationship to reality - I heard a female voice ask, "Are you all right?"

My mind was going at breakneck speed, as I lay on the seat, smelling an acrid odor.

"I can't move," I said. "Can you get me out of here? I smell something burning. You'll have to reach around me and undo the seat belt." I could talk and my mind was clear. I knew I probably shouldn't be moved, but all I could focus on was escaping the burning smell.

I don't know how I was moved. I don't remember the face of the lady who placed me on the road. I ended up lying on my back, looking straight up. People's faces and body parts moved into my view and out again. All I could do was move my eyes. Yet

I felt very in control of my emotions. I was aware of the events that were occurring around me. I didn't feel lightheaded. I didn't feel any pain, except for the intense burning sensation in my neck. I whispered, "If you go in my purse, my driver's license and medical card are in the center section of my wallet."

The woman went to get my purse, and exclaimed "There's a dog in the car!"

I had forgotten about poor Jordan. "His leash is on the front passenger seat. Put that on him to get him out," I said.

An unknown man called the police from his car. Eventually I saw a policeman step across the K-rail from the other side of the road. I mumbled to him, "It wasn't my fault. A truck was going to hit me."

He spotted Jordan and said, "I'll call animal control."

The lady who had gotten me out of the car, a total stranger, quickly said "Don't worry, we'll take care of your dog and get him home." I felt great relief knowing Jordan would be safe and in caring hands, not relegated to a place where he could possibly be euthanized.

There seemed to be several people around me by this time.

"Look, this liquid is going to run down and get her wet," someone said.

"There's a blanket in the back seat of the car. You can use that," I replied.

The burning smell was the coolant running across the hot engine and moving towards me.

Suddenly I started thinking about my other animals at home - two dogs and two cats. I lived alone. What would happen to them? Who would take care of them? I told the lady the names of two co-workers. I even told her their work telephone numbers. They'd take care of Shadow and Whisper (the dogs), and Smokey and Tasha (the cats).

After what seemed like a long time, an ambulance came. A huge collar was fitted around my neck and I was lifted onto a gurney and put in the ambulance. I don't remember most of what the paramedics did but I noticed they didn't put in an intravenous line. 'That must mean I'm not too badly injured,' I thought. 'Maybe I'll be OK when I get to the hospital.' When they asked me which hospital I wanted to go to I was surprised. I figured that sort of decision was made automatically. Suppose I had been unconscious?

I said quickly "Scripps, there on Genessee Avenue." It was the closest hospital and I knew it had a Class One trauma center. I had seen rescue helicopters land there when I was at work and doing some of my lunchtime runs.

Once at the hospital, things happened around me. All I could see was the ceiling. There were questions about insurance. My card was with me somewhere.

A nurse asked, "Who should we call?"

I gave the nurse my friend Jim's name and work address. He and his family lived only a half-mile from my house and we'd all become good friends. I had met Jim Newman sixteen years earlier at a computer conference in Ft. Lauderdale and we had stayed in touch ever since. For a while I only saw him at the annual meetings but his current posting was in the San Diego area. I think I was hoping that all my problems would evaporate as soon as Jim arrived.

Then I was left alone and I became very afraid, lying on a gurney in a curtained section of the emergency room. I couldn't see anything going on around me. It felt like it took hours for anyone to come look at me. As I lay there I was having more and more trouble breathing. My diaphragm didn't seem to move and my chest barely rose up and down as I tried to breathe. Each breath became harder to draw.

I heard a doctor and woman patient behind the curtained room on my right. They were talking in very slow calm voices about symptoms that seemed insignificant and minor to me. Had she had any other dizzy spells? Did they trouble her or interfere with day to day activities? Were there any fever or cold symptoms?

In a weak voice, I moaned "Can't anyone help me? I'm having trouble breathing."

Finally, a doctor came. I told him about the burning pain in my neck and not being able to move. He examined me to see what I could move or feel and where I had pain. I had no contact with my body from my chest down. When he moved a toe or foot, I couldn't sense anything. I was sent to x-ray.

When I returned to the ER, I was asked if I was allergic to any medications.

"No," I said.

An IV line was started. Two people stood by looking for signs of allergic reactions.

"Here are a couple of hives on her stomach," one of them commented, "but everything looks good."

All I knew was that I couldn't move. Later I found out I was being given a fairly new treatment for spinal cord injury, administered intravenously. It was only an hour and a half after the accident when the steroid, methylprednisolone, was started on me.[*] The steroid infusion was continued for a full day.

My whole existence seemed to be reduced to a tiny sphere around me. I was slid into an MRI machine sometime later. The machine didn't seem to be as small and confining as I had heard it would be. Lying on my back, all I saw was a stainless steel doomed roof.

Two neurologists looked me over and studied my test results. They said I had sustained a spinal cord displacement that showed up clearly on the x-ray. One of the doctors pressed my skin with a dull pin to determine sensitivity to pain. Only my upper arms, shoulders and neck felt the pin. I had no sensation of

---

[*] Administered shortly after an injury, large amounts of methylprednisolone can help prevent secondary damage in the spinal cord caused by the body's response to traumatic injury.

even communicating with my legs and I was unable to move my arms.

As if nothing was wrong, I found myself talking with a nurse who sat with me. I told her I worked nearby, at General Atomics (GA). She was impressed by the fusion experiment I'd been working on and that it was my job to keep the computers running.

"You've had an amazing career," she said as if we were chatting at a cocktail party.

But the truth of the situation kept intruding: I had a spinal cord injury of the C5 and C6 cervical vertebrae - my job was all over. My life was all over. How would I ever find a way to live like this? What would make me want to go forward now?

Finally my friend Jim arrived. I was so glad to see him. Now I was not alone. I was moved to the ICU and he stayed with me the rest of that long, hellish day. He held my hand and placed his hand on my upper arm where I could feel his presence. He talked to me and stood nearby so I could see him. He made me feel like a living person again, not just a body in a hospital bed.

Traction was tried. Gardner-Wells tongs were attached to my head. I felt points dig into my forehead and the side of my face, then some pulling sensations. More weight was added and more pulling. But nothing magically snapped back into place.

An operation would be necessary and since I was in such good physical condition, with no other injuries besides some bruising, the operation was scheduled for the next day.

Bone would be taken from my hip and used to fuse the C5/C6 vertebrae together. A metal loop would be placed over both vertebrae and some wire strung to keep everything stable, using a Codman Ti-Frame and Codman titanium soft wire cable.

Dr. Williams, a neurologist, would do the surgery. She was a tiny woman, so small she had to stand on a stool in the operating room. I was terribly afraid and wanted her to fix me, yet like the scientist I had always been, I told her I would like to check her credentials before agreeing to the surgery. She said fine. She would come back in the morning. Then she told me it would take many months for me to heal. She said I probably would remain paralyzed, perhaps regaining only a fraction of my former abilities.

Death felt like it was very near. I didn't want to live in my current numb, paralyzed state. It felt like my body belonged to a stranger. I wondered why I hadn't died in the car, rather than being left with a functioning brain with no body. I wasn't sure how well I would do in an operation. I knew that spinal cord surgery was dangerous.

Jim and I talked about such things as paying the bills. I told him about Jordan and gave him names and telephone numbers of people who might help. I gave him the name of a friend who could keep an eye on Ameego. I gave him my boss's name and number and the number of my half-sister, Lana Perry, who lived in Baltimore. I told him where to find my hand written will. We agreed he'd return in the morning with a notary public so I could legally give Jim power of attorney for me.

Bizarrely, that entire day I felt in control of my mind. It was easy, deciding what to do, since I didn't feel like I was personally involved and there really was not much choice. Every fact and every bit of information stored in my brain seemed instantly accessible. I remembered names and phone numbers, where each medicine for the dogs was stored, the color of the box with the extra checks in it. Every thought came to me with amazing speed. It was as if my mind was moving at breakneck speed, reviewing every aspect of my life.

That night, I lay immobile, my mind in a drug induced trance. I remember nothing from that evening to the next morning. I wasn't feeling the pain in my neck. I had no feelings in my body. I wasn't afraid. I simply didn't feel like I was alive.

The next morning when Jim arrived I said, "Let me die rather than exist as a vegetable." I saw no real reason to struggle. In the durable power of attorney for healthcare, I had Jim mark down that I didn't want any life-sustaining or mechanical equipment to be used if I was going to die shortly.

Oddly I was obsessed with the fate of my three dogs more than my own condition. Jim told me that house sitters had been arranged and that Jordan was safe.

Sedated, I was wheeled to the operating room just after noon. Anesthesia was started at 1:15 p.m. Access to my vertebra was through the muscles at the back of my neck. The operation started just before 3 p.m. and was finished at 6 p.m. There were no complications or unexpected problems. It had been impossible to assess exactly how much damage had been done to my spinal cord, but the cervical vertebrae were put back into alignment. Only time would determine how paralyzed I would be.

I SPENT SEVEN days at Scripps hospital in the intensive care unit and it all passed in a druggy haze. I remember very few things distinctly. People from my office came to visit but I don't remember talking with them.

I do remember Jim. He was at my bedside everyday. I can't remember any of our conversations, only the calming feeling that came from his presence. I felt secure, knowing he was in charge of my life.

My hair kept getting tangled in the thick soft collar around my neck. A nurse managed to cut it with me lying down and not moving. I was much more comfortable when it was removed.

I was lying very still and my ability to breathe was reduced, putting me at risk of getting pneumonia. A pulmonary doctor with a soft kind voice asked me to breathe and blow into something. I couldn't do much, but I tried. The diligent care in the ICU spared me from this complication.

A physical therapist came often, to move my arms and legs. He was young and handsome and I enjoyed looking at him.

He kept reminding me how important it was to move my limbs through their range of motion so that the joints would stay free and the muscles and tendons flexible. I had little thought of using my arms, legs and hands but I was happy for the physical activity and the company.

The records indicate that the physical therapist moved me from my bed to a blue chair four times. The back of the chair could slowly advance me from a lying to a partially raised position. It must have taken a great deal of preparation to get me ready and I must have been apprehensive about the pain that accompanied any movement. Yet, to this day I have no recollection of the 'blue chair.'

A social worker came to see me several times. She made notes in my chart but I don't remember her either. 'Patient appears to be in good spirits yet still verbalizes fear and anxiety.' Was I being criticized by this faceless figure because I had not adjusted to a life of paralysis in three days?

The man who had been my primary physician for five years talked with me once on the phone. He was very distant, as if he was afraid of what had happened to me. That conversation made me feel even worse. I knew my old life was over. I was wrapped inside a body I could not move and I didn't know what would become of me.

Dr. Williams, my neurosurgeon, made sure I was released to the Sharp Rehabilitation Hospital, located in central San Diego. Sharp's rehabilitation center treated spinal cord injury, stroke, and brain injury patients. Dr. Williams knew it was the best place in the area for me.

I was transferred from the Scripps ICU to Sharp Rehab about 11 a.m. on July 16, eight days after the accident. I was terribly afraid to leave Scripps. Any change in my environment was frightening to me. I had no idea what to expect in a new place. I was afraid to ride in the ambulance alone. To help relieve my sense of panic, Scripps let my friends, Nancy and June, ride with me in the ambulance. I knew Jim was following in his car as well.

I was settled into a room at Sharp off the nurses' station. There was one window and two beds. I was given the bed near the window. There was another woman already in the room. My TV was mounted 15 feet away on a wall. It had a remote control and a speaker that allowed a patient to watch TV without bothering the other room occupant.

Of course I could not operate the TV. I couldn't even operate the bed controls. The bigger issue though was how was I to use the call button. At Scripps a nurse was always nearby so I didn't need a call button. But here the nurses were much further away. I became more afraid as I realized I had no way to summon help if I was in trouble. Everything becomes a big issue when you are lying inert in a bed in a new place.

Because of the small amount of physical therapy I had received at Scripps, I could now move my right arm slightly. With my arm resting on my body, I could bend my elbow and move my forearm about five inches up and down and I could push my elbow towards my side. A special call button was installed on my bed. It stood upright and had an easily moved plate that I could push by a minute movement of my elbow. This plate became my lifeline and my connection to the world. I felt so relieved to have this tiny modicum of control, it made me weep.

Then I was alone. I felt abandoned, vulnerable and frightened. What if I couldn't move my arm or the plate slipped too far away from my elbow?

Finally I slept a little. The TV hummed gently on low. However it didn't take long before I felt terrible. My neck throbbed. The rest of my body seemed very upset. My stomach was queasy and my insides felt on edge and not right. Even though I couldn't feel pain, my body felt as if it was on fire and a raw burning sensation took over. I had received medication frequently at Scripps, but in this new place there was nothing. I pressed the call plate. A nurse came, and I implored "Where are my medicines, I need my medicines."

She went away to check, and I lay there in my bed, in agony. I could see a clock. I noticed how the light changed in the window as the afternoon wore on. I pressed the call plate, again, and again. Each time, a nurse would appear, say something like 'I'll check into it,' or 'We're working on it,' and then she'd disappear. Finally, about 5 p.m., a nurse appeared with a white cup full of pills. There had been a mistake in my transfer. My prescriptions had not been sent along with me. It had taken the staff at Sharp all afternoon to get the orders for the medicines.

In a short period, I received six Tylenol for pain, three antibiotics, four valium, three Nizatidine (to keep my stomach from bleeding or developing ulcers), two narcotic painkillers and Maalox for my churning stomach. I quickly took the pills when they were brought, and finally dozed off as the drugs entered my system.

During that drugless afternoon the nurses and staff thought I would be a difficult patient. I felt as if my fears about leaving Scripps had been justified. That day was one of the worst of my life. It felt almost as bad as the day of the accident. What more was waiting for me in this new place and how could I be rehabilitated when my body wouldn't even move?

On Wednesday July 17, 1996, my first full day in the rehabilitation hospital began. I didn't know what to expect. I woke up feeling sick to my stomach and not interested in food. A tray was brought to me. I told the nurse I wanted to be left alone when she came to feed me. I had been in a disconnect from the world at Scripps, because I was in a haze of drugs. Now I was more aware of my surroundings and my body than I had been before and it was a rude awakening. The drugs had been cut down and the haze was lifting.

My new doctor came to see me about 8 a.m. Dr. Casey Herman had a pleasant manner and a soothing voice. He was about 45 years old. He seemed out of place with his hippie-looking shoulder length gray hair. He seemed like someone I could trust. I felt so afraid and alone that his presence was a relief.

"The first days will be devoted to evaluating your condition and capabilities," he told me. "Then we can start down a path of work that will lead to your release back into the world."

The very idea of getting out of the hospital seemed impossible and absolutely terrified me. I needed to be where there were many people around to care for me. I told him how afraid I was to even think of leaving, especially since I lived by myself. He explained that a whole team of people would be helping me to readjust. My fears were normal he told me. Eventually I would feel differently. In spite of his perkiness I was not convinced.

He was concerned, however, about my not being able to eat. I told him my stomach was churning and boiling. I felt like a giant was punching me. He said an IV would be administered for a few more days to keep up my strength.

"But you can't rely on an IV. It will limit your movement. If you really are sick enough to be kept in bed, you will have to go to a nursing hospital because the insurance company will not let us keep you here if you can't participate in the rehab activities."

It felt like a veiled threat. I pictured myself amongst a crowd of old, dying, toothless, smelly people.

I stayed in my room that day, with the head of my bed slightly elevated, while one professional after another came to talk to me. The pin test was done again. With my eyes closed, or not looking, either the head of the safety pin, or the point would be pressed against my skin, just enough to make a small indentation or dimple. Then the invariable questions, "Did you feel anything?" I kept saying "No," "no," "no." Only when the pricks were being made on my upper chest, arms and shoulders could I feel the normal sting of pain. A few places on my hands I felt a slight prick, but not real pain. Yet when the head of the safety pin was pressed against me, I could feel it more frequently.

I later learned sensations are carried to the brain in different sections of the spinal column and although they seem related, the pain from the prick, and the pressure from the pinhead traveled different routes to my brain. I could even feel pressure sensations on my legs and my torso but my feet were mostly numb. Sometimes I could not tell when they were being touched.

Another measure was made of my toes, legs and fingers, called proprioception. Did I know where my body was, without looking? Did I have a sense of my own body and its position?

I remembered reading Oliver Sachs' book, <u>The MAN who MISTOOK HIS WIFE for a HAT</u>, and one particular section had remained in my mind because it had frightened me so: a young, healthy, athletic woman awoke feeling strange and within three days found she could barely move. When she was tested she did not know where her body parts were located. When I read the passage, I had looked down at myself. I couldn't imagine anything worse than not being able to sense my own body, not enjoy the movement of my body. The chapter was entitled "The Disembodied Woman." Now I knew exactly how she felt. I was disconnected from my body and the connections were ruined. My mind was fine, but my body weighed me down like an anchor. I wanted to discard it for a model that worked or better yet, get the old one back.

During the proprioception tests, the examiner cushioned my foot in his hand, then slowly moved a toe up, down or left it in place. Sometimes I couldn't tell which toe was being manipulated or even what foot was involved. About half of the time I correctly identified which way a toe was being moved but I felt like I was guessing. The sensations weren't obvious. My body was a distant thing that only sometimes sent signs to me. It did appear that I had some proprioception, which meant I might get more as I healed. Now I was slightly better than when I was lying prone on the freeway. Then I thought my legs were bent, rather than stretched out straight on the asphalt.

My hands were examined last. I concentrated on my fingers as they were moved, blocking out other sensations around me. Although I am right handed, my left hand was more alive. I could identify each finger as it was manipulated. My right hand felt more like a guessing game.

The therapist asked me to move my arm and to push or pull her hand. Most of my movements were slight, and many of the assessment numbers were zero, on a scale of zero to five. When my right arm was lying on my stomach, I could slide it up towards my head, then slide it back down. I was able to move my left arm about 3 inches towards my head but then it was stuck. I could not move it back. My fingers had no resistance against the therapist's hand. I put lots of effort into trying to move but it was frustrating to be working so hard and still be able to do so little.

Pain, pressure, proprioception. These became the central elements in my life. It felt as if my world was reduced to nothing. All I had was a head that functioned properly. But my head was useless without my body. I was helpless and there was nothing I could do about it. How could I have a life worth living?

No one told me I would never walk, but the message was clear. Everything being done and said was to prepare me for a lifetime in a wheelchair, with limited upper body mobility. Nothing was done to test my legs. I didn't even feel connected to them. They made no involuntary movements. They just lay flaccid on the bed. They flopped so badly that a special boot was fitted and Velcroed onto each foot. The boots were rigid and held my feet at right angles to my legs. Otherwise the foot would fall down and eventually line up with the rest of my leg – termed foot drop. I didn't know why foot drop was so bad, since I never expected to walk again.

A social worker introduced herself and let me know she was there for any problems.

An occupational therapist talked a little about how she would work with me.

A recreation therapist stopped by to give me a few encouraging words.

Someone from the cafeteria came. We looked at menus and she wrote down what food to bring me for the next week.

A neuropsychologist talked with me for a while. She asked if I was depressed. What did she expect? A perky, bubbly, well adjusted quadriplegic? I told her my mind still seemed to be moving at the speed of light, as if the accident had just happened and I was pumped full of adrenaline. I kept going over and over the scary events on the freeway.

"The extremely fast paced mind seems to happen to most people right after a spinal cord injury," she said. "It will probably take a few weeks before your mind returns to its normal pace."

My immediate medical crisis was over. I had cooperated with everyone, but I wished they would all go away. Or better yet, I wanted to go away. Being dead would be easier. My mind would not have to struggle from within the cage my body had become. The thought of suicide crossed my mind, but there was no physical way I could do it. Even if someone put a gun in my hand, I couldn't hold it or pull the trigger. Why wasn't I killed in the accident? That would have been so much easier. Then I realized I didn't want to die; I just didn't want to be alive.

When lunch came, the smell was revolting. It made my stomach do flip-flops. I was designated a 'feeder' so a nurse came to feed me. It took a long time to get even one or two bites into my mouth and the nurse had many other duties. After a short time, she left. The food sat next to my bed, cold and unappetizing.

I was wearing a thin nursing gown, open up the back and tied at the neck. I could see my hips and blue paper diapers through the gown. At Scripps, an indwelling foley catheter had been placed in my bladder and it drained all the time. At Sharp this was gone. The injury had caused me to lose control of the sphincter muscle that opens and shuts during urination. The muscle was permanently paralyzed closed, so I could never pee normally. A catheter would have to be inserted periodically to drain urine from me. The female nurse gently explained the procedure. She'd use a sterile kit each time, inserting a catheter and draining urine into a container. Then she (or he) would press on my lower abdomen to help empty my bladder.

I didn't feel anything. I didn't feel the tube as it moved into my body. My bladder never felt full or empty. The procedure is called intermittent catheterization. In hospital-speak terminology, this became a "cath." I needed diapers because sometimes my bladder might uncontrollably spasm open. There were more problems associated with my injury than I had ever imagined.

I was exhausted from interacting with all the new people. My neck was so painful I didn't try to move my head at all. Someone turned the TV on and off for me, adjusting the volume. An IV was put in my right arm but for some reason wasn't seated properly. It seemed to jab me. It hurt and I was annoyed that the needle entered my body in one of the few places where I felt pain. Just my luck, I thought.

I slept fitfully for a while. Then came the p.m. medications. I was rolled over to a new position, propped up with pillows and left again. More fitful sleep, then a cath and repositioning. A few hours later, rolled over again. Later, another cath. Then morning medications. Then breakfast was brought in. The night was over but it had not been restful.

I tried to avoid talking about being depressed, but I worried about my animals to anyone who would listen. My first concern was that someone was talking care of them. My next was about their futures.

I HAD NO notion of what to expect when rehabilitation started. It was my third day at Sharp. I tried but could only eat a bite of the breakfast that the nurse tried to feed me. After breakfast, preparations for getting me into a wheelchair began.

The IV was removed from my arm. The nurse wrestled thigh-high white stocking up my legs while I lay there, lifeless.

I saw a pile of ace bandages but couldn't imagine what they were for. There were four of them: one set was wrapped around each of my lower legs from ankle to knee, and the other two were wrapped around my thighs, from knee to groin. The nurse pulled them very tight. I lay limp, unable to help. A long piece of elastic, about 10 inches wide was stretched tightly around my torso and fastened with Velcro. This was an abdominal binder. I looked down at myself. I looked like a mummy. All these wraps were needed just so that I could sit up.

The compression around my legs and body helped to keep the blood from settling in my legs and abdomen and ensured that oxygen would get to my brain. When lying in bed, my blood pressure was 90 over 60. I learned that lowered blood pressure was caused by lack of function of the valves in the veins, making it difficult to maintain pressure.

Once I was wrapped, a layer of real clothes was put on me. The nurse buttoned on a blouse and pulled on my pants. I felt like an obstacle, being rolled back and forth, trussed up like a turkey and then dressed.

I had no way to support my body in a sitting position. None of my muscles worked. I was afraid of falling headfirst onto the floor. My safety was entirely in the hands of the nurse, who was tiny. Even though I am small, I didn't think the petite Indonesian nurse could move me to the wheelchair.

"Are you ready? Here we go, nice and easy," she said as she elevated the head of the bed. Then she smoothly swiveled my body around. My feet fell over the bedside and she raised my upper body to an upright position.

"Are you all right? Not dizzy?" she asked. "Let me know if you feel faint." She kept her hands on me to prevent me from tipping over.

I felt slightly faint, but didn't say anything.

A wheelchair was already positioned against the bed, its seat at right angles to the mattress. The nurse leaned over me, squeezed me between her arms and rotated me into the wheelchair seat. It amazed me that someone so small could move my dead weight. To keep me from sliding in the wheelchair, a strap was fastened around my chest while large wheelchair arms supported my sides. I was glad to be safely seated.

The nurse wheeled me down the long corridor to a large room that looked like a gymnasium. My mind was still rushing like a train as I took in all the sights of the room. It lacked the antiseptic smell of a hospital and had a pleasant feel to it. There was a seating area for visitors, six large mat-tables, four tables with chairs and an exercise corner with various pieces of equipment. The ceiling was high and the room was bright. Large windows on two sides looked out onto a patio and a grassy area.

Rehab followed a general pattern. It started with occupational therapy (OT) in the morning, followed by group exercise sessions or work on the exercise equipment. Then there was a two-hour break at lunchtime, with physical therapy (PT) in the afternoon. Sometimes recreational therapy or pulmonary therapy was scheduled for the afternoon. Occasionally there was a lecture about problems and the care of quadriplegics.

I noticed several women seated in wheelchairs at the institutional-style tables. I saw a man in a distant corner, lying in a reclining wheelchair. I was dismayed when I saw his chair back raise up, then move as he blew into a tube. I knew immediately he was more severely injured than I was. I had conflicting thoughts of being luckier but also of being terribly unlucky to even be in this room. I didn't know how to relate to the other patients. I hoped that we could help each other without constantly being reminded of our injured bodies and minds. I saw patients and therapists working on mat-tables. I wondered how the weight equipment at the far end was used, and exactly how I would fit into this place. It seemed a friendly atmosphere, with everyone chatting and occupied with therapy tasks. Still I felt like a lump as I was rolled into the room. I was apprehensive about everything.

The head occupational therapist, Marilyn told me I needed to learn as much about my body as possible, so I could eventually direct my own care. This seemed an overwhelming responsibility to me since I could barely move. I didn't have a clue about what needed to be done but that was quickly changed. My first lesson was about lay-backs and pressure sores.

"When you are in a wheelchair," Marilyn said, "you need to be aware of how long you sit. Any prolonged time can result in pressure sores. You have to be sure you are sitting up properly, not slouching or leaning against the sides of the chair. Each hour you should request a lay-back for 20 minutes. If we don't remember, it's your job to remind us."

The first lay-back was a great relief. Marilyn sat on one of the mat-tables and tipped my wheelchair back about 45 degrees. This took pressure off of my butt and distributed it evenly across my back. I was tired from the mental and physical effort of interacting and happy for the chance to drift away for a while.

There were two more lessons that first morning. The first was about tenodesis. I hated the sound of the word immediately. Tenodesis is a way to manipulate hands. The occupational therapist demonstrated by raising her forearm, then letting it fall rapidly to a beanbag on the table. As the arm extends, the fingers naturally make a small curl, without any conscious muscle activity. If an object is between the fingers, rapidly raising the arm causes the fingers to curl tighter, possibly raising the object. Then she helped me move my arm, aiming at the soft beanbag. Sometimes the bag ended up resting between my fingers and palm but the entire experience was exhausting and demoralizing. It made me realize how little I could do with my arms and hands. I was relieved to do the next lay-back. I closed my eyes and tried to be anywhere else but in a wheelchair.

The hour before lunch was reserved for arm strengthening, using the weight equipment. I was too weak for the activity and was seated at a table on the other side of the room where I used a special machine. My right arm was Velcroed onto a small rectangular board with casters which reminded me of a skateboard. The end away from me had a line running into a box. The box contained a mechanism that provided resistance when the line was pulled. The box was positioned to my left. I was to roll my right arm out toward my right side and back, pulling against the resistance. The therapist set the mechanism to a very low level of tension. Since I was working on a smooth table, there was little friction from the casters. By moving my arm on the horizontal tabletop, I did not have to oppose the force of gravity. The board practically moved by itself when touched. Yet I had to pull, back and forth, using great amounts of energy, just to do this simple task. I pulled and pulled against the cord. I was able to move my arm about ten inches. Until this point, I had been a lifeless object, but this simple maneuver made my body and mind rejoice at once again being able to do a physical activity. I actually began to enjoy the little I could do.

I was so exhausted when I got back to my room that I hardly noticed the scary transfer into bed. I had no interest in the lunch brought to me, yet the fear of being sent to a nursing hospital loomed over me. I had to eat. I made myself take a few bites when the nurse came in to feed me. Then I rested and slept during the two-hour lunch break.

The neurosurgeon had put in orders that I was to wear a hard Philadelphia collar on my neck during activity out of bed. When the nurse started to put it on, I protested. During the morning, the collar had made my neck hurt, and the thought of aggravating the bones in my neck was physically sickening. The collar felt like a stretching device to push my head off of my shoulders. It made me feel like the bones, which had been wired back together, were being pried apart. After a few phone calls the nurse got permission for me to use the soft collar as long as there was no pain.

As soon as the soft collar was in place, it was time for my afternoon round of physical therapy. Another transfer, bed to wheelchair, and another long push down the hall to the gym. I was positioned next to a large mat-table. It was about 22 inches high, eight feet by eight feet, and covered with foam and vinyl. The physical therapist who came over to greet me was named Mandy and I liked her immediately.

"I'm going to transfer you to the table," she said. "You can lay flat and I can range your arms and legs." I felt very secure in her hands. She effortlessly moved me onto the table.

She moved my arms and legs, stretching the muscles and tendons and working every joint. I tried very hard to pay attention, to sense what part of me was being moved and in what direction. I had always disliked massages and other people fussing with my body. Perhaps I had skin that was a little extra-sensitive. All that sensitivity was gone now and I was able to relax with Mandy working on me. I found I liked having my upper back rubbed. It was one part of my body where my sense of feel was almost normal.

I also discovered that Mandy and I had a mutual love of animals. I told her I had successfully trained my dogs using positive rewards and treats. She told me she had a pot bellied pig at home. I laughed and was delighted. We launched into ways she could use positive reinforcement to train her pig, Bo. How odd, yet how comforting, it seemed to me to have this perfectly normal conversation when everything around me was so strange and frightening.

Life seemed full of these bizarre juxtapositions. I had so many things in common with Mandy but an accident had separated us into the healthy and the injured, and brought us together.

Later I found out all the patients felt the same way I did, caught as we all were in this new world. We were an uncommon lot, being four newly injured women. Eighty percent of spinal cord injuries happen to men, usually under the age of 35.

Automobile accidents, diving and guns cause most injuries. The injuries seem to split between paraplegia (where only the lower body, below the waist, is affected) and quadriplegia (where arms, legs and trunk are impaired). It was unusual for a rehab center to have only women, and so many at the same time. The four of us had an immediate common bond, but we were too scared to talk about it yet. That would come later.

Casie was 19 and had been in an auto accident; Lisa was 68 and had also been in an auto accident. Trish was on her way home from her college graduation and had gone with friends to a river swimming spot. There she'd had a diving accident. We were all quadriplegics.

I was happy to fall into the rehab routine. It alleviated my need to think about anything. After the first few weeks, I became accustomed to the various therapies. Since it was very tiring, I went from one activity to another and snoozed unthinkingly between times. During the day this worked well for me. It was the evenings and the endless nights that were so oppressive and disturbing.

Jim managed to stop in, if only for a few minutes, almost every night. He was the one element of my life that had not changed and his visits made me feel secure and connected to my old life.

"The dogs are doing well," he told me. "Two friends are taking very good care of them and the house. Jordan was sick for a few days after the accident but the vet says he's fine now."

Jim had even talked to one of my stable friends, who agreed to keep an eye on Ameego. I smiled as I thought of my horse.

For now, I was safe and secure, and alone, here in the hospital.

Chapter Two

Rediscovering my Big Toe and Learning to Move, Inch by Inch

MY TEETH ALWAYS felt fuzzy when the nurse brushed them. The first task of occupational therapy (OT) was to brush them myself. But my hands worked poorly and even lifting my arm up high enough to reach my mouth was difficult. I could not even grasp the toothbrush. I could barely hold the toothpaste and there was no hope at all of unscrewing the cap!

At 9 a.m. the nurse had me dressed and into the wheelchair when Jeanie, my occupational therapist, came to my room. She put a device around my hand called a U-cuff. It had a soft padded portion to go in my palm and was fastened around the back of my hand with Velcro. There was a narrow slot where Jeanie inserted my toothbrush.

"The only one who has to use your toothpaste is you," she said. "I will unscrew the top and you can leave it off all the time. Why bother to squeeze the toothpaste onto the brush? Just hold up the tube and squeeze a little directly into your mouth."

I struggled to press a little toothpaste in my mouth, managed to move my right arm around a little and brush at my teeth. It was by no means a complete job, and I had to stop several times when I was tired. Jeanie removed the brush from the U-cuff, put a little water in a glass and helped me change my position so that I could rinse my mouth. She congratulated me but it seemed like I had done only a minimal part and I could not have done even that without her help. The whole operation had taken an hour. Again I thought 'I'll never function on my own. I will need people taking care of me forever.' I was tired and just wanted everyone to go away and leave me alone.

There was little time to rest however before I was taken down to the gym, where two days a week a young woman, also a quadriplegic, came to lead us in 'wheelchair aerobics.' Francine was in her thirties, quite attractive and usually sitting in a long skirt in her manual wheelchair. She brought a tape player with rousing music and led us to punch, flap, and otherwise move our arms and shoulders. We also rolled our heads and necks, stretched and tried to relax. Her enthusiasm inspired us.

I noticed her fingers were curled under and did not seem to be particularly useful. I marveled when I learned Francine lived alone, drove her own car to the hospital, and pushed her manual wheelchair up the sloping sidewalk to our exercise room. Maybe there was hope for me after all.

Francine also taught us to play 'volley ball.' A string was stretched out and tied about three feet high. We lined up across from each other on opposite sides of it. A balloon served as our ball. It was a hit and miss game, mostly misses of course. An occupational therapist and a few volunteers were kept busy retrieving our bad shots. Still we cheered for each other and tried to be supportive. When I first tried to play, I couldn't move or control my arms. To help me, each arm was placed in a sling, hanging from a metal pole. This allowed me to push my arms forward and backward without having to hold them up. Occasionally, the therapist would loft the balloon directly at my hand. Then I could actually hit it to the other side of the string.

It was difficult for me to see my body struggling to play this simple game when I remembered the many friendly games of volley ball I had played on the beach or in gymnasiums. I then had been a valued team member and could scurry around to save many shots. I still felt like an athlete, but my eyes told me I wasn't any longer. In the several weeks since the accident, all my muscles had atrophied.

Soon I graduated to the weight machines. I used to dive into physical challenges, but now I didn't know how to begin. Leather cuffs, lined with sheepskin, were buckled tightly around each of my wrists. A ring on the cuff was attached to the ring on the weight bar with a clip. I was now sitting in my wheelchair, with my arms suspended above my head, looking something like a cartoon of a prisoner in a dungeon. I tried as hard as I could to pull down the bar but I couldn't budge its lowest weight of ten pounds. With the weights totally disconnected, I could move my arms down towards my body. I didn't think this was much of an accomplishment, but it was a place to start. I pulled a few times and rested. Then a few more times and rested. I felt like a piece of meat in a butcher store stretched out between the bars.

I waited for help and then I was attached to another place on the overhead bar and pulled some more. Then I was hooked up so that I was pulling from in front of my knees. It took a long time to go through all these motions. In an hour's time I managed to completely tire myself out, even with rest breaks and a 20-minute lay-back. I was disheartened by how hard it all seemed but at the same time it felt good to be doing something physical with my body.

I couldn't help thinking about when my biceps popped up out of my upper arms. One hundred pound bales of hay and 50 pound bags of grain had provided me with great upper body workouts. Now I could barely move. Still, watching the others gave me hope. Lisa was moving a stack of several weights. She immediately became my model and got my competitive juices flowing again. I wanted to beat her in our side-by-side exertions. I never voiced my competitiveness though, since we were all balanced so delicately in our minds. Comparisons and failure were too hard to bear. But it was here, connected by machines and our injuries, that we started to get to know each other.

Lisa looked strange, moving around in the middle of the machines, carrying her own metal headgear - a large halo pinned to her skull and shoulders to stabilize the area where her neck was injured. "Don't we look a mess, with our great new clothes?" I said.

"Try getting something that works with a halo," Lisa said. "My daughter Cathy has been getting things at the thrift store, and cutting a big hole up the front to fit over all my head gear."

We were afraid to discuss anything important so we kept up a cheery banter. Voicing our fears might make us face the horrific disaster that had befallen us.

After a few sessions with the weights, my arms were stronger and brushing my teeth became easier each week. I needed lots of help, but it no longer took an hour.

Next I had to learn to dress myself. We started with tops. The nurse had already put the abdominal binder and leg wraps on me. I was sitting in my wheelchair. Jeanie untied the string holding my hospital gown and held out a tee shirt to me.

"You need to get your head through the proper hole and then work on your arms," she said.

She helped me get my arms and head into the body of the shirt. I felt like a turtle. The extra-large shirts Jim had brought me had plenty of room and once inside the garment, I squirmed until my head was sticking out. My arms were still folded against my body. By maneuvering each arm separately, I managed to wiggle my hand to the sleeve and poke it out.

"You'll be able to dress yourself soon," Jeanie said. "You did a good job. It will get easier."

My unmoving legs were a different problem.

Because my legs had no involuntary muscle contractions they put me at great risk of developing blood clots. The pumping action of healthy moving leg muscles keeps blood flowing back to the heart. The lack of involuntary movement was a reaction to the shock of the accident, causing my body's systems to shut down. With my slowed circulation, blood could easily pool. The pooled blood could thicken and clot, possibly causing a fatal stroke or heart attack. Consequently each morning, before my legs were put in their stockings and ace bandages, the nurse circled a tape measure around the largest part of my calf and recorded the measurement. The measurements were compared from day to day. In order to prevent clots, I received three shots a day of Heparin (a short-time acting blood thinner). Three shots a day may sound uncomfortable, but I received the shots in my abdomen and only knew it was happening if I watched the needle slide into me. I felt no pain.

Perhaps one of the most difficult parts of recovery for me was that I felt so alone. The other ladies were surrounded by their families: Lisa, by her husband, daughter and son-in-law; Casi by her sisters and parents; Trish by her parents and sister; and Rosaria (who arrived at Sharp at the end of July) by her beautiful two year old daughter, her husband, mother and brother. I was blessed to have Jim. He took care of my house, the mail, bills and other concerns.

There are no words to say how much the support of my friends helped me deal with the slow, often depressing job of rehabilitation. During my two and a half months at Sharp, I had at most five days when no visitors came to see me. I thought that after several weeks no one would come to visit me but I was wrong. Friends turned out in numbers I could never have imagined.

A few nights during my first week at Sharp, so many people came to see me they could not all fit in my room. They spilled out into the hallway. Someone had the brilliant idea of setting up a visiting schedule and a secretary from the San Diego Supercomputer Center volunteered to keep it. Friends from work had to call her and get on my schedule before they could come to see me! She faxed me the roster for each week and the nurse taped it to the wall next to my bed.

Lying in my bed after visiting hours I was so overwhelmed by the love and caring of my friends and co-workers that I often found myself crying.

Each visitor pitched in to help me eat. I found that I could usually get down some soup and bread so I began to request this entry on my menu selection for every day. If my soup was really cold by the time my visitors arrived, a quick trip to the microwave down the hall fixed the problem. A friend would slowly spoon soup into me, placing bread pieces where I could reach them, while keeping a conversation going. It seemed a very natural and caring process. I did not feel awkward, and my friends liked helping me. Sometimes I felt like a little baby being fed, but I didn't let this thought intrude.

Later, when I could hold a fork in the U-cuff and lift food to my mouth, I still needed and accepted help. Just raising my arm from tray to mouth was tiring. I was no good with a spoon and soup would spill on everything. It could take me 45 minutes to an hour to eat a small amount of my dinner. The nurses were relieved that I was eating and that my friends could help me as the nurses did not have the time I needed to be fed. The people who came to be with me did more than just warm my spirits. They were absolutely essential to my health.

When my friends saw my poor appetite, the food and drink began to arrive. I'd told Jim to pass the word that I didn't want flowers. My unmoving body lying in my bed surrounded by flowers would seem even more like a corpse. Soon Jim had to purchase two small wheel-about plastic caddies for all the thoughtful gifts and food that arrived. I was pleased to share my bounty with my visitors, the other patients, their friends and the hospital staff.

Most of my visitors were the men I'd worked with and with whom I had contact on a daily basis. Some were people I barely knew, but they had heard about the accident. I had expected my close friends, especially the women, to come but I had thought there would be some conspicuous absences. There were none. Since the room was cheerful and did not smell antiseptic, everyone was comfortable being there with me.

Some people came to see me again and again. On return visits, many brought their children along and sometimes even strangers. People wanted to share their own stories and so I heard about back injuries, hand injuries, car accidents, unemployment, relationship problems and the general vagaries of human existence. None of this was presented as depressing. These were problems that had been overcome. The sharing felt deep and sincere to me and because of it I was able to voice some of my own fears. I did try however to keep the great hurdles of my recovery from overwhelming my visitors.

Two strangers who were brought to see me had suffered spinal cord injuries. They could now walk. They both told me to keep up my hopes because one never knew what might happen.

I learned that many people I thought I knew were not as simple or two-dimensional as I'd believed. I had seen one man, a physicist, so absorbed by his job that he seemed to have little interest in unscientific things. On a visit, he quietly revealed he was the custodian of his autistic brother and planned to assume his brother's sole physical care when his parents could no longer cope. No fanfare, no big deal. Just not the man I thought I knew.

One evening I had just a single visitor. We chatted amicably before he surprised me with his story.

"Not many people know," he said, "but I tried to commit suicide. Obviously I wasn't successful but I found out so much about myself and everything around me, that I now believe it was the best thing to happen. I am now so glad it didn't work."

"I don't know if I want to be dead or alive," I said, nearly in tears. "Dead would be easier. Being alive for me now is so much work. Look what little I can do. I don't want to live like this. I'm almost not a person, just a thing that lies here with a talking head."

"You don't know what is coming for you and it might not be so bad. You just have to hang in there and wait. Forget about suicide. I'll be here if you need to talk. Lean on me. I didn't have anyone to help me in those dark moments, but I'm here if you need me."

I was overcome with emotion, since I hadn't really talked to anyone about not wanting to live. We talked about living and life. He didn't have any answers, except that life wasn't so bad. He urged me to accept my current situation and to look toward the future with some hope.

When he left, I sank into the mattress thinking 'Wow! People are amazing. They've been so good to me. I just have to keep going, and see what happens.'

About this time I moved to the other bed where I could see outside. By turning my head an inch or so and shifting my eyes, I could see sunlight, some blue sky and puffy clouds. I could escape from the room and maybe fly with a passing bird.

Rosaria Lopez, a lovely young girl, about 20, was wheeled in to be my new roommate. She had become progressively stiffer over a few days so that most of her body was paralyzed. Her doctor did not know if she had multiple sclerosis or myolitis, and two years later they were still not sure of her diagnosis. She had come into the U.S. from Mexico with her father. She was a legal immigrant at that time, but after her father's death, her status became unclear. Fortunately, she had a job that provided her with the care she now desperately needed. She had baked the luscious pies at a local Marie Calendar's restaurant. Although her English was minimal and I tried to use some of the Spanish I had learned long ago, the language really didn't matter. We had a common bond. The words were not important. Our bodies had similar problems. We could compare what was being done to us. We became close friends, lying in beds in the same room. We ended each day with:

"Palm, I love you."

"Rosaria, I love you. Sleep good tonight."

These simple words expressed all our shared worries and concerns, with the hope that tomorrow would be better.

Rosaria made five of us, five female quadriplegics.

THE SAME DETERMINATION that got me through my schooling played an enormous part in my rehabilitation. Although I experienced mood swings and occasional dark depressions, I made myself concentrate on the progress I was making.

Since none of my lower muscles moved, there was no way for me to get digested food out of my large intestine. My sphincter muscle was paralyzed shut. In a strange way this wasn't so bad since I had no sensation of what was happening but it meant that every morning a nurse had to insert a suppository. About thirty minutes later, the suppository would cause spasms in my lower intestines and then the nurse would position me on my side and manually removed the stool. I always disliked this 'bowel program' although there was no pain.

I accepted the rolling, dressing, undressing, washing, examining, prodding, poking and pulling as if it wasn't happening to me. I am convinced that not thinking, not caring, not minding was a device of self-protection.

Learning to sit up on my own was a major job. This was made more difficult by my hands. My bent fingers would not open so they couldn't be placed on the mat-table with fingers spread open. Mandy, my physical therapist gently moved me from lying on the mat-table to sitting on its edge. While holding me up, she helped me place my arms out to each side and slightly behind my body. I braced with my clenched fists, knuckles pressing into the mat. In spite of my years of athletic activity, because of my spinal cord injury I now lacked any trunk muscles for support. Once Mandy had gotten me into this position, she had to help me balance my upper body. My arms and body tired quickly, but I began to develop some strength and balance. Eventually I could sit for several minutes at a time. It may have looked like a small step but it was a major move towards developing my strength and a measure of independence.

So many of the things I had always taken for granted were almost impossible now. I had little control over my weak diaphragm. I had to relearn how to cough. A weak cough would allow fluid or phlegm to build up in my lungs, resulting in pneumonia. I learned to inhale as deeply as possible and then cough while Mandy pressed inward and upward on my upper abdomen with the heel of her hand. When my new cough began to sound like it came from a normal person I actually felt a sense of accomplishment.

There was breathing to be remastered. The first afternoon session of pulmonary therapy, I blew into a small white tube. The therapist said the resistance would help to strengthen my lungs and breathing muscles. My breathing ability was tested by my blowing into a tube, as hard and as long as I could. I huffed and puffed, but not much happened. Because my breathing was weak, so was my voice. When I talked others had difficulty hearing me. Sometimes my voice would 'catch', as if something was stuck in my throat. Even now, I occasionally have a 'sticky' voice. The therapist gave me other breathing exercises to practice in bed. I practiced – breathing in for five seconds, breathing out for five seconds. I did this for longer and longer periods of time, up to 12 seconds. Another exercise was to say each vowel, holding the sound for as long as possible.

We, 'The Fearless Five' (there were just five female spinal cord injured patients active in rehab at that time), had fun doing Pulmonary therapy as a group. We were positioned in a semi-circle, sitting in our wheelchairs. A dartboard with Velcro was placed about 6 feet away in front of us. With a small blowgun, we aimed light Velcroed ping pong balls at the target. Rosaria's breath was so strong that the ball flew well past the board. Lisa could hit the target, and sometimes the ball even stuck to it. My puff, however, resulted in the ball falling on the floor in front of my legs. Casi and Trish had the same problem. Still, we had fun trying together.

I had noticed one in-patient who was vent-dependent. He had been hospitalized for months, and did not participate in our regular activities. Usually I saw him sitting in the hallway near the nursing station. From my room, I could hear the loud alarm when his ventilator stopped. I was grateful I could breathe on my own. I was fearful enough without having to live with the constant threat of a ventilator failure. I now understood more about the fragile position of Christopher Reeve, who had almost no movement.

After a few weeks the nurses asked me if I wanted to be given a shower. I was afraid but the other ladies urged me to give it a try.

"It's really very enjoyable," I was told, "and it feels great to get your hair clean."

I decided to be brave and try it. Shortly after dinner one evening a special gurney was brought into my room. It was a flat plastic slab with upward sloping sides. Two nurses maneuvered me onto it, covered me with a towel, and rolled me into a special shower room. The water was turned on, the temperature was adjusted and then the nurses turned the hand-held sprayer onto me. Although the steamy atmosphere of the room was very pleasant, I couldn't feel the water. I had no warm liquid sensation of water on me until the spray reached my shoulders and face. Then it felt good. Having my hair washed thoroughly and hearing the squeaky clean sound it made was wonderful. The nurses were gentle and even seemed to enjoy a bit of splashing. They had donned plastic coveralls to keep their clothes dry. But while being brushed, soaped, scrubbed and rinsed, I must admit I felt like an automobile in a car wash.

I was carefully dried. One towel was wrapped around my head and another towel was draped over me for transit back to my room. Once in my room a thin hospital gown was put on me and I was moved into bed. One nurse stayed a while and partially dried my hair with a blow dryer.

About ten minutes after the nurse left, I started to shake. Soon I was shaking uncontrollably. I didn't know what was happening to me. I pushed my call plate and an aide came. I was scared. She called a nurse and before I knew it several people were gathered around my bed. My temperature was normal. My blood pressure was measured. There were no obvious signs of a problem. A nurse did a cath, in case my bladder was overly full. Someone brought in a hot blanket from the clothes dryer and placed it over me. Twenty minutes later another hot blanket was brought in. Finally I stopped shaking.

I had been cold but I had had no feeling of being cold. My body seemed to be reacting without my awareness of what was wrong.

I learned several important lessons that night which are still relevant to me. Over most of my body, I can not tell if water is hot or cold, which means I can burn myself without even knowing it. Because my hands do not properly sense temperature, I have to test water temperature with my arm. It seems like a dirty trick that the same path that transmits pain in the spinal column also transmits temperature sensitivity. My roommate Rosaria was in an even worse predicament as she could sense temperature only on her face.

I didn't know I was chilled until the cold had seeped into my body and I'd begun to shake. Much later, when I was able to be outdoors, I found I could not tell when I was getting overheated. My body no longer perspires when I am hot, which means I must take extreme care when temperatures are over 80 degrees. I have to carry a spray bottle, wear a water-retentive scarf, wear a hat, stay out of the sun and generally curtail my hot weather activities. I have learned to anticipate temperature conditions that threaten my well being, but I am only somewhat successful.

After that first experience I was understandably leery of taking another shower. The nurses took to automatically throwing several blankets in the dryer when my shower was started and they immediately covered me up when I was back in bed. The problem was solved, except I never got over feeling I was being run through a car wash.

I was awake quite often during the night, my mind spinning through the problems I was facing. I wouldn't take any drugs to help me sleep, since I was already taking enough to stock a pharmacy. Instead I counted backwards, 99 to 0, until I lost track and dozed. Usually I made the countdown 4 or 5 times before I got sleepy, with my mind making many diversions along the way.

My stomach was still giving me problems. I had little desire to eat during the day. It constantly felt like a giant hand was squeezing my stomach, which felt full of glass shards. After three weeks, Dr. Herman admitted that my constantly upset stomach perplexed him. My doctor friend, Francine, gave me the name of a gastrointestinal physician. He was small, balding, and talked like a record spinning too fast.

He said, "I'll give you a prescription and everything will be all right."

I nodded but thought it sounded too good to be true.

The next morning, a new pink pill appeared in my little white cup. By mid-day I was feeling better and by the middle of the next day, I was hungry. Although the drug Prilosec had been around for some time, it was relatively unknown. Once the pill began to work, I could eat and begin to gain some strength.

Every three weeks, just after breakfast, I was taken to a patient-clinician conference. It seemed like an inquisition. Dr. Herman, my occupational therapist, my physical therapist, the social worker, the insurance coordinator, and the neuropsychologist sat on one side of the large conference table. My side of the table stretched out like an abandoned beach, with just me sitting there. I took a deep breath as I faced everyone. I felt less than a 'real person' for how real could I be? I was so needy. I could not function as an adult. I was more like a helpless baby - one who would never grow up.

I was reminded of the many meetings I had conducted at work, where I was the only woman in a sea of men. I relied on that earlier composure to get me through those patient-clinician conferences. I talked a little about how I was feeling, both physically and mentally except I didn't bring up my negative feelings - the wish to be dead or thoughts of suicide. I figured 'who wouldn't be depressed in my situation?'

"Well, that's all for now," said Dr. Herman when it was all over. It was strange to realize that my progress was a work activity for these people. By the end of each meeting, a plan was laid out for the next few weeks, with specific goals and activities. Although my welfare was of great concern to everyone, the formality of the meeting overshadowed their warm hearts.

One morning after several weeks, the nurse came into my room with a new wheelchair. I was told it was never to be called an 'electric chair' – it was a 'power chair.' Mine was scaled to my size, with a joystick control for my stronger right arm and hand. Suddenly I had a great sense of control over my life. In my new chair I could move around independently. I felt like a water skimmer on a calm pond, quietly appearing and disappearing. Although I bumped into the bed, the door and the hallway walls learning to maneuver it, I was thrilled with the chair. It was like learning to drive all over again. I drove to the gym, the longest distance I had traveled alone since the accident. I practiced riding my new black steed during OT and PT. Aside from the joystick, the chair had a separate control, which allowed my back to recline. I could do my own lay-backs! It made me feel like I was a bit more responsible for my own destiny. My first wheelchair pressure mark had disappeared and I was determined to avoid ever having another one. I was relentless at watching the clock and suddenly becoming supine. It was a terrific feeling to have some control over my life.

More wondrous things were about to happen to me.

Near the beginning of August, my legs started to move around on their own. Sometimes they twitched a little and other times they kicked out like a professional soccer player's. It was both exciting and problematic. My transfers from bed to wheelchair became dangerous. My legs could kick out at any time and cause the nurse to lose her grip on me. On particularly bad days one of the stronger male aids or nurses had to help with my transfers. Since my muscles were contracting on their own, the heparin shots used to diminish the blood-clotting danger were stopped.

Around this time my numb hands began to feel like they were full of pins and needles. They also began to feel exceedingly cold. Friends brought me gloves, which I wore all the time.

My body was a foreign thing to me now, and I did not know how to react to it. If someone bumped me, or if I rolled over a rough spot in the wheelchair, my body jumped and spasmed unexpectedly. I had to learn to anticipate these reactions and be ready for them. It was like learning a new dance, with ragged steps and halts, and lots of mistakes.

It was hard to watch my legs jump around and not be able to control them. It seemed that just as I was becoming accustomed to my numb body, it was changing. These changes were not what I had anticipated.

I knew the swelling and injury to my spinal column was healing but still some of the side effects were unexpected. I never knew exactly who I was or where I was. Then one morning, when I awoke, I knew that my left thumb had come alive. I could make a little circle with it. It was also much more sensitive when I touched an object. I noticed the feeling around my ribs was different. The abdominal binder suddenly felt tight and restrictive. Strangely enough, I couldn't tell when I was or wasn't wearing it but it felt like unknown hands were always squeezing me.

I wanted all the weird sensations to go away but I was also hopeful that my body was improving so that I could do simple things. Maybe I would have the strength to eat normally, at least with my left hand. Maybe I would have enough sensation that every bump was not a dangerous threat.

Then one evening while I was lying in bed watching TV, my left leg started its most recent routine: the knee bent a little, my ankle flexed and my toes curled. I had gotten used to this slow periodic movement of my leg, usually in the evening. The movement repeated itself every 12 seconds. It reminded me of the first time I had taken snow ski lessons in Pittsburgh. After an evening of being out in the snow, a quick supper, and a tired dive into bed, my legs had jumped around. They had been trying to practice the snowplow or the stem christie, which I had just learned.

The constant flexing of my leg made it hard for me to concentrate on the TV. I kept noticing it, waiting for it to stop. It was like a hiccup, where you wait for the next one, hoping it would forget to come.

In some attempt to intervene, I concentrated on my leg. I envisioned an electrical wire running down from my head, along my backbone, branching into my left leg and ending in my toe. Each time my toe bent, I scrunched up my face pretending I was sending a signal to it. I did this over and over again, every 12 seconds. I don't know why I tried this mental control that night. It just felt like the right thing, and after many years of athletic activity I had learned to listen to my body.

I became tired after 15 or 20 minutes of this mental activity, and was relieved when my leg stopped its jumping. I went back to watching TV and tried not to think about what I had done.

But I had to try again. About half an hour later, I shifted my gaze back to my big toe. I stared at it, so I could make a mental connection, like soldering wires together. I squinted my eyes and said 'now move big toe.' I watched and watched because if it happened I wanted to see it to be sure.

I felt something click inside me. Then it happened. I moved my toe! I yelled out loud, "I did it, I moved my toe. It moved, I moved it."

My roommate, Rosaria, looked over at me, smiling. "Oh Palm, that's wonderful. You are good. It's so good. You will be OK."

It was August 18, 1996. Only Rosaria and I knew.

I was afraid to try again; maybe it was just a freak thing. I wanted desperately to walk, to be normal, to escape from this bad dream but I was afraid to taunt myself with unrealistic hopes. I knew disappointment would be too much to bear.

The next morning, when Dr. Newman made his rounds, I wanted him to see me move my toe. I was afraid he would warn me about getting false hopes, but I had to try.

"Can you move the sheet off of my feet and look at my toes?" I asked tentatively.

We both watched as my left big toe moved back and forth at my command. Without another word, he placed his hand on my right quadriceps and asked me to move that leg. Although I concentrated and tried, nothing happened. He did the same with my left quadriceps and then with my abdomen. Nothing seemed to happen, yet he straightened up and smiled at me.

"You are going to be able to walk," he said.

I was holding my breath. A big smile appeared on my face. I let out a long sigh. I had wanted to hear those very words, but didn't think I ever would.

News spread quickly on the hospital grapevine. All the nurses and therapists came to see me, not just my nurses and therapists, but all of them! Their smiles were warm. They told me how happy they were. Good news was rare and everyone was delighted to share in my good fortune.

I was one of the lucky few. Most quadriplegics never use their legs again. I didn't want the other patients to feel left out by my sudden accomplishment and was glad to find they were as delighted as the staff had been.

I smiled all that morning. I envisioned the old me walking, skipping, running and laughing. I had reason to hope. I was determined then to work even harder to get better. My body was no longer the enemy. It was on my side again.

I HAD MANY dreams during my fitful hospital sleep, but one stands out in vivid detail. I was lying on a cot in a large dark room. Other people were sleeping in the room; it reminded me of a dormitory. I needed to get up to go to the bathroom, but I couldn't. My legs were paralyzed. No one was awake to help me. I became agitated as I struggled to sit up on the edge of the cot. Then a beam of light appeared at the door at the far end of the room. In the dim light I saw my mother coming toward me. "I'm here, honey," she said. "Everything will be all right now. I can help you." As she reached my bed, I stood up and she led me hobbling towards the door.

I awoke abruptly, feeling both sorrow and joy. It was so wonderful to see my mother, but at the same time I knew she was dead. It was thirty years since she'd died, yet she was a real person in my hospital room. I missed her so then. I needed her strength, her love, her presence. She could have helped me. She could have saved me from the real nightmare of my life. I cried because of my love for her and I cried because I knew it was just a dream of seeing her and of walking again.

My therapy routine continued, soothing me with the same people and the same activities each day. OT focused on my hands and doing everyday tasks. I slowly attempted new things. I was too afraid of leaps and bounds. I played with two year-olds' toys, manipulating putty, picking up rings, blocks and small objects. I threw beanbags into wastebaskets. I played cards with the thick, large variety used by the elderly. Money was simply beyond my grasp. I could almost manipulate dollar bills, but coins were impossible.

I tried my best, even though it felt like it wasn't good enough and would never be good enough. Progress was so slow, but it was progress. I was no longer classified as a 'feeder' and I had advanced to using the normal call button instead of the super sensitive plate.

I tried to write my name, but couldn't recognize my own scratchy signature. Then I shortened my signature to three letters, 'P He,' and became a new person.

In one of my progress conferences I said I wanted to try using a manual wheelchair. I felt strong and bold the first time I sat in one. I could be like a paraplegic if I was pushing my own chair. Quadriplegics think paraplegics have it easy and paraplegics envy people using walkers. Someone is always better off or worse off. The first afternoon, I tentatively put my hands on the wheelchair push ring. My twisted fingers didn't allow a grip, so I used my palms instead. When I pushed, I found the chair moved easily. I slowly wheeled around the gym, moving like an aimless snail. I expected the same scenario the next day when I tried the manual chair again. I was overwhelmed with disappointment. It was all I could do to move five feet. I later learned that the chair had a mechanical problem and was difficult for anyone to move. What a relief! I continued to use the power chair out of my room but spent time in the manual chair every day.

Mandy had already heard the news about my big toe. She was beaming when I arrived at our PT session that afternoon. She gave me a big hug and told me we needed to add exercises to get my legs working.

We continued on techniques for transferring between wheelchair and bed. I never mastered the slide board. But later, when my legs had a little strength, we practiced a standing transfer. Mandy stood in front of me and grasped me under my arms. I tried to stand as she pulled me up and rotated my rear to the mat, then lowered my upper body so that I was sitting. I had a little strength in my midsection and could sit upright for 5 or 10 minutes, using my arms like tripods for support.

Just about every session, Mandy had me work on the technique for rolling over. As my body grew stronger, I felt I should be able to do this, especially since my legs were no longer completely paralyzed. Lying on my back, I stretched both arms out to my right side. Then I swung them violently over my body, pointing to my left. At the same time, I rotated my head and shoulders left, hoping that the lower part of my body would follow. One afternoon, I tried 3 or 4 times. My legs seemed like wet noodles that were stuck to the mat. It didn't matter that my upper body was twisted like a pretzel. My legs were not going to follow. Mandy gently pushed my hip over.

"Let me help a little," she said. "It's a hard thing to do."

I burst into tears. "I don't want to be helped. I want to do it myself."

I never cried. I always kept up a good face but suddenly I had run out of masks. I knew how important this maneuver was because rolling in bed would help prevent pressure sores. I lay on my stomach and hid my face in my bent arms and sobbed. Mandy let me cry, then we moved on to something else once I had quieted down.

News of my reaction must have reached Dr. Newman because he ordered a new mattress for my bed. It was placed on top of the regular mattress and was made up of small (4 inch by 4 inch) cells. A motor pumped air into the cells. Half of the cells inflated for a few minutes, then deflated and then the other half inflated. This clever mechanism varied the pressure points against my body, even though I didn't move.

Although Mandy encouraged me, never giving up on my legs, my visions of walking down the hallway faded. There were no sudden changes. Moving one toe was a long way from standing on my own two feet.

We began again. With me lying on my back on the mat, Mandy placed a slippery board under my heel. I wore socks that would slide easily on the board. I was supposed to slide my leg out to the side and back. I concentrated, envisioning the movement. My neck muscles tightened. My shoulders hunched. I used every muscle in my body that I could muster. The first few sessions, my foot moved a few inches, while Mandy guided and helped me. 'If I can barely do this, how can I ever walk?' I thought. But I was determined and would not give up.

Mandy encouraged me to lift my heel up, just an inch up above the mat. When I couldn't do it, she said, "Here, start this way. I'll raise your heel and then you hold it up."

Success finally came, an inch at a time. We worked on tiny little leg movements, adding inch to each hard-earned inch. It didn't seem like walking, but I was heading in the right direction.

I needed to be able to stand if I was going to walk. With no leg muscles and very low blood pressure, this was not so easy. A medieval looking metal device, called a standing frame, stood near the middle of the gym. While seated in my wheelchair, a strap was wound behind my knees and another wider one behind my butt. Then I was ratcheted into a standing position, my knees braced so that they could not collapse. The first time I was cranked up was scary. The view from five feet high seemed new and expansive. I was held up for 10 seconds before being lowered back into the wheelchair. In time, I could stand for a minute or two. I found I had to distract myself by talking to Mandy, otherwise my head felt light and dizzy.

On one occasion, expecting the usual reaction, my head lolled and I said, "Mandy, let me down. I'm losing it."

It turned out my abdominal binder was not pulled tightly around me and as a result my blood pressure plummeted. After a rest, the binder was pulled tight. Then I could stand for a minute, like a trussed turkey. It was disheartening to think that I still needed all the leg wraps and binders in order to maneuver. Mandy told me my body would adjust. Naturally she was right but I was tired of waiting.

The last chart before my discharge from Scripps had an ominous notation – 'possible bladder infection.' I was unaware of the problem, but had been given Ciprofloxacin to treat the infection. Before antibiotics, many people who survived their spinal cord injuries died of pneumonia or bladder/kidney infections. As I write this, many bacteria are becoming more and more resistant to antibiotics.

One big problem was that my body no longer sensed the early stages of infection. I couldn't feel any discomfort or burning sensations from my bladder. I couldn't distinguish the early signs of a fever. My numb body no longer reacted to its own warning signals.

As it turned out, the indwelling catheter at Scripps had provided a ready pathway for bacteria to enter my bladder. The intermittent cathing, with sterile wipes and tubing was supposed to prevent this problem but the world is not perfect and the female anatomy makes bacterial contamination quite easy.

I was only dimly aware of the symptoms of a bladder infection and dismissed the problem as something that happened to other people. Then one afternoon, I started to feel hot and logy. I didn't want to move. By evening, I had a temperature of 104 degrees. The nurse at first admonished me for ringing her again, since she had just taken my temperature and it was near normal. When she saw the new reading, things changed in a hurry. A technician came and took blood. A portable x-ray machine rolled in and pictures were taken of my lungs. Another cath was done and the urine sample sent for analysis. The quick actions and especially the x-ray machine alarmed me. I knew something was seriously wrong but I felt so sick I really didn't care. I oscillated between being alarmed and feeling like maybe this was a way to just give up and die.

The next day I was weak and ill. I had been started on antibiotics the previous evening. The first antibiotics given are always a hopeful guess, since it takes the lab two and a half days to get test results on which drugs are effective. My physician friend Francene called. I told her I was sick and I didn't know what was happening. I said I wouldn't be much fun to visit.

"I'm coming," she told me. "I'm going to find out what's going on."

Francene arrived that evening. She had the nurse pull up all the test results on the computer, asked to have them printed out and brought the results to my room. She went over every parameter. We talked at length about bladder infections and my symptoms. From the data she determined the antibiotics were working. I would be fine in a few days. I was relieved at her analysis, especially since the hospital staff had kept me in the dark. This was at least the third time she had come to my rescue in the hospital. I felt so fortunate to have her as a friend.

Another evening, after my visitors had gone, my bed was lowered flat. I thought about the next day as I waited for sleep. Suddenly, I felt short of breath. Why did I seem to always get sick at night? I tried to draw air into my lungs but my diaphragm barely moved. I called for a nurse who listened to my wheezy voice and then called for help. The head nurse, who was responsible for all three shifts, was about to go home. She stayed to take care of me, first measuring my blood oxygen count, then taking my blood pressure and my temperature. As a precaution a cath was done and then a suppository and bowel program. Finally, I could lie flat and breathe. It turned out to be a simple problem. My abdomen had been too full. It had pushed on my diaphragm and my weakened muscles couldn't do a proper job of getting oxygen into my lungs. Since the protective mechanism of pain and sensations were gone, I had not gotten the proper signals from my body.

The lack of normal body-to-brain signals is a very serious problem for quadriplegics and paraplegics. It can lead to strokes and death. I found out during this period that when something went awry with my numb body, my blood pressure could rise rapidly. My body could react in this way to something as simple as a hangnail or as critical as appendicitis. This reactive high blood pressure and associated headache is termed "autonomic dysreflexia." Autonomic dysreflexia is quite uncommon (except in quadriplegics and paraplegics) and even most nurses are unfamiliar with it. During my second week at Sharp, the staff taught me about the problem and gave me an explanatory warning sheet to carry with me when I left the hospital. I now know that whenever my blood pressure rises rapidly, it is probably a sign that something else is wrong with my body.

I was scared and discouraged when all this happened to me. I realized I might suddenly become sick and quickly die because my health was so fragile. I wasn't afraid to die. It might even have been a relief, but I wanted to leave my affairs in order.

I had saved money over my entire working career. If I made it home and continued to recover I would need that money. I had a sketchy hand written witnessed will. I asked my good friend Jim to bring me a small tape recorder so that I could revise the will and create a trust. During the late afternoons, when it was quiet in my room, I dictated into the recorder. Eventually Jim took the tape to a trust specialist and turned it into an official document. I signed it with my new scratchy signature. I was relieved to know several charities that protected animals and open land would benefit when I died.

At this time, one of my tennis partners recommended I see a lawyer. The day the lawyer came I was in pain, scrunched up in my bed, trying not to move. He was able to ask enough questions to get the general facts about the accident. After he left he did some of his own research. When he came back, he said he was willing to take the case on a commission basis. I agreed. He returned with a written contract. It was a relief to know someone was looking into this horrific accident, which had effectively ended my previous life. Brian seemed serious, optimistic and sincere.

Although it felt good to have resolved my affairs, I was not optimistic about my future. I had always been a worker and not a quitter, but my condition was so fragile that I found it hard to hold onto hope.

Chapter Three

A Fighter Since Birth, My Early Years

MY MOTHER'S ABILITY to bear children was dubious. She'd had two miscarriages not long before her pregnancy with me. I was born six weeks early (on September 23, 1944) and faced an uncertain start as a premature baby. My 3 pound 12 ounces dropped perilously to 3 pounds one ounce.

My father took a picture of me being held by the delivery room nurse when I was three days old. The nurse was so impressed with my fighting spirit she sent him a letter about my delivery.

'When I saw her,' she wrote, 'I was certain that I would not need the crib after all, because Pamela was not only blue or purple – she was positively black! She seemed to not breathe at all.'

After delivery I was a fragile baby and had to be protected. My parents installed a large glass window in my nursery so friends could admire me through the glass. I am grateful for that early fighting spirit, because I believe it has been part of my ongoing will to survive.

My mother had two children from a previous marriage. She married my father Harry in the middle of the depression, August 8, 1933. Both Mom and Dad worked to become financially stable. My father had suffered a nervous breakdown but no one in the family, either then or now, seemed to know anything about his illness, although he had been hospitalized a few months. He was only recently released when mother began seeing him. My father had a quick but restless mind and he seemed unable to focus on anything for an extended period. He had trouble holding jobs and had spells when he was not functioning. During one long period he was fixated on photography, and during another he wouldn't go further than six blocks from our house.

My father was a handsome, charming, intelligent but strange, uneasy man. After World War II, he opened a used car lot and he spent hours there, doing everything himself. He acquired the cars, worked on their engines, sold them, and kept all the books. I never knew if the business was successful, or why he finally closed it down. Afterwards he worked for a nearby Oldsmobile dealer as head of the used car lot but that job lasted only a few years. Between jobs, he didn't work. My mother had to find office jobs to keep money coming. She often impressed on me the need to get a good education and be financially independent. It was a lesson I learned well.

My parents very much wanted to have children. They had purchased an unfinished bungalow in the northeast section of Baltimore, before I was born.

I was a sickly child during my early years, but a turning point came when I fell in the goldfish pond one cold spring morning. I was trying to push the grass mower, rocking it determinedly, backing it up, when I fell into the water. My mother saw it happen and ran out to get me. She swore that she had the clothes off me before the water had even reached my skin but shortly thereafter I came down with pneumonia. I didn't feel very sick and could revel in all the special attention I got. I stayed on a couch in the living room, sleeping, watching TV, and eating, for an entire week. Penicillin was ineffective so I was given the new drug aeromycin. That drug changed my young life. It ended for good the fight for survival that had occupied my first five years. I bloomed into a healthy, active, little girl.

Although I was short, very slight, shy, and unsure of myself around other children I became a tomboy. I loved jumping over hedges, climbing in a forbidden cherry tree, splashing in the sprinklers, hanging from the bars of a jungle gym and playing in the grass, dirt and mud. The five neighborhood children my age were all boys, so it seemed completely natural for me to run, jump, climb trees and play ball. My father encouraged my boyish activities and indulged me as his only child.

When some of the neighborhood boys picked on me, my father taught me how to box. He knelt down on the floor and told me to hit him with a pair of padded maroon-colored boxing gloves. At first I was reluctant, but when I realized I would not hurt him, I started to swing.

One chilly afternoon, I taunted the neighborhood bully. I urged him to come close and hit me or call me names to my face. When he did, I took one swing and hit him on the nose. My punch sent him running home with blood all over his face. After that, I didn't need to use my new skills again. I became a respected member of the neighborhood. My father was as proud as I was that I could take care of myself. I always felt best when I could say "I can do it myself."

I would use these words again and again as I struggled against paralysis.

My mother loved animals and shared this love with me.

I had many pets: parakeets, hamsters, ducks, chickens, turtles, gold fish, chameleons, frogs, Dutch rabbits, and white mice (up to 15 and all of them loose in the basement on at least one occasion!)

On the Saturday before my 13th birthday, I was visiting with 89-year-old farmer Crown, waiting for mother to pick me up. Mother sat smugly, as she called for me to come to the car. She had a surprise sitting in her lap - a gray fuzzy female miniature schnauzer puppy. I gathered the little dog up into my arms. She was all mine, and I immediately loved her. I named her Schotzie.

An amazing sequence of events began with this gift. A local breeder, Jeanne, agreed to help me learn to groom Schotzie and then show her. I showed Schotzie myself, from Connecticut to North Carolina. Either Jeanne or my mother drove to the show grounds. I got to see many new cities and places on the East Coast as I handled Schotzie all the way to her America Kennel Club championship. I also showed her at Madison Square Garden in the Junior Showmanship competition. Schotzie slept on my bed and stayed by my side. She was sweet, self-assured, and worshiped me. She and I had a special bond that was obvious, both inside and out of the show ring.

It was my father who first brought horses into my life. I was just four years old. His interest was in the racetrack, not riding and over an eleven years period, he owned several thoroughbreds. Although these horses were not of good stock, my father still fancied himself a horseman and loved spending time looking over racehorses and talking with trainers.

My father took me with him on one of his trips to the Hilltop Stable. He was going there to see a particular thoroughbred. The stable rented horses to the public, and also served as a lay-up place for racehorses that needed a break from the track. It was love at first sight. I immediately felt at home in this new place. The air was different, sharper and more pungent, filled with the smell of hay, new cut grass, and animal manure. My little girl visions of a perfect farm in idyllic surroundings materialized before my eyes.

Although he didn't ride himself, my father taught me to ride. His directions were simplistic: pull on the reins, say "whoa" to slow down, and kick with your legs to go faster.

That first day I was allowed to ride Rocky. He was a large old horse who could hardly walk. I rode him in circles in a small ring. I wasn't afraid to be sitting high up above the ground because I trusted this huge gentle creature to take care of me. I remember smiling in bliss as we went round and round. I still have a picture of me perched on top of him, in my plaid shirt, striped pants and black cowboy hat. I was exactly where I belonged.

After a short time I could ride around the ring by myself. My father then bought me a medium sized (14-hand*) pony, dark

---

* A horse is measured from the ground to the withers, the place where the neck joins the back. One hand is four inches, derived from olden days when farmers placed hand side-on-side to brown, named Skipper. In reality, the pony was too big and strong for me, but since he was mine I thought he was perfect. In fact he was cantankerous and mean. He couldn't be trusted and he didn't like to be ridden. His favorite trick was trying to scrape my leg against the fence but I easily lifted my short legs out of danger. He did throw me once though, high up in the air. When I hit the ground, I followed the emergency instructions my father had drummed into my head. I rolled and rolled to stay away from his feet. I rolled so far, I almost ended up outside the ring. I wasn't hurt or even scared. I was more afraid that I might not be allowed to ride again. Skipper went too far when he almost kicked my father's head. He was sold and I worried that I would not be taken back to the stable.

My father had seen my delight when I was near a horse and soon I had my first real pony. I named her Twinkle Toes because her light colored hooves shone in the sunlight. She was a brown and white pinto pony, 12 hands tall. She came with a black Western saddle and bridle. Her back was taller than my head when we first met, and it was a long reach from the ground to get up onto her but it was on Twinkle Toes that I learned how to ride. At first I was limited to riding in a ring while someone watched. Occasionally an adult would walk with me on a short ride through the narrow trails and tall trees. I learned to canter and ride securely, using my balance and quick reactions to make up for real skill. My father and I were probably closest to each other during this period.

When Hilltop Stable was crowded out by the sprawling city of Baltimore, my parents found the Crown farm not far from our house. Twinkle Toes was moved there. For some reason, my

---

measure a horse. Assumedly the width of the average hand is 4 inches. For further measurement, a hand is broken into inches, so that a 14.3 hand horse is 14 hands and 3 inches or a total of 59 inches (4*14+3.)

father no longer took me to ride. Now my mother did. I rode for many years at this 100-year-old farm.

I was allowed to ride on my own with an older girl on weekends. There were large pastures with narrow beaten tracks around the edge where we cantered and pretended to be competing in races. There were miles of trails through the woods. We would set up tiny brush obstacles and jumped over them, or stop and sit with our feet in a stream while the ponies grazed. In late spring, we carried paper sacks and picked wild blueberries. One year, a golf course closed down, and we got to ride on its grassy rolling hills, pretending we were surveying grand southern plantations.

When I was 12, the city was again closing in and the Crown farm had to move much further away. The new property was larger with 50 acres, two barns, three grassy rolling pastures, two streams and a pond all surrounded by forests of tall oak trees. Even though I only rode on weekends I felt like I was in a countryside paradise.

Due to my father's sporadic employment, my parents did not have enough money to keep Twinkle Toes. But she stayed at the farm for a while and I continued to ride her. During this time, Twinkle Toes had 3 babies. I loved each one dearly. Later, after Twinkle Toes was sold, I rode a pony that belonged to Minnie Crown.

His name was Mr. Rhythm. He was the largest horse I had ridden, standing at 14.2 hands. He was beautiful, with slim elegant lines and a sparkle in his eye, and I was the perfect size for him. Mr. Rhythm and I traveled many miles, up and down hills, and into the nearby river.

Though a teenager, I was treated as an adult who could deal with all the horse gear and horse dangers. I was trusted to behave smartly and take care of myself.

I felt very lucky to have had a pony of my own when I was so young. I realized having a pony was a special privilege and I knew my parents scrimped on their own pleasures to make me happy.

My father taught me how to read the racing form. I loved the numbers and the small print telling about each horse's past performances. I sometimes got to go to the track, even on school days. I studied each horse in a race, bent over the Racing Form, picking out a likely winner. I was fairly successful and people sitting nearby in the stands started to ask me for my choices. My logical mind enjoyed the challenge, and picking a winner was very exciting, especially if I had a $2 ticket on the horse! When our own horse's race came, I followed Dad to the paddock to see the jockey hoisted aboard. Mother sewed our racing silks, which were florescent pink with blue chevrons on each arm. I could spot those silks anytime, even from across the track, in a cluster of other horses. When our horse won, I ran with Dad down to the unsaddling area, and got to stand near the horse so our picture could be taken.

One winter, our racehorse, Fancy Dan, was stabled in the big Crown barn. He was getting old, and was recovering from a racing injury. I was warned to stay away from all the racehorses since they were unpredictable and dangerous. However, Fancy Dan had a wonderful personality and I knew he enjoyed any attention I gave him. I would often sneak into the stall to brush him. This rebellious act seemed not so bad to me, as I instinctively could tell that Fancy Dan was really a pussycat and safe to be around. One day when the adults were gone, I saddled him up and rode him around the barnyard. He was very tall as I sat high up on his back. I was a little afraid at first but Fancy Dan behaved perfectly. I never did tell my parents what I had done because I didn't want to be banned from riding.

Usually though I was very careful and tried to stay out of trouble. Like most riders, I had my share of accidents. I fell off numerous times over the years, was kicked and stepped on by horses. I simply pretended it didn't happen and tried not to limp or act injured. I didn't want anyone to worry. I wouldn't be put off by a little pain or a scary situation.

I did a good job of covering up the bumps and bruises. When I was 41, my horse Salty stomped on my right foot and I had it x-rayed. My arch was swollen and black and blue. I was concerned that I might have to limit my riding, and almost talked myself out of the ER visit. The emergency room doctor reported that the bone by my big toe was broken - he could see it clearly on the x-ray. Since Salty hadn't stepped anywhere near my big toe, some other horse stepping on me 30 years earlier must have made the break. The doctor was a bit disappointed that I didn't need treatment, but I was pleased to know how well I had done as a kid.

FROM THE BEGINNING, school was easy and I was a good student. I fell in love with algebra and I knew I wanted to continue studying similar subjects in college. Because of my love of animals, I also thought I might like to become a veterinarian.

In tenth grade I started a three-year College Preparatory Class. Eastern High School was an all-girls public school, located 8 miles from my house and I walked a mile to catch public transportation every day because I never wanted to miss a minute of my classes. There were no fluff courses. I studied English, Spanish, political science, history, mathematics, biology, chemistry and physics. I excelled in algebra, advanced algebra, plane geometry, solid geometry, trigonometry, analytical geometry and calculus and I graduated with an A average. I had little contact with boys during these years and didn't date or even go to my high school prom.

I knew my parents couldn't afford 7 years of college and vet school so I decided to major in mathematics instead. I wanted to go to Johns Hopkins University because of its good technical programs and high reputation as an engineering school. But no females were allowed in the regular 4-year technical curriculum.

I located Carnegie Institute of Technology (CIT), not far away in Pittsburgh. CIT lured me with Technical Drafting, Physics, and many Mathematics specialties and during my junior year of high school I applied to Carnegie and was accepted into the School of Engineering.

One year at CIT cost $2000, a huge amount of money but both of my parents encouraged me to apply. I naively assumed there was enough money for me to go to college.

I wanted to be able to take care of myself and not depend on anyone for my financial security. I was driven by this need and had confidence I could do anything I set my mind to do. I was issued a work permit at 15 and worked in a credit agency on Saturdays, and summers between my junior and senior year of high school.

Then the week I started my senior year of high school my father fell ill. He complained of chest pains and saw our family doctor, who did an EKG and exam. All the results were good so mother and I were relieved. But on a Saturday morning, my father still did not feel well. He told me he was going to go back to bed to sleep some more.

Later that morning, my mother was downstairs and I was upstairs in my room reading, when the phone rang.

Mother yelled up to me "Can you crack the bedroom door and tell your father that he has a phone call?"

I walked down the hallway and opened a narrow slit in the door, but after a few calls of "Dad, Dad, phone for you," when there still was no response, I yelled down to mother "He's not moving around. Should I go in and wake him up?"

Mother immediately ordered me to "Get downstairs and go outside. I'll take care of it," in a stern unyielding voice.

I stumbled down the steps in a daze and went out back, into the sunshine, thinking, knowing 'He's dead. What is going to become of us?' I knew that my father was dead. It was September 9, 1961; he was only 48 but he died from a massive heart attack. I was sad at his loss and afraid for the future. It was the first time my world turned upside down. Two weeks later I had my seventeenth birthday.

Suddenly the life I had anticipated was not to be, yet I never cried. Probably because I was afraid to let my emotions out. Although I was sad about my father, I was also mad at being abandoned by him when he should have been taking care of mother and me.

My mother was left to deal with my father's chaotic business affairs. He had excluded mother from any of the financial aspects of their marriage. Mother had not even written checks nor did she know how much money was in the bank. (Not much, as it turned out.) There was only one small life insurance policy. Mother arranged for us to live in my half-sister Lana's house. Mother used the life insurance to help with the remodeling. I became insecure about everything.

My immediate concern was college. My aunts, uncles and grandparents pressured me to go to work after high school, to help take care of mother. Fortunately, my mother did not agree. She wanted me to attend college and to live away from home while doing it. But with no money, I didn't know how this would happen.

I applied to University of Maryland and asked for financial aid. I also sent Carnegie information about my father's death and asked for financial aid. U. of Md. offered me a 4-year full scholarship but Carnegie responded by saying the School of Engineering was very competitive and I would have a better chance to receive a scholarship from the associated Margaret Morrison Women's College (M.M.) Margaret Morrison awarded a Bachelor of Arts in Mathematics, and had some classes in common with the School of Engineering. But I wanted a B.S. degree, not a B.A. from some women's college! Carnegie Institute of Technology still lured me. However, I applied to M.M., was accepted and offered a two-year scholarship of $1500 each year. Mother kept encouraging me to try for what I really wanted. I chose to attend Carnegie and M.M. Fortunately, I won an additional two-year scholarship of $500 per year from my high school, so the expenses of the first two years at Carnegie were covered. After that I would be on my own. I would then have to rely on working and government loans.

The summer after graduation, I moved with Mother into our remodeled quarters at Lana's house. Even though we had our own private rooms with a little kitchen and separate bath facilities, I was not comfortable in the house. For mother, it was a wonderful place, and I know she was happy there. She had family, her dogs and her garden. For me it always seemed like a temporary roost.

I worked full time that summer, saving every penny for college expenses. I did repetitive and boring tasks for a small manufacturer of cameras, monitors and other electronics equipment. I soldered resistors and capacitors onto printed circuit boards and when these were done, drilled holes into newly manufactured printed circuit boards.

When I headed off to college I felt very shaky. I knew the responsibility for my future rested on my own shoulders and I didn't know if I was up to the task.

In the fall of 1962, I arrived at CIT. I was enthusiastic about entering the college experience but I missed my mother, my two dogs, and my horseback rides around the countryside. There were no inexpensive and convenient places for me to ride in Pittsburgh but at least I could be with mother and my two schnauzers when I went home for holidays.

For me, being in M.M. was too much like attending high school. I longed for the more rigorous curriculum of the College of Engineering. The first day of analytical geometry (which I had already taken in high school) pushed me over the line. A small, dark Indian man started off with some equations on the blackboard. He intoned, "ve ned to scare the ixes". (With a thick accent, he was trying to say square the X's.)

In an act that amazes me in retrospect, I went to the registrar and totally rescheduled ALL of my classes. I signed up for Calculus I, Western Civilization, English Composition, Physics I, Chemistry I and Chemistry Lab with the students and teachers in the College of Engineering. I became one of twelve women in a freshman class of over 600 men. I was afraid but I plowed ahead anyway.

I worked very hard but the physics class was a thorn in my side. Everyone attended one large physics lecture session and then broke out into small sections to review assigned problems. My section was taught by an older man who ran his class like a military institution. Each student had to stand to ask or answer questions and always use "Yes Sir," "No Sir." On one occasion, when I was answering a question, the teacher's true prejudices came out. He said, "No girl should be taking up space in the physics class. You should be home where you belong." I cringed at his words and shrank back into my seat. I needed a B in order to maintain a required grade average and I wasn't going to get any sympathy from this teacher. A bad grade might mean I would lose my scholarship.

I spent outlandish amounts of time studying and working all the physics book problems, even the unassigned ones. The points I accumulated on homework assignments, the midterm and the final were enough to give me the B I needed. But the teacher gave me a C. Even the course professor would not override the grade. I learned life was not always fair and that prejudicial attitudes could win out over hard work.

I spent the long Christmas holiday at home, happy to have two weeks with Mother. I studied over the vacation and worked as well at a manufacturing plant. I was determined to get my education and knew I needed the extra income.

Finals were difficult and I needed a B- average to keep my scholarship. My first semester average was slightly below this, because of the C in Physics, but I made up the difference during the second semester.

My advisor was dumbstruck to learn that I was taking all my classes in the College of Engineering, but agreed that my scholarship would still be valid as long as my grades were up to the required minimum.

I worked in the office of an electronics company and saved all my money the next summer. My relatives had little schooling, and were critical of my attending college. Neither my mother nor father had graduated from high school. I was told a girl did not need a degree. I knew how unique my mother's attitude was and I appreciated how much she did to support me.

Over the summer, I had decided that I could get my degree a semester early by overloading one course each semester. I didn't leave myself much time to enjoy college but it saved me the cost of one semester.

In my sophomore year, my roommate Betsy started dating a graduate student in Chemical Engineering. She introduced me to his student helper, Ned Henline, a Chemical Engineering major. Ned was a sophomore and a 'commuter,' coming in for classes every day from a Pittsburgh suburb. We were both shy and quiet and he too was focused on getting a good education. We struck up a close relationship almost immediately.

Soon after our junior year began, we decided to marry. We picked out a small engagement ring and had it sized. I was very happy the night he slipped it onto my finger. Rather than make a big announcement, after getting back to the dorm for the 1:30 a.m. curfew, I was silent, but kept my hand in a prominent place. When someone finally noticed the ring, we all ran up and down the hallway howling in excitement. Mother had met Ned several times and was happy for me.

I was in love with Ned, and we planned to wed in January 1966, as soon as I finished all of my classes after the first semester of senior year. Ned would finish his classes a semester later in May. He wanted to stay at CIT and pursue a Ph.D. in Chemical Engineering. I would become the breadwinner. I looked forward to our being together and believed we would be happy.

I was trying in every way to earn money and be frugal. During my junior year I did clerical tasks and worked for an economics professor putting data into a computer program and processing the data.

The summer of 1965 I lived at home with Mother and worked while Ned worked in Ohio. Mother said I could have $1000 for the wedding and could keep whatever I didn't spend. Her gift spurred me on to plan a small no-frills affair. My roommate would be my maid of honor, and a friend of Ned's would be best man. I found a German baker who would make us a tasty but inexpensive wedding cake.

That summer I made my own wedding dress and several suits that I would need as a working woman. My mother was right there to help when I was having trouble with a difficult pattern. She had been making her own clothes my whole lifetime, including many of my clothes.

I made a full-length brocade wedding dress, with satin at its princess waistline and a flowing detachable train. I also made a blue satin bride's maid dress for Betsy.

I purchased invitations and addressed them all. Plans for the wedding were complete when I returned to school in the fall of 1965.

My last college semester seemed to be passing smoothly, with exams and then the wedding falling into place. Ned and I found a second floor flat that we would rent starting in January 1966. Never mind that it was upstairs from a Polish couple who cooked cabbage all the time.

It all ended with a crash in mid-January. Ned found me one day between classes and said his father had been taken to a hospital from his mechanics job at a bus company. We dropped everything and drove to the hospital. We waited silently with his mother. When the doctor emerged from between the double doors he said softly "I'm sorry." Our wedding was just a few days away and the atmosphere was filled with gloom. Ned's father was buried a week before our wedding. It was a horrible way to end my college career, and an even worse way to approach a wedding.

Except for Ned's mother, none of his relatives attended our small wedding in Baltimore. Snowflakes blanketed us as we drove away, headed for Pittsburgh. The next morning, at our overnight stop along the Pennsylvania Turnpike, the car had disappeared under a mound of clean white snow. Ned and I laughed and played baseball with a broom and snowballs before driving the rest of the way. I was happy and hoped the worst was behind us.

WHEN I FINISHED college, I was at the right place at the right time. I knew I didn't want to be a teacher, but I wasn't sure what I could do with a Bachelor's Degree in mathematics. I had taken two computer courses at Carnegie and I fell in love with the simplicity of solving a problem using a programming language.

Only a few large companies were starting to use computers and I was ready! I barely had to look for a job. With only two college computer classes under my belt, Alcoa Aluminum hired me as a programmer. My job was in the Economic Analysis and Development Department, which didn't give me a clue about my new work. I learned this was an operations research group that did the forecasting for sales and profits for all of Alcoa's products. Most of these predictions came from computer models. My male peers all had Ph.D.'s and had never worked with a woman. But they helped me learn to feed my punched deck of cards into the computer. The work was fun and I got paid to do it!

My mother was very proud of me. She stayed with Ned and me in our small apartment when she came to attend our college graduation ceremony in May 1966. We enjoyed this chance to be together again. I was quite sad when she had to return home.

I focused on my new career and started to pay off my college loans while Ned received a fellowship for graduate work in Chemical Engineering. With my job and his stipend, we had enough to make ends meet.

When opportunity knocks, open the door, my Grandmother Rokel would have said. I received a letter from Carnegie and was amazed to read that the Mathematics department was offering me a place in the Masters class, along with a teaching assistantship, starting September 1966. I hadn't even applied and here was this whole new opportunity to consider. Even though I liked my job at Alcoa I gave notice and entered graduate school in the fall.

I made the right decision.

Graduate work was much harder than undergraduate work and I felt the pressure immediately. My class was small, 12 students with only 3 women. I taught a recitation class of freshman Calculus twice a week and I was petrified my first day of teaching. My voice cracked when I realized that some of my students were older than I was. But I enjoyed passing on my love of mathematics and my self-confidence grew.

In November, my mother had gone with a tour group to Mexico City, and I looked forward to hearing all about her experiences when Ned and I visited her over Christmas. Because my own course load was heavy and the subjects difficult, I would have to do most of my work over the Christmas break, and during early January, just before finals. I had purchased presents at bargain sales, throughout the year, had everything wrapped and under our small tree in our apartment, just waiting to be transported to Baltimore for the holiday.

Then a bomb fell on Sunday, December 18. It was the worst day of my young life. Lana, my half-sister, called and told me our mother was in the hospital. She had just come out of the operating room and was not doing well. I raced home to Baltimore.

Lana drove me directly to the hospital from the airport. Mother was in the Intensive Care Unit. The nurse let me see her for just a few minutes. She looked terrible, with tubes everywhere and her skin ashen gray. But the worst thing was she smelled like she was already dead, a terrible sweet-sour odor of death. Her only words were "It's no good, it's no good. You take the elephant." I was almost sick sitting there next to her. When my time was up I staggered from the room, my stomach in a tight knot and my breathing shallow. It was to be my last visit with my mother.

The hereditary ailment, Raynaud's disease, ran in my mother's family. My Grandfather Rokel and Aunt Gertrude had it. I had seen mother's fingers turn totally white during cold weather or whenever she handled cold items from the refrigerator. It is a blood vessel disease that causes the small arteries of the hands and feet to contract suddenly, cutting off the blood flow. The return of blood to the fingers and toes is extremely painful. The lack of blood caused my mother to develop ulcers and later gangrene at the tips of her extremities. Several years earlier, she had undergone a sympathectomy, an operation where the nerves that control the caliber of the arteries are severed to lessen the pain. It had worked to relieve the pain in her hands.

Mother had entered the hospital in mid-December although she hadn't complained to me, nor mentioned any upcoming treatment before the Christmas holidays. Her doctor tried an experimental drug to help her symptoms. But it didn't work. Another sympathectomy (for her feet) was performed. Looking back, I think that the doctor made a bad decision. My mother began to bleed internally. By the time I saw her, she had already received 11 pints of blood. Her heart and body failed from the strain. Mother died soon after I arrived.

Ned drove down from Pittsburgh in time for the service, but even his arms around me didn't lessen the pain. My grief was overwhelming. I couldn't focus or think. She had been my best friend. She understood me down to my little toe, and now she was gone. I was unprepared for the emptiness that came over me with her death. The future looked blank and hopeless without her.

In less than eleven months Ned and I had lost two parents; only his mother remained. I closed down my mother's financial affairs, and painfully sorted through her things.

Four months after she died, I received a bright postcard, written in her distinctive hand. It had been mailed during her trip to Mexico.

It has taken me many years to deal with Mother's death. I miss her to this day. She left such an empty place in my life. I was used to thinking of her opinion, through her perspective. She was almost always in my thoughts.

I only realized later how angry I was at her for dying. I was disappointed that she didn't share her problems with me, that she hadn't given me any clue how badly she felt physically. I was mad because she wouldn't stop smoking, which would have helped her symptoms. I was disappointed that she couldn't describe her Mexico trip to me. All I had was her journal of the trip but reading it only caused me pain because she was gone.

Because of my auto accident, I am now very sympathetic to the emotions she must have been feeling at the end. When she said 'it's no good,' she knew her body was failing and she was going to die. I did 'take the elephant.' It is a yellow glazed statue, with a crackled surface, about 12 inches long and 14 inches high. It was a favorite piece of mine as a girl and I proudly keep it on display now. I consider myself blessed to have been loved so totally and unselfishly by my mother.

Ned and I drove back to our Pittsburgh apartment, to a Christmas tree with presents under it, still waiting to be delivered to my mother. I quickly unwrapped them, trying to keep the sobs from overwhelming me as I thought about what had not been. I had wanted to establish some small Christmas traditions for Ned and me, but for the next 5 or 6 years Christmas reminded me only of death and sorrow.

I couldn't study over that horrific Christmas break. I did the best I could, but everything was difficult. School seemed irrelevant. I received a B in three classes and one C.

One spring day, I opened a letter addressed to me from the Department of Mathematics. I wasn't surprised at its message. My assistantship would not be renewed. I needed to take at least two more courses, and possibly four, as well as write a thesis in order to receive a Masters degree. That would require another year in school and I just didn't have the heart for it and I couldn't afford to stay without financial aid. Even though my professors knew about the death of my mother, they apparently felt little sympathy.

I was forced into a new phase of my life. I found a job at Westinghouse Nuclear Energy Systems, in Monroeville, Pennsylvania, as a programmer. I worked in a department that kept track of the various pieces of equipment needed to build a nuclear power plant. Because I was on the ground floor of an exhilarating new field, there was a lot to learn. I began to enjoy the work.

When the department reorganized, I became a part of the corporate Management Information System. I wasn't sure what that meant, but then neither did my new boss, who knew nothing about computers. My group's job was to develop a system that would allow the computer to automatically generate all the paperwork needed to build a nuclear power plant. We had to develop a construction schedule, generate purchase orders and track the actual plant building. It was an extremely ambitious project. I attended a one-week course in COBOL programming and became 'an expert.'

Unfortunately, there was no way to make an expert out of my boss, so when the Mathematical Analysis department had an opening I applied there and was hired. My boss intervened saying the job I was working on was too important and I couldn't be transferred for several months.

Working with him was too frustrating. I finally said I would quit if I couldn't be released to the new job. Finally the higher-ups decided I could finish up some short-term tasks and transfer to the new group.

The move turned out to be a very important one in my career. The new department was composed of men with Ph.D.'s in Nuclear Engineering, most of whom had attended Carnegie. The group developed and ran various codes that analyzed what happened in the nuclear core of a power plant. A wonderful man, named Dr. Richard Evans, headed up the group. His soft voice made everyone feel good about his or her job, even though he spoke seated in a wheelchair. He had been injured as a teenager and was a paraplegic. Yet he had completed his doctoral work. He ran a large group, and he traveled extensively as part of the job. I never felt strange or awkward with him and have thought of him often since my own injury.

It was a relief to be so involved in my job and to forget some of the recent painful events in my life.

In the summer and fall of 1969, Dr. Evans and my supervisor urged me to finish my Masters degree. Ned would receive his Ph.D. in the spring of 1970. This meant there was only spring semester for me to complete my requirements before Ned and I would most likely move away from Pittsburgh. I didn't think I could finish in time. I needed two semesters of Complex Variables to fulfill the course work requirements, and I had to write a thesis.

As it turned out, the department had changed during the time I had been away. The thesis requirement had been dropped and the Complex Variable requirement was waived. I needed to take only two courses to complete my degree.

My employer, Westinghouse, paid my tuition and allowed me to attend classes in the afternoon. They kept me on as a full time employee, albeit with a slightly lighter workload. I am forever grateful for the support I received and the encouragement from my wonderful department.

I was awarded my Masters of Science Degree in Mathematics in June 1970. This opened up opportunities I would not otherwise have had as a young woman working in a man's world.

Ned finished his thesis in the spring of 1970. He applied for jobs far and wide, and accepted a position in Naperville, Illinois, a western suburb of Chicago.

I had a wonderful job in Pittsburgh that I didn't want to leave, but I also looked forward to moving on. Most of our friends still relied on parents for financial help, with money for a car or the down payment on a house, but there was no such luxury for us. We would have to make our way alone, with just each other.

Chapter Four

Pam Before – Early Jobs and Horses Reenter
My Life

DURING THAT FIRST month in our new home, when Ned and I moved from Pittsburgh to Chicago, I concentrated on getting us settled in, but I felt like I was standing still. One evening when Ned arrived home from work, he left a briefcase in one spot, shoes another, tie another, and jacket another. Even though he hadn't really made a mess, I felt like everything I had accomplished that day, namely having a spotless house with everything precisely in place, had been ruined. That's when I knew it was time for me to get back to work!

I had sent an application to Argonne National Laboratory (ANL) before leaving Pittsburgh, along with strong letters of recommendation. I wanted to work there. Argonne had a small group called the Code Center. They gathered programs associated with nuclear reactor analysis and made these programs available to other institutions.

Finally Argonne interviewed me and told me I could start work in the Code Center. Argonne did not usually hire people with Bachelor's degrees, so the effort I'd put in getting my Master's degree was already paying off. I loved the informal research environment at Argonne and was glad I had waited for the job.

After two years I applied for a position in the High Energy Physics Division which was even more interesting than my work in the Code Center. My immediate supervisor was Trish Jones, a woman near my age who had a M.S. in Physics. She helped me get my feet on the ground, learn the ropes and do the job. I became the division expert on using the local and remote computer systems.

I worked with the first remote terminals installed in our building. This was cutting edge technology at the time. Even so, I could enter 3 command lines on my terminal screen, get a cup of coffee and return to the terminal, long before the commands had been processed. Computers kept changing and I found I loved the challenges of the new technologies.

The Argonne site was about 1500 rolling acres, much of it covered with trees and woods. I didn't get much exercise sitting behind a desk so I decided to take fast walks at lunchtime, no matter what the season. I only stayed indoors during heavy rains.

In spring and summer, the area was beautiful and green. I walked a short ways across my parking lot to reach country-like grounds that reminded me of the places I had ridden on horseback as a teenager. My path took me across a bridge over a small stream and through dense woods on a narrow trail. From the bridge, I lingered in the sun, watching dragonflies defend their territory, perching on branches and then buzzing intruders, their iridescent colors glinting in the light. Sometimes I saw muskrats swimming silently, trying to be inconspicuous as they built mud nests along the edge of the water. Once I entered the woods, I was alone.

In fall, I would detour to the broad lawn with tall walnut trees. I picked up bags of walnuts from the grass and took them home to parcel out to my backyard squirrels throughout the winter.

In late fall, I sometimes came unexpectedly upon a white deer on the wooded trail. These deer had been introduced to the site and were quite numerous. The smell of a buck was strong, musky and thick. At this time, the males were aggressive and on the lookout for receptive does or other rival bucks. I retraced my steps rather than confront one.

Once it began snowing, I rarely saw anyone else, as the wooded path was hard to find. But I loved the serenity and new face snow put on the familiar place. My love for the outdoors came back to the surface and I found myself working with more enthusiasm after each short foray outside.

I never felt totally at home in Chicago. The weather was something to endure. The first winter, there was a week where the temperature fell to -25 degrees Fahrenheit every night. During that cold spell, either Ned or I went out in the middle of the night and ran the car engine to keep it from freezing up. Our townhouse had no garage. During the summer we suffered through one week where the temperature rose to one hundred degrees every day and the humidity was near 100 percent.

Eight months after moving to Chicago, Ned and I were able to purchase our first home. It was a nice three bedroom single story home with basement on a pretty wooded lot. My dogs could really stretch their legs here. By then I had several miniature schnauzers along with Buttons, my mom's West Highland White terrier. I put up a bird feeder in the back yard, kept a pair of binoculars on the windowsill and became hooked on bird watching. With my trusty Petersen's Field Guide I could identify most of the birds that stopped by for food.

I already was a confirmed animal lover, but one day while leafing through a catalog which arrived as bulk mail, I found a new exciting area to study and took a class in Ethology, the study of animal behavior. Animals were observed in the field rather than a laboratory. The class taught methods of field study. I watched videos and took notes on behavior every 3 minutes, developed behavior categories, drew diagrams and measured distances between animals. I was in heaven with this new discipline. I knew of Jane Goodall's work with chimpanzees and had even attended a lecture by her in Baltimore, so I was well inspired.

Best of all, the class included eight weeks of field study at the Brookfield Zoo. I considered either wolves or zebras, particularly since my knowledge of dogs and horses would help me. Zebras won out though because they were visible all the time and did not have dens or inaccessible areas. I looked forward to each Saturday of observation. I prepared a crock-pot of vegetables and beef to cook during the day, and then spent eight hours standing in front of the zebra enclosure. Male and female ostrich and sitatunga deer were also in the enclosure, so there were very few dull moments, at least to my mind.

I longingly thought about a new career in animal studies but I couldn't just drop my marriage and education for a totally new endeavor. I was too committed to my marriage to consider such a change.

Ned and I now had only one living parent, his mother Talia. Before I met Ned, Talia had a kidney removed because of cancer. Unfortunately, her cancer reoccurred while we were in Chicago. Ned flew home to see her several times and was with her when she died. When he returned to Chicago we were both orphans, on our own and alone, but together.

Then in May of 1972, Amoco sent Ned to Japan on a business trip. After three days, I found a local horse rental stable and called them. New riders were required to attend several sessions to assess their abilities. I made a reservation for the upcoming Friday evening.

As I arrived, the sweet smell of hay and the sound of moving horses energized me. I had not been on a horse for almost ten years. My mount was well behaved as we walked, trotted and cantered, and even jumped over small obstacles about 18 inches high. Five women about my age were riding. They were regulars and made me feel welcome. I became one of the Friday night regulars and a member of the ladies social group. We went to a late dinner after every riding session at a nearby restaurant or at one of our homes.

There is something about communicating with a horse, which I needed. This contact I had with horses was so different from my technical world of scientists and computers. Riding became very important to me.

I had learned to ride mostly by balance and had no formal training. I had jumped over little logs on my ponies but nothing more than that. In Chicago I developed new riding skills. I learned to do a sitting trot, very quietly, with no bouncing. I learned how to feel the horse's movement with my seat, to post on the correct diagonal and to cue the horse into cantering on the correct lead. I grew more confident at jumping and sometimes rode the horses that were difficult to jump, with good results.

Some of the ladies in my riding group decided to travel to San Miguel de Allende in Mexico. (We took trips in 1973, 1974 and 1975.) Howard Black's Esquela Equestre had about 20 horses and former members of the Mexican cavalry taught lessons there. We stayed at the Atascadero on the hillside outside the city. The hotel had many rooms, with one wing clustered around an inner courtyard. Green grass and exotic bird-of-paradise plants were just outside. The sun beat down in the high desert atmosphere. It was a wonderful contrast to Chicago.

Mornings started with an hour long lecture on aspects of riding and horse care. I had never heard of dressage (from the French, meaning "to school"). The horses at the Esquela knew basic dressage movements. They responded to very small commands to walk, trot and canter. They also had been trained to do a few maneuvers such as shoulder-in and half pass, where the horse moves and bends his body. With dressage, I could be a partner with a horse, doing elegant movements. I discovered I had a knack for it. When shoulder-in was demonstrated by one of the instructors, it was like a light turning on. I immediately got my mount to perform the movement smoothly and easily. (Of course, it helped that the horses already knew what to do!) At the Escuela, I learned to do shoulder-in, haunches-in, turn on the forehand, flying changes of lead at the canter, and we all watched the head instructor do piaffe and passage.

We also jumped in our morning session, did some drill team riding and went for a trail ride, with the Mexicans carrying side arms! After a large late lunch, if we still had any energy left, we could ride some more. Afternoons were a bit more casual, and we tried our hands at vaulting onto a horse as it circled a person controlling him with a long line. I was limber and light, and could easily vault onto the cantering horse. We also jumped over obstacles bareback with our hands raised out to shoulder height, sliding around on the slick hair. Sometimes we tried our riding seat on the rope-strung bucking barrel with a teacher at each end, trying to shake us off. In the late afternoon, after siesta, we usually walked into town and browsed the shops, returning for a late dinner. It was pure bliss.

These three trips developed my deep commitment to riding, horses, and dressage. Little did I know how much this training on horseback would mean to me years later when I was paralyzed.

ON THE EVENING of August 26, 1996, I kept my eye on the TV. I shushed the visitors in my hospital room as the introduction for Christopher Reeve began. As he rolled out to the microphone at the Democratic presidential convention, I held my breath. I now knew a lot about the problems he faced every day and I was awed by his courage. I had even dictated a note to him, telling him how much I admired him and how happy I was to see him out in the world, fighting for all of us with similar injuries. His efforts may actually lead to treatments or therapies, which can help me and others like me. In November I received a short personal note from him, with the annotation '(Dictated).'

> *Thank you for sharing your personal experience with me. You know firsthand the challenge one must meet when faced with a serious health problem. I truly appreciate you sharing your story with me and your show of support at this time in my life.*
>
> *I wish you well and truly appreciate you taking the time to write to me.*

The other thing I had in common with Christopher Reeve was our love of horses. Seeing him on TV and knowing the history of his struggle after his riding accident, made me think about the first horse I purchased all for myself.

My trips to Mexico had developed my deep commitment to riding, horses, and dressage. In 1975 I started to read advertisements and contact barns and trainers in western Chicago, looking for a horse to purchase. Most horses were easy to eliminate with just a cursory look, but on July 6, 1975, at a barn that trained horses to jump, I found a horse that almost perfectly fit my bill. I was shown Salty by the stable hand, Joe. Salty was a quiet animal. He had been trained in just the basics of walk, trot and canter and would jump over a low pole. I went back to see him another time, unexpectedly and with friends, so that I could see him in the barn, being saddled and handled. (This would eliminate the chance that he had been worked very hard earlier or had been given drugs to make him appear quiet and calm.) He appealed to me partly because of the kind expression in his dark eyes. Even though he was expensive, I made up my mind to get him.

What I didn't know was that horse stables and hunter jumper shows in the Chicago area were often associated with the Mafia. On occasion when the 'wrong' horse was winning a competition, that horse might be found the next morning with a broken leg. The people in the business could be very cutthroat. A friend who owned several horses told me to be wary of everyone. I talked to Salty's handler, Joe. I had seen Salty's original registration papers as a thoroughbred (i.e. race horse) to be sure he was really registered and then I offered to purchase him contingent on a successful veterinary exam at the Naperville clinic. I knew that only a vet representing me would give a fair examination of the horse.

People at Salty's barn had told me Salty was being trained for a career on the racetrack. I knew that racehorse training started when the horses were about eighteen months old. I also knew that the hunter jumper barn was not equipped with tracks and starting gates needed for young racehorses. Joe told me I could use any vet except the Naperville Clinic. I finally said "no deal," even though I really wanted Salty. I was very wary of the whole situation.

Joe called me a few days later and said that I could use the Naperville clinic. Rumors were afloat that Joe's barn was in trouble with the IRS. I suspected the owners needed money. I wrote up a very explicit pre-purchase agreement, made a down payment and Salty was taken to the clinic for examination on July 14. The vets did their usual tests, including leg x-rays and a blood screen for drugs. Salty came up clean. The vets also thought he was suitable for dressage work. I had myself a horse!

Joe delivered Salty to his new home at Rock Ridge stables on July 24. A short time later, Joe disappeared. Then shortly after that, the IRS raided the barn where Joe had worked. Fortunately for the horses, they were all moved out the night before the raid occurred. I was worried about my marginal dealings with the Mafia. All I wanted was to have a nice horse of my own.

On August 19 I received a certified letter from a Mr. Earl Winnor. He wondered if I knew anything about his horse Hightop Grey, who had been stolen from him by his horse's trainer. If I had Hightop Grey, would I bring him back? Hightop Grey was the registered name of Salty. I had had his thoroughbred registration papers signed over to me. I didn't know how Mr. Winnor got my address, but I knew I didn't want to talk with him. I was suddenly afraid that Salty might be stolen from me if his whereabouts were known. I took the letter to a lawyer, who did a little research in antiquated horse laws and found out when an owner gives original registration papers to a trainer, and the trainer is selling horses, the trainer has carte blanche in all transactions. My lawyer wrote to Mr. Winnor telling him to deal with the trainer for any criminal acts. Nothing was said about my owning the horse or where the horse might be. I heard nothing more. What I think happened is that Mr. Winnor hoped I was some naïve young woman and he could get back the horse and still keep my $3000 purchase amount. As it turned out, the large barn and breeding facility Mr. Winnor owned burned down within a month. Rumors flew that the place was heavily insured.

Even though Salty was a light gray color, not the brown or black I had originally envisioned, I loved every inch of him. I spent endless hours brushing and currying his soft summer coat, cleaning his feet and combing his mane and tail. He was a rambunctious, energetic horse and quite a handful for me.

Five weeks later on August 31, I learned a hard lesson of horse ownership. My brand new horse was hurt. Salty was very lame on his left hind leg, and the hock joint (equivalent to our elbow joint) was swollen and hot. On Sept 11, a friend trailered Salty back to the Naperville Clinic. The vets diagnosed a pulled peroneus tertius tendon in the left hind hock. The treatment was rest, cold soaks and lots of hand walking. Over the weeks, as I walked him, it was difficult to keep his feet on the ground because he had so much pent up energy. It wasn't until November 1 that I was able to ride him again and an additional six months before Salty was totally sound.

By this time, Ned had become involved with aerobatic airplanes. After a few flying lessons, he went on to get his private pilot's license. Then after lessons in a dual biplane, he had purchased a single seater Pitts aerobatic plane.

The horse and airplane activities were expensive, but we still were able to save money and were not living above our means. We were very focused on our careers and were not thinking about having children yet. Our marriage seemed stable. We enjoyed activities together, and also had our separate interests. Each winter we traveled to a western ski area and enjoyed a week of good snow and steep slopes. In the summer Ned ran, while I often accompanied him on a bicycle.

Although I hated giving up my job at Argonne, when Ned decided to take a job with Rockwell International in Canoga Park,

California, a suburb of Los Angeles, I was pleased. I was more than glad to move my horse away from Illinois where I would not have to worry about the Mafia.

Los Angeles seemed quite exotic to me. Moving was complicated since we had to locate a place for my dogs, ourselves and an airfield and hanger for the Pitts. I also needed a stable for Salty.

The airplane was flown out to a hanger at the Santa Paula airport, a small facility in Ventura County. Salty was shipped several months later to a nice stable in Canoga Park, in the San Fernando Valley. We rented a small three-bedroom house in Simi Valley where I could have my dogs.

I began looking for a job, but with little success. The economy was very slow early in 1976. I scanned the newspaper everyday for the names of any company that could use programmers. I sent out resumes. I visited nearby offices and filled in applications. There were no jobs.

I had no friends, and very little to do. When Salty arrived, looking a little bedraggled, I was very happy to see him. He neighed and was calmed by my presence, once he came off the van. He had broken his halter during the four day trip, and cut his right ear, which was bloodied and had a nasty looking sore. The vet cleaned the wound and Salty got some antibiotics. He ended up with a notch in his right ear for the rest of his life.

I met a new friend, Doreen Thayer, at the Canoga Park stable and we took to each other right away. She helped me develop an 'eye for dressage,' the skill of recognizing when movement and paces were done correctly by the horse.

I loved the weather in Los Angeles. The sky was a brilliant cloudless blue every day. It was a great place to get into dressage, since there was so much related activity nearby. I was familiar with many dressage movements based on my stays in San Miguel de Allende, but I had to learn all about tests and levels. I took dressage lessons at my stable then rode Salty in a schooling show, doing two Training Level tests. (A dressage test is similar to the compulsory figures that used to be required in figure skating. Each test consists of a series of different movements and figures, done at the walk, trot or canter. Training Level tests were the easiest. The tests become more difficult as they progressing through First, Second, Third and Fourth Level.)

At the Bell Canyon show grounds, I entered Salty in a class that judged his suitability for dressage. I also rode him in a class where my potential as a dressage rider was judged. I was thrilled when I received two blue ribbons. This confirmed my desire to learn as much dressage as possible with Salty.

The Los Angeles area was a hotbed of new interest in dressage because Hilda Gurney, who lived in the San Fernando Valley, had won team gold and individual silver metals in the 1975 Pan American Games on her horse Keen. At the Montreal Olympic Games in 1976 the pair placed fourth individually and helped bring home the team bronze. I was fortunate enough to take lessons from her, and share in the excitement of this growing sport. I watched her ride her thoroughbred horse, Keen, at local shows.

Doreen and I took our horses to a few shows together. After one long rainy week, when we hadn't been able to ride much due to slippery footing, we headed up to Arroyo Grande, about five hours away, using Doreen's truck-trailer rig. We had arranged to stay at a private stable and were almost there around midnight, on a very dark night, but near the top of a steep and slippery hill, the rig just didn't have enough power to make it. We unloaded two jittery horses using flashlights, and led them about a half mile to the stable. We retrieved the trailer later, when it was empty and could make it to the barn. It's a wonder we survived.

Our show rides weren't particularly good that weekend as neither horse was in the mood to listen. Both had too much extra energy. Before returning home, we pulled into a quiet spot near Pismo Beach and unloaded the horses, anticipating a trail ride on the dunes and beach. The white sand looked very inviting and we led the horses to some deep soft spots. Both of them lay down, rolled, and wallowed in the sand, enjoying the opportunity to scratch their itchy skin. After brushing them, we saddled up and rode South in the dunes just back from the water. Both horses were frisky, but the deep footing and sand mounds calmed them down. It was a wonderful ride in the sun and when we turned back towards the trailer, we rode on the flat hard sand of the beach. Both horses behaved, ignoring all the cars, trucks, and people who were traveling along the beach. Neither horse particularly wanted to get in the water, since they were afraid of the breaking waves. When the horse trailer came into sight, both horses nickered and recognized it as their homeport. The weekend was my first long excursion with Salty and the ride along Pismo Beach was one of the most memorable rides of my life.

Ned continued his interest in airplanes and aerobatics. He sold the first plane and began to build a more powerful Pitts Special from a kit. I preferred the peace and quiet of riding my horse and having four feet on the ground. Salty and I were a perfect team.

Chapter Five

Life Away from the Hospital – Going Home

THE SHARP REHAB facility had a large training room equipped like any regular kitchen - sink, stove and refrigerator. However the counters were lower than in most kitchens and the bottom cabinets had pull out shelves so we could reach inside and get things from wheelchair level. It was given a homey feeling by the addition of curtains on the windows. We five women gathered there in our wheelchairs one afternoon to make chocolate chip cookies, although I have to admit the therapist did most of the work. She had already started the oven, assembled all the ingredients and the utensils when we arrived. We were to do the measuring and mixing. We took turns stirring the batter. I had to wedge the bowl between my legs and a cabinet and then use both arms and both hands to turn the spoon. When it came to adding the egg, we all looked to Lisa. She was the only one among us who even had a chance of getting just the egg, no shell, into the bowl. She hesitated, then held the egg and gave it a great whack against the bowl. She managed to get most of it into the cookie mixture. We all cheered. We struggled to stir in the egg and the chocolate chips, working as a relay team, passing on the bowl when our arms got tired. The therapist helped get the pan in and out of the oven. The smell was tantalizing. It was the first time any of us had sniffed a just-baked item since our accidents. As the chocolaty scent drifted out into the gym, the staff showed up to share in the spoils.

One afternoon, Jared Bend, a recreation therapist at Sharp, had us gather in front of a TV set. Jared had been a quadriplegic in a manual wheelchair for over 20 years. He always seemed to be in motion. His cheery 'How are ya!' never changed. He was an inspiration because he loved life. He wanted us to see other quads doing interesting activities. The tape he ran for us showed men wind surfing on special boards and water-skiing. Another segment showed a man bouncing up and down rough trails in a special 4-wheel all terrain vehicle. These people were enjoying themselves and it was amazing to watch. I was sure I would never be able do these strenuous activities. Instead, I wondered if I would ever be able to master the VCR machine as adroitly as Jared did.

Because I had always looked at people in wheelchairs with pity and didn't see disabled people as individuals, I assumed everyone would look at me the same way. Facing the world therefore was frightening. I didn't want to expose myself to the stares of strangers, their heads turned away pretending they didn't see me, making me feel like I was not a part of the human race. It was easier for me to stay safely hidden inside the hospital.

But we had no choice. We had to go out and face the world. It was inevitable and necessary. Our initial outing was the movie, "First Wives Club." It was also our first time sitting on a wheelchair lift attached to a van. My power chair, with me in it, weighed about 300 pounds. The mechanism slowly hoisted me up. It was also my first car trip since the accident and I was nervous, especially when the van got close to large trucks or busses.

Our recreation therapist purchased the movie tickets while the five of us tried to remain anonymous, huddled together in our wheelchairs. I was glad to get into the dark theatre, where no one would be able to see me. Accommodation had been made for wheelchairs but talk about bad seats! Our chairs were wedged against the back wall. Still the movie was fun and it was wonderful to forget about my condition and just laugh. When we returned to the hospital, it was dark outside. I realized the hospital had become the only place I could live without fear. I had enjoyed the movie and going out, but I was glad my existence had been cloaked by darkness. I hoped no one had noticed me.

Our second trip took us to the organ pavilion at Balboa Park for a free public concert. The afternoon was perfect, mild and clear. Sun filtered down through the trees surrounding the band shell. The manicured lawns of the park were deep green, filled with picnickers and couples holding hands. The seating area at the pavilion had rows of long park benches, overflowing with young children, parents and the elderly. The air had the feel of a holiday celebration.

We unloaded from our vans about two blocks from the pavilion. We made a somber procession, in our black wheelchairs. I didn't want all of those people to see me. I feared I might inadvertently bump into someone with my heavy power chair. I knew that children could sometimes be especially cruel. They might make fun of me, or call me names.

Fortunately, Jared Bend led us down the long center aisle. He did wheelies in his chair and gave all the kids the high-five. By doing so, he provided the icebreaker we all needed. After his antics, I was able to relax. I enjoyed the music from the huge pipe organ as it vibrated through the air. I even managed to smile and say hello to a few people.

Once back in my room though, I cried. I wanted to be like all those other normal people. I wanted to be like I used to be. Life was so easy for all of them. Why was I the one who had to be trapped in my body, injured beyond my worst imaginings? I remembered a young woman who had jogged by the pavilion. That should have been me, but never would be. Pam was dead. The person I knew, the person I had been for 51 years, was gone. It felt like I died just then and I cried for the person I would never see or be again.

Still we had to go on – keep learning, keep trying, keep living. Our last outing was to a nearby Italian restaurant. Friends and relatives accompanied some of the other patients. Trish, who was in a large power chair, couldn't even get in the front door and had to go past the dumpsters and trash cans to enter through the kitchen. We were gathered around a large round table, our wheelchairs dominating the room. I felt very conspicuous. But the food was a nice change from the usual hospital fare. I was proud of myself for handling my own fork and eating unaided. At least I could take care of myself after someone had helped me put on my U-cuff and had cut up my food for me.

But again I was even more relieved to return to the hospital. Everyone knew me there. I didn't have to worry about insensitive stares. In the hospital I knew how people would react to me and how each day would unfold. There were no unexpected hurdles. It was a safe place but I couldn't stay there forever, even though I wanted to.

I seemed to be the only one desperately afraid to leave the hospital. Then a wonderful thing happened. My nieces, Emma and Sally, children of my half-sister Lana and only a few years younger than I was, announced they were coming to see me. I felt a totally new feeling when they arrived; someone had come to take care of me, family who would not abandon me. I realized that I had done a pretty good job of holding myself together in the hospital alone but I saw that the other ladies had many of their fears relieved by loving relatives.

Emma and Sally were concerned about my return home, and also about the placement of my animals, since they realized how important this was to me. I had not found permanent homes for the dogs, cats or for my horse, Ameego.

Emma fell in love with my little Lakeland Terrier, Whisper. I knew how charming he could be, with his sleek body and his ability to curl up like a little leaf in your lap. I was happy to let Emma take him home with her to Baltimore.

Shadow, my special rescued dog, my one-quarter wolf dog, was another problem. She needed frequent dips for her skin and antibiotics when the infection got out of control. But we had been through so much together, I felt I couldn't abandon her. Suddenly, it flashed through my mind that some friends had a place near the stable, and a fenced yard for their two Rottweilers. I knew I was asking a lot, but I called Marilyn from my hospital bed. I expected her to defer, wanting to check with her husband.

Instead she said, "Pam, certainly, we'd be glad to take Shadow for you. There's plenty of room and you can come and visit her."

I wanted to hug her over the phone.

Then a riding friend agreed to keep my golden retriever, Jordan, along with her King Charles Spaniel. Jordan was always the perfect dog, a gentleman with impeccable manners. His stay with my friend would be temporary, as I wanted to have him with me when I went home.

I got an idea about Ameego. He had been bred and raised by the woman I had bought him from. When I purchased him at age five, she had been embroiled in a divorce and didn't have time for a second horse. But that was 10 years ago. I had seen her occasionally when I rode Ameego as she kept a horse in a corral just down the hill from mine. When I reached her on the phone, she instantly said that she'd be happy to take Ameego back and she didn't want any money to take care of him either. In fact, she said she would purchase him from me, which she did a few days later, for one dollar.

All these arrangements happened in about a week. I couldn't believe that all my animals (Whisper, Jordan, Shadow and Ameego) would be in good hands. Before returning home to Baltimore, Emma and Sally brought all three dogs to the hospital courtyard. I sat in my wheelchair and felt so happy to have them lick my hand. It was such a relief to me that I did not have to abandon them because of my awful situation.

My two cats were fine and were being fed at my house. The house sitters moved out after the dogs found their new homes, but someone continued to stop by and leave food for the cats.

I had to focus on my future. I felt very unsure about my ability to play a part in determining my own fate. Circumstances seemed to flow around me, sweeping me toward eventual release from the hospital.

Much of the time I felt like Humpty Dumpty when he fell, the pieces left on the ground. I had felt like a hollow shell when my marriage broke up, but this time I couldn't be glued back together. I thought of myself as 'not real.' I wasn't sure exactly what that meant but I felt I was not a whole person anymore. Pieces of me were missing. I couldn't function or live without enormous amounts of help. It seemed all my relationships with other people were overwhelmed by my disability. I was no longer an attractive, self sufficient, interesting female member of the human race who could live and move around on her own.

Then one evening in my hospital room I got help from an unexpected place.

At General Atomics, everyone who swam, ran, biked, played tennis or did some physical activity kept track of one another. I had seen Jeff near the locker room many times. He was well built, athletic, slim and good looking. We had done walks together, when he was recovering from a virus and I was dealing with a troublesome back.

One evening, he arrived in my hospital room without warning.

"Pam, what are you doing here like this? Let's get going," he said.

Being firm, but also gentle, he pulled me forward and kissed me. He kissed me deeply, probing my lips with his tongue, with desire and sincerity. I was suddenly transformed to another place. I felt emotions rise in my throat as I enjoyed the kiss. It was a revelation to me that someone could desire me and my miserable body. Jeff was not making some inappropriate pass at a helpless hospital patient; he was breathing life back into my soul. He knew it too. Those few short moments are etched deeply in my memory. Maybe I wasn't a real person yet, but I was getting there.

This thought fortified me as I faced another difficult relationship problem.

There had been other relationships since Ned – one lasting for ten years – but none of them worked out. A more recent gentleman friend, Henry, appeared in my room one day. I was so scared of being alone. I was wary of the problems Henry and I had when we dated before my accident. When Henry offered to move back in with me if I married him and gave him $10,000, my decision was easy. I was sad to see him leave, but I needed to be in control of my own destiny. I would find a way to do it alone.

BOTH MY OCCUPATIONAL therapist and physical therapist visited my home, to see what modifications it would need for me to live there. Fortunately, my house was on a single level, with wide doors and a wide hallway. Most of the outside doors would work with just a small ramp. The exception was the eight-inch step in the garage. The bathroom would also be a problem, but the master bath could be transformed with a roll-in shower. Jim worked on some of the preliminary plans for that modification.

It would be necessary to hire people to live with me and care for me 24 hours a day. I had no insurance to cover this expense. People who were hired through an agency cost between $10 and $30 per hour. That could amount to more than $262,000 per year, much more than I could pay. I needed to find individuals who could work directly for me.

I had interviewed many job candidates at GA and was usually pretty good at assessing someone's personality and capabilities. Except now I felt overwhelmed. Getting it right was a matter of my life or death. The situation became more pressing as my discharge time approached.

Dr. Newman delayed my release so that some more intensive therapy could be done on my legs. The insurance company extended my time a mere five days, giving me a little more breathing room to find help.

The word went out for help over the Internet. Someone heard about my plight, and sent information about a nurse who might be interested in the position.

Darlene's nursing credentials were up-to-date but she was not currently employed. She was taking a break from the emergency room and said she would love a job like mine. She could work seven days a week, for a reasonable fee plus room and board. Her friends in San Francisco gave her a very good recommendation.

She drove to San Diego and, after an interview, I told Darlene I wanted to hire her, but would first want to validate her nursing certificate and check references. A few phone calls later, when everything checked out, she seemed the perfect solution to my predicament.

Jim had already started putting my house in order. I arranged for Darlene to meet him there. The house hadn't been properly cared for since the accident. Cindy, who had house cleaned for Jim, would put things in order. Cindy had been dependable in the past, in spite of an earlier problem with drugs. The house wasn't really ready for Darlene yet, but she said she didn't mind sleeping on the couch and she even volunteered to help with the cleaning chores.

In the middle of all this activity I had my fifty-second birthday. I was so worried about going home that the event seemed insignificant. I didn't want to celebrate being alive in my condition. I had always envisioned growing old in a stately, active, energetic way. There were mountain trails and open deserts I had wanted to explore and since I had been taking good care of myself, I felt like I had earned this vision.

But at this point I saw myself in a wheelchair, like a cougar in a cage, eyeing territory he no longer could reach. Living was an effort. Every day was a physical and emotional struggle. Seeing normal people tantalized me with their easy movements and their under-appreciated abilities. I hoped no one would remember my approaching birthday.

But they did.

I don't know who the ringleader was but at 7 p.m. on the evening of September 23, a secretary from work marched into my hospital room, carrying a cake with candles. Twenty other people followed her.

It was nice to be remembered. Cards and a few small packages landed on my bed. A plate with cake appeared in my lap. I was sitting in bed with the head raised, a task I could now do myself. The plastic fork was light and so I could eat my cake myself, with no help and no U-cuff. I was pleased to share my accomplishment with so many friends. But I knew that by the next day the problems of going home would resurface.

Suddenly life seemed to be going very fast and everything felt out of control. Jim had gone to a few neighbors, to let them know about my accident. He told them new faces might be seen going in and out of my place. My neighbor Eva, who I knew only slightly, had offered to keep an eye on the goings on at my house. She came to visit me in the hospital. We had barely known each other before the accident.

Just before I was due to come home, Eva went over to check on things one afternoon. She knocked on the door but when no one answered she looked through the window and saw Darlene lying on the couch. No amount of knocking or calling seemed to get a rise out of her. Darlene appeared groggy. She'd heard the noise but didn't react. Both Jim and I suddenly suspected Darlene was using alcohol or drugs. Later, when we questioned her, she said she was really sleepy and hadn't slept well the proceeding night. She seemed fine by then, and told us she didn't drink or use drugs. I asked her to do a drug test and she consented.

Jim and I decided a quick, unannounced trip to my house might be a good strategy. Just before my departure, the doctor gave his OK. Jim bumped my manual wheelchair up over the small step at the front door and pushed me rapidly from room to room. It was impossible to tell if anything was gone because so much was moved around for the cleaning. The house felt strange to me but Darlene seemed all right.

I would be going home for good in three days. A hospital bed was ordered, a portable potty, and a shower bench. I was fitted for my very own power chair. I wouldn't be getting one that automatically reclined (too expensive for the insurance company). A more portable manual chair, I would have to purchase myself. I was fitted for it and Sharp lent me a manual wheelchair until mine could be delivered. Arrangements were made for a nurse to come to the house several times to see how I was doing.

The bright light in all this was that Emma, my niece, was going to come to California and stay with me for a week while I got settled into a routine. My release was scheduled for September 27, a Friday. I don't know how I would have faced that day without her by my side.

I discussed my hesitations about Darlene with Dr. Newman saying, "Suppose she isn't dependable. What happens when it comes time for a cath? I can't do anything."

"That would be a problem," he said, "what with the risk of dysreflexia and high blood pressure. You would have to go to an emergency room, and that would take time. Perhaps the best thing would be to send you home with a foley indwelling catheter until you know how everything works out."

I was worried about overall care, in particular the dreaded bowel program. Then two of the male aids, Tad and Mike, agreed to come to my house for two hours each evening to take care of this procedure. One or the other would come, depending on their schedule at Sharp. This would give me a chance to see how Darlene worked out.

On Friday Jeff brought his pickup truck, to take me and all of my accumulated possessions home. I would have to return to receive occupational and physical therapy as an outpatient. But I was going home to live, after being in the hospital for 82 long days. I was afraid and wary but I thought I could make it.

I expected to feel a sense of comfort when I was pushed through my very own front door but instead I felt like I was walking into a stranger's house. "Oh no," I moaned, "where is everything?" I didn't even realize I was holding my breath and turning a pasty gray color as I looked around.

It seemed that every piece of furniture was moved or missing. Pictures hung in strange places and many were sitting on the floor stacked against the wall.

Cindy had done her house cleaning magic, but to me, it was distressing. She had rearranged the furniture in the family room so that half of the room was totally empty. The front hall seemed desolate. One living room wall had been a carefully arranged collage of pictures and paintings but now only a few of the paintings were up. Everything was out of kilter.

I knew it would be hard to come home, but I thought I knew what to expect. It took me 6 or 7 months to find a foot-high doll my mother had crocheted which used to sit on my bureau. Also missing was a small doll Mother made for the top of my Christmas stocking, the white lace dress draped around the side of the sock. A beautiful multi-color blue hand hooked wool rug that she made me disappeared and was gone forever. These missing things upset me when I needed my mother's comforting memory most.

To Cindy's credit the house was clean and as it turned out, the large empty space in the front room was a perfect place for my hospital bed. Placed in the center of the house I could be part of daily activities. On the tile floor, I had enough strength to move the manual wheelchair. It would be many months until I could push the wheelchair across a carpet. There was a TV across from the foot of the bed, and a table within reach.

Emma went through the empty larder in the kitchen, went shopping and came back with bags of groceries. Her nephew, Jason, had come with her from Maryland so we had a full house.

By mid afternoon I was exhausted from all the activity. I was thankful to be transferred to my new hospital bed.

By the third day, I was glad to be home. Jordan had been brought back the first evening and now stayed by my side. Smokey the cat had jumped up on my lap the first day, but my other cat Tasha was afraid of the wheelchair, and ran away from me.

'It's not so bad,' I thought. 'I can get out the back door onto the patio and watch the birds come back to their feeders. I can see the green grass and feel the breeze from the ocean.' I rolled the wheelchair up to my own dining table. I didn't have to eat hospital food. I could eat without help (after the food was cut up and the u-cuff was on my hand). I could answer the portable phone, when it was on my lap. I would be all right. I didn't taunt myself with the things I couldn't do.

Jeff had made ramps for the front door and two back doors. My wheelchair had easy access to the hospital bed, dining room and kitchen. I didn't have a call button, which made me afraid to be alone all night. Jim came up with a clever solution, using a wireless doorbell. He taped the button to my bed, and Darlene kept the ringer next to her at night.

The Telephone Company gave me a special phone. By pushing a wireless button, which was attached to my bed rail, a dial tone was activated on the nearby speakerphone. After five seconds, an operator would come on the line, and could place calls for me. All I had to do was talk!

My neighbor Eva had gone up and down my one block cul-de-sac gathering a list of everyone's name, address and telephone number, and when they were usually at home. She also arranged for a few neighbors to come over to the house on different days of the week just to chat and to make sure I was all right. I got to know all my neighbors. Eva and I became close friends.

Emma headed home to Baltimore. We had set up everything imaginable to keep me safe but I knew I would miss her. Darlene had been alert and had passed her drug test. Yet when Emma left I was apprehensive. Darlene and I would be on our own together.

PATIENCE HAD NEVER been one of my long suits, but I knew Darlene and I had to work together. I couldn't get out of bed in the morning until I had help and I was waking up at 6 a.m. Darlene was a night person. I had to be content to watch TV and wait for her. I also had to get used to Darlene's cooking and resist the urge to have everything done my way. The one unbending rule was she had to smoke outside.

I was really afraid of being caught in the house during a fire. During the day I had a chance of getting outside if I were in my wheelchair, but if I were in bed, I'd burn up. Maybe I over reacted, but I had additional smoke detectors installed in every bedroom.

For the first few weeks, we did well together. Then on a Tuesday evening, when it was time for me to get ready for bed, everything changed. At first all the bedtime preparations proceeded as usual. Darlene changed my foley bag to the big one needed for overnight. She helped me maneuver a heavy long sleeve tee shirt over my head, and then rolled me to get on the long sweat pants I wore at night. I was always cold so I was bundled up like it was January in Alaska, even though the San Diego nights in October were mild.

When we were almost done, Darlene began to slowly pull a wool sock onto my left foot. She seemed distracted. Then she picked up the other sock, and started pulling it on the same foot. It was as if she didn't notice I already had a sock on that foot. She was moving like a character in a slow motion movie.

I said "Darlene, it's OK. Are you all right? Here, sit on the bed next to my legs."

She slowly lowered her hips to the mattress. Then she slid off the side of the bed and disappeared onto the floor. The room was quiet. I could hear her gentle breathing but I couldn't see her and I couldn't move myself enough to get her in my sight.

"Darlene, are you all right? Darlene, tell me, are you OK?"
There was no answer.

I was helpless and a prisoner in my own bed. I had dreaded just such a situation. I pushed the telephone button, read Eva's number from the list on the wall, and waited while the operator made the connection. My heart was in my mouth, but I tried to keep my voice calm. After many rings and no answer, I had the operator call Jim. He was home.

"I'll be right over," he said, "but it will take me a few minutes to get there."

Those minutes seemed like hours. During that time, Darlene had gotten up and gone to her bedroom. I didn't see her, but I heard her feet. She had turned off a hallway light. She was like a zombie.

As Jim unlocked the front door, I told him, "I'm all right. I think Darlene is in her room."

He came back from her bedroom after a few minutes.

"She's groggy and incoherent and won't wake up. She seems OK – no fever, or seizures, nothing obviously wrong, but I couldn't get her up," he said.

We decided that it was safe to leave Darlene alone for the night, but it wasn't safe to leave me alone. I needed someone to get up and roll me over at 3 a.m. I was afraid Darlene would stay in her groggy state, and might even be that way in the morning. I was afraid to be alone, and it was 11 p.m. at night.

"You know, Don lives alone, and nearby. Maybe he would be able to come and stay over night with me. He can roll me over. Then we'll see if there still is a problem in the morning," I said.

Don didn't seem to mind being roused in the middle of the night. He gathered up a few things and arrived about a half-hour later. Jim and I explained the situation. Don said he would be sure I remained safe. He would get up at 3 a.m. to reposition me. He settled onto the queen couch in the living room, about 30 feet from my bed. Amazingly, Darlene showed up on time to roll me over, although she didn't say anything and didn't seem to be quite with it.

The next morning, it must have seemed strange to Darlene to find Don in the house. Don stood by my bedside and Darlene near the foot of the bed.

"Darlene, do you remember what happened last night?" I asked quietly. I wanted to yell and shout accusingly, but I managed to control my emotions.

She shook her head. I told her about her slide into oblivion.

"I don't know what it could be," she said. "I've never had a problem."

It was a delicate situation. I needed Darlene's care, and I didn't want to antagonize her. At the same time, I needed to replace her. I felt like I was walking a tightrope. I sucked in my breath and tried to stay calm and in charge. I told Darlene that she could stay in the house as consultant, with room and board and very reduced pay, if she helped train the new person. She agreed.

I placed an ad in the paper and several people called. I did mini interviews over the phone. A nice sounding man arranged to come over in the afternoon. Dave had a mellow voice, was good looking, tall and slim, with sandy colored hair. He told me he was almost finished taking a 12-week course to obtain his Certified Nursing Assistant (CNA) credential. This would allow him to work as a caregiver in private homes. He liked to cook and to keep house. He had his own apartment and seemed too good to be true.

"I can't work 7 days a week, but maybe 4 or 5 would be good," he said.

I realized that a caregiver who had no life other than living in my house was probably not a good idea. That meant I still needed another person. With two caregivers, we could get some relief from each other. Dave had his own life and a dependable car. I needed helpers to be able to make shopping trips, do outings with me, and eventually take me to Sharp for out-patient therapy.

I asked Dave if he was gay. He said yes.

"But I am really afraid of getting HIV and am practically celibate. I'm very careful and just tested negative two months ago." His sincere open answer and volunteered information convinced me of his honesty.

I told him he was hired, assuming all of his references checked out. I thought, 'this certainly was easier than I had expected. Maybe everything won't be so bad after all.'

The ad was still running in the paper when Darlene answered the telephone and talked to someone for a few minutes. She came running to me and passed me the receiver.

"You've got to talk to this lady. She's perfect. She knows just what you're going through. You've got to hire her," she said.

Cheryl arrived later that afternoon. She was a tall, good-looking girl, with long blond hair. She was bubbly, talkative and charming. Her qualifications were a bit shaky, but her desire was real.

She had been in a bad car accident in February 1996 that had hospitalized her for a month. She had been unconscious two weeks of that time. She had a head injury and broken bones in her arm and back but she had made an amazing recovery although the scars on her arms and shoulders were still red and angry. She had just started working part-time at a nearby Eddie Bauer store.

She wanted to work a few days a week for me and continue her job at the store.

"Pam, I know how it is for you. I can help. I couldn't walk right away either," she said. "We can get better together."

I was charmed by her and she had one other credential, which she neglected to mention: she had studied and received an EMT certificate (Emergency Medical Technician) just a few years earlier.

The references for Dave and Cheryl both panned out. I felt lucky to find people so quickly. I hoped that it wasn't a little too easy. I had been warned that hired help might be undependable, have drug or alcohol problems, might steal money or things from my house. I was at their mercy. I couldn't see them all the time. I couldn't get into their bedrooms because of the carpets. I had to give them money for shopping and other necessities so I had to trust my instincts and see how things worked out.

Dave and Cheryl started their 24-hour shifts two weeks after Darlene's fall. In the interim my friends rallied around. Someone slept on my couch each night. Don stayed on weekend nights and several men and women from work took turns during the week. Between Dave, Cheryl and Darlene, my care at home was good. At least I felt safe. I was able to stop the evening visits of my two Sharp caregivers.

Then everything seemed to go wrong again. Jim bowed out of his full time duties of paying my bills. I began opening bills and making out checks but this was very difficult, both physically and mentally. I had to fight against each envelope.

When I opened my October AT&T Master Card bill, I found there was $2500.00 due! I had several active credit cards but none had been used while I was in the hospital or since I came home.

The details of the bill showed $400, $500 and $600 amounts withdrawn from my account at several ATM machines in Pacific Beach over a period of 10 days.

I was very upset. I immediately called AT&T and was telephone tagged to someone in the fraud department. The lady was very helpful and I worked with her for several weeks as the story unfolded. I had never used my credit card to get cash, so all these transactions at ATM machines should have raised red flags at AT&T. As it turned out AT&T had called my home once but did not leave a message.

I told the lady at AT&T I was a quadriplegic in a wheelchair and couldn't possibly have made the withdrawals.

"I'll order up the camera tapes for those dates and times," she said. "Then we can get a picture of the culprit."

About 4 days later, Cindy, who had done the house cleaning, came to see me. She was not my favorite person at this point, since I'd found many of my precious keepsakes missing.

"Can I talk to you in private?" she asked.

"Sure," I said.

"I don't know how to say this," she said. "I stole your money."

After a pause I said, "Why?"

"It just felt so good to walk around with some money in my pocket," she answered.

"Well, do you still have the money?" I asked.

"No, I spent it on things for me and I gave some to my friends."

She didn't want me to tell Jim. He had setup a file of my paperwork in his house, and it had a folder marked Credit Cards. In it was an extra credit card, with a PIN number attached. Cindy had stolen the extra card and used it to get the money.

She left, promising to get some of the money back. I called AT&T and told them what had happened. It was decided to wait and see what Cindy would do. Then I called the police, to make out a report. AT&T needed this for their records. I told the police about my automobile accident and paralyzed condition, and how Cindy had stolen money from me using my credit card. They were less than sympathetic.

"Yes, lady, it looks like a crime, but since you know who did it, we can't do anything. It's a civil matter. You got to take her to court." They wouldn't even make out a report.

A few days later, Cindy came back to me with $1100. She said she couldn't get any more.

"I'll send this money to AT&T and then it's up to them," I said. "What you did was pretty unthinkable. It's like stabbing me in the back. Don't you think I have enough problems already?"

The theft qualified as a felony, but she was not charged. AT&T arranged for her to send them $100 a month, but I'll bet she never made the payments. I never saw Cindy again but learned about eight years later she committed suicide.

Chapter Six

Home Therapy Geniuses and Facing old Friends

AFTER I WAS out of the hospital, I was entitled to a month's occupational and physical therapy in my home.

I don't even remember the name of the first occupational therapist who came to me. What sticks in my mind was her obsession with my bathtub. She decided I should work on techniques of transferring from my wheelchair to my shower bench, which extended over the edge of the tub. According to her I could scoot across the bench and end up in the tub and take my own shower, all without help.

At first it sounded like a reasonable goal to me, but I simply did not have the strength needed to get into the tub. My usual routine was for the caregiver to undress me while I was sitting in my wheelchair. Then I was lifted over the edge of the tub and onto the bench. The shower head was on a long flexible hose, and I could do some soaping and rinsing while the caregiver watched and then did my back, legs and feet. I was lifted back into my wheelchair, with towels wrapped all around me. My large cushy blue bathrobe was warmed in the dryer before I was wrapped up in it. Yet with this new occupational therapist I spent 4 or 5 of our sessions sitting in the bathroom, eyeing the tub the way a climber studies a mountain. I wanted to do it but I couldn't attempt the climb.

She couldn't help me with the one practical question I had for her. My CD disc player was easy to use from my wheelchair. It had large buttons that I could push. I had several books on CD I wanted to listen to, but I couldn't get the CD cases open. I could have asked my caregivers, but the point was to learn to do it myself. She tried several techniques with me but with no success. Oddly, by the last of her five covered visits, my fingernails had grown long enough that I could pry the CD cases apart.

My physical therapist was much better. The first time Dale came to my house we were both happy and sad to see each other. The previous year, we had been on the same weeklong camping trip into Canyon De Chelley, in Arizona. Dale remembered me as one of the strongest and fastest people in the group. Now I was essentially immobile.

We talked a bit about that trip, but it was too bittersweet a memory for me. Dale could see how hard I was trying to hold back tears. She knew all the exercises I'd done in the hospital so we quickly started. Later, she added new exercises, as I grew stronger.

Many of my leg exercises were still done while I was lying on my back. I tried, straining with every muscle, to do a little more each session. Many times I tried so hard that I aggravated a nerve in my neck. Dale was particularly good at helping me learn to relax and use just the required muscles. She taught me to reposition my head so that the nerve would not be pinched.

Dale understood who I had been and I was really sorry when our month was up.

In the tradition of my pre-accident athletic training, I practiced all my exercises everyday. Then in November when I changed to a different insurance sub-group in order to stay with my Sharp doctor, the fluky rules of the insurance company gave me an unexpected bonus – another month of home PT and OT. This miracle brought Angie and Vivian to my door. They worked together as a team, their therapies complementing each other.

Vivian was tall, businesslike, and looked like a fit outdoor person. Angie was about my height, with dark oriental eyes, and a quick smile. They spent the first hour with me going around my house, assessing what I could and couldn't do. I was delighted with them.

I was asleep in my bed near the front door the next time Vivian arrived.

She said, "Well, looks like you're rested up. Let's start right here in bed. How about working on rolling over."

I still had not been able to roll over by myself and didn't think I had the strength. But I wanted to do it.

"First of all, let's get rid of those moon boots on your feet," she said. "You're moving around so much during the day that you don't need to wear them now. And let's try raising the head of the bed a little bit. Then you can use your arms on the side rails to help you turn your body."

Vivian could read me like a book. I maneuvered myself a bit, trying to work out exactly how much to raise the bed and how to use the side rails. Soon I was able to roll myself over from one side to the other. It was a revelation!

"And since you are there," she said, "let's work on getting you out of bed altogether."

"By myself?" I asked. I didn't want to get hurt and I also was afraid of trying too much and becoming discouraged.

"Don't worry, we'll do everything safely. You are going to be surprised at how much you can do!"

She helped me sit up on the side of the bed. I couldn't do the whole transfer without help, but she showed me how to position the wheelchair and myself, using my arms to support my weight, resting my feet on the floor, and then sliding into the wheelchair. She helped by giving me light support under my arms so I couldn't slip down onto the floor. The bed mattress was a little higher than my wheelchair seat, so gravity helped me as well.

That hour with Vivian passed in a flash and I felt like a different person when she left. I wouldn't need anyone to get up and roll me over at 3 a.m. anymore! If an emergency occurred while I was in bed, I might be able to get into my wheelchair myself.

From that day on, whenever I was in bed, the wheelchair was always located in exactly the right place for my transfer. My bedside TV had a unique feature of two timers: one to turn it on at a pre-selected time, and another to turn it off. I set the ON time for 3 a.m. and the OFF time for 3:10 a.m. That gave me enough time to wake up, maneuver my body over, helped by the light from the screen, and then go back to sleep. My caregivers received a huge gift after Vivian's visit: they were able to sleep through the night.

On November 18, Vivian said, "Let's do some walking."

I trusted her ability to assess my capabilities. We put on my gait belt (a webbed belt about 3 inches wide that was buckled tightly around my waist). Vivian stood facing me, holding firmly onto the belt.

"Rest your arms across my shoulders and lean on me," she said.

Then she stooped down and slowly stood upright. I was glad that she was strong as I leaned heavily on her while I stood on my own feet.

"Keep your legs straight and push them forward as I back up," she said.

I tried to walk for the first time. I moved like a stilted mechanical toy, but I moved forward a few feet. My caregiver kept the wheelchair directly behind me. Vivian held me as I sat down heavily to rest. We did it one more time and I WALKED another five feet. I was completely exhausted from moving just 10 feet on my own but my endorphins were pulsing and I was high. It was one of the most memorable days in my life. Suddenly my dream of walking again seemed possible.

Vivian had brought in a set of bicycle pedals. They protruded from an 8-inch by 8-inch stand and had a small knob to adjust the resistance. I sat in my wheelchair with my feet held to the pedals by Velcro straps. The first day I did a few revolutions, very slowly and stopped. Then a few more. Stop. I couldn't go fast and I couldn't pedal for long because the nerves to my legs just stopped working and I lost contact with my legs and feet. Sometimes my heels moved rapidly up and down, out of my control, like a sewing machine gone haywire. This condition is called "clonis" and is caused by nerve signals bouncing up and down the spinal column. This usually occurred when my legs were tired and ready to quit.

I worked on the pedals for five minutes everyday, pedaling and resting. I always tried to increase the time before my legs gave out on me. I remembered my weeks of pedaling around New Zealand and Canada. Back then I liked the feeling of working and going somewhere. Now, I told myself, I was headed to a place where I could walk again.

I was getting stronger. Vivian and I did our walk together but never more than 10 feet. It was awkward for her walking backwards and leaning forward made me walk in an unnatural way, as I was dragging stiff legs that I couldn't pick up.

"A set of parallel bars would really help you," Vivian finally said.

I had seen them at the hospital. They had all kinds of adjustments and looked very expensive. Then my friend Jeff volunteered to make me a pair of parallel bars sized just for me. We talked about the measurements. Jeff, with his mechanical engineering background, said he would come up with something. He designed bars twenty feet long, with supports at each end and the middle. He made the whole apparatus from plumbing pipe. All the pieces cost about $200. Don Edwards and Jeff bolted them down on the cement patio in my backyard. Within a week I had a set of my very own parallel bars to work on whenever I wanted. I was so thankful for my wonderful friends!

On the cool afternoon of November 25th, after 5 minutes on the pedals, Vivian positioned my wheelchair at one end of the newly erected parallel bars. Holding onto my gait belt, she helped me hoist myself to a standing position. The wheelchair was pulled back while Vivian stood behind me. I slowly moved forward five feet, shuffling my feet while leaning on the bars and supporting myself with my arms. After five feet I was done. I stood shaking while the wheelchair was pushed up behind me. I was near tears. I had the best setup possible and I still couldn't walk. But Vivian was not discouraged. She told me next time would be better.

Two days later when Vivian returned, things had changed. I had used the pedals and done my other exercises in her absence. Vivian followed me as I stood at the end of the bars. She held my gait belt as I started to move. I moved easily, from one end of the bars to the other. I was stiff and jerky but I managed to walk twenty feet! I couldn't believe it!

"What happened?" I asked Vivian, as we beamed at each other. "I didn't suddenly become stronger in two days. How come it seemed so easy today?"

"Your nerves are reconnecting and starting to work again. They need to relearn how to do things. But they'll get better with each repetition."

I was so happy there were tears in my eyes. Although I didn't trust how my legs felt because they didn't feel as if they'd hold me up, I still wanted to walk. I wanted to go places on my own two feet. I had imagined that walking would feel like it used to feel, but it didn't. I realized I would have to learn to use my legs the way they felt now, even if they never were what they had been before.

I continued to exercise everyday. Many days I went through my routine twice. I competed with myself, trying to walk more steps or do more leg lifts each time. My caregivers, Dave and Cheryl, learned to help me walk using the gait belt and the parallel bars.

I knew that I was lucky to have been an athlete before the accident. I had enjoyed hard physical work. Now I would work harder than ever before. I realized my mental toughness was even more important than my physical abilities. I was going to recover through shear force of will.

Vivian helped me figure out how to transfer from my wheelchair to a regular dining chair without arms. I was beginning to feel like a real person at the table. The wheelchair could be pushed out of sight, and I could use my own fork, as long as there was nothing more solid than mashed potatoes on my plate.

When Angie came to work with me she said, "Let's get those hands working. That's what you want to do the most, isn't it?"

So we started. Angie knew all the little exercises to move each finger. We ran through them, using putty, small objects, nuts and bolts.

"How adventurous are you?" she asked me. "Are you willing to try different or strange things?"

"I'll try anything, no matter how strange or weird," I said.

Angie's oriental heritage gave her an open approach to new experiences that the average therapist would not have. Consequently, we tried many things to get my hands working. If the results were good, we continued for a few days. If not we moved on to something else. I had used heat on my hands at Sharp, by burying them in warm sand. Angie suggested I use my rice bag[2] instead. After I had warmed my hands on the rice bag for ten minutes, Angie massaged them and tried to stimulate their movement. After a while I could begin to straighten my fingers. I could even curl them about half way closed. They always seemed to work better after Angie's touch. Later, they would revert to their cold tingly state. In the meantime, I could turn pages in a book, or perform tasks previously impossible. I often wore gloves during the day and always at night so that my hands did not feel like useless lumps of ice or keep me awake with their unpleasant sensations.

---

[2] Rice bags are wonderful and easy to make. Fill a large tube sock with about 3 pounds of rice. Stitch closed or tie a knot in the top. After 2 or 3 minutes in the microwave, it's ready for use and stays warm for about 60 minutes. It's a great hand warmer on a chilly night, helpful when draped around a stiff neck, or put under the bed covers on cold feet.

Angie again surprised me one day by suggesting we try ice on my hands. She knew my hands were always cold and uncomfortable.

"OK," I said, but I was not looking forward to this new experiment.

Angie took an ice cube and rapidly slid it down the inside of my forearm, along the tendon to my wrist. As she repeated the movement my fingers curled closed when the ice reached my wrist. I never understood why or how, but I was able to close my fingers better while she did this. I concentrated on each movement, trying to make the connection from my head to my fingers, hoping that later the connection would still be there.

Several times she brought a vibrator and used it to stimulate movement in my hands and fingers. That seemed to help as well. For several days I did my hand exercises with magnets strapped to my hands. We even strapped magnets to my shoes but I will have to say I was never sure if these made any difference.

Angie did all of these things in an attempt to startle and activate nerves that were barely working. Even the magnets may have lined up nerve cells so that pulses could flow between them, and eventually to my brain.

While Vivian continued working with my legs, Angie provided backup with my arms and balance. They were a well-practiced team. She helped me become confident about getting from my bed to the wheelchair by myself. Angie pushed and pulled on me when I was sitting in my wheelchair to help me work on my strength and balance. This quickly paid off because after a few weeks, I didn't need the belt around my chest to keep me upright in the wheelchair. She even took the arms off of my wheelchair so that I had only the back for support. She made me reach to the side for objects and bend towards the floor. She challenged me with arm exercises, done in sets, called "proprioceptive neuromuscular facilitation" (PNF). These exercises had me doing arm movements from one side of my body to the other. I'd start with my right hand held loosely down at my side and then raise it up so that my right hand was above my left shoulder. At first, when I tried to move my arms in a new way, they would get tangled up or just not go in the direction I wanted. I had to think about doing each exercise, then concentrate during the first few awkward attempts. Sometimes it took 5 or 6 tries before I could do a movement smoothly.

I made great progress with this dream team. I wished they could come more than three times a week, but it wasn't possible. We had a long break over Thanksgiving. I was so pleased that my stories about running in London, Paris, Sydney, and San Diego inspired Vivian to get up early on Thanksgiving morning and run the Turkey Trot 10K Race. I couldn't be out there cheering for her, but I could enjoy her run vicariously. Afterwards Vivian gave me her 10K tee shirt in honor of my inspiration. I was touched.

Thanksgiving was my first holiday home in a wheelchair. My running buddy, Karen, was having a large dinner with her family and I was invited, along with Dave, my caregiver. We each brought something. I told Dave how to assemble and bake my Grandmother Rokel's special bread pudding. A beautiful table was set on the back deck of Karen's uncle's house, which overlooked the mountains east of San Diego. It was a warm and sunny day and was one of the first times since the accident that I was able to forget my physical condition. I transferred to an ordinary dining chair, surrounded by loving people and a wonderful meal. I felt real hope. My life wasn't over, as I so often feared. It had been transformed into another kind of existence.

NOW THAT THE crisis was over, I was afraid my old friends would forget about me. Everyone would get on with his or her own life, and I wouldn't be a part of it. I didn't want to be isolated at home, but I didn't see any alternative. I no longer worked with many people everyday, as I had before. I didn't interact with hospital staff or other patients either. Instead, I was stuck in my house trying to make a new life out of the remnants of my old one.

I tried not to mourn as some of my old friends drifted away because I found the bonds I had with some of my existing friends became stronger.

My friend John from GA tried to visit me once a week at lunchtime, usually bringing a few other people with him. Sometimes he brought me special dishes made by his wife. Sometimes he would pick up a hamburger or smoothie for me. I looked forward to his lunchtime visits, hearing new gossip about work, and being included with a group of people who were a part of the real world. John made it possible for me to be a little bit of the person I used to be.

While I was in the hospital, no one had taken care of my yard. Toward the end of my hospital stay, one of my GA visitors asked me about it.

"I guess it will get along without me for a while. The sprinklers go off automatically, so everything should still be alive," I said.

Frankie said, "Well, I'll go over and give it a check." He got directions and Jim left the gate unlocked for him.

Once I was home, Frankie began coming over at least twice a month, usually on Saturdays to work in the yard. He didn't have much money or a high paying job or fancy position at GA but he gave of himself, with his own two hands. Even though he worked 5 days a week, had his own house to care for, did all the housekeeping, shopping and yard care for an aunt who was in a wheelchair, he still came and puttered in my yard for 4 or 5 hours, cutting grass, trimming bushes, pulling weeds, sweeping and cleaning. He was a wonderful generous man.

It became a regular routine for Don Edwards to come over every Saturday afternoon. Don invariably brought an armload of groceries and cooked a wonderful meal. Usually Frankie, Don, Darlene and either Dave or Cheryl was there. Sometimes Eva from across the street joined us. Sometimes other friends dropped by. Don always brought enough food for a crowd. We passed the time laughing and telling stories. A feeling of camaraderie and caring floated in the air around us. I was so lucky! Their company helped me keep my spirits up and kept me looking toward the future.

All my tennis buddies wanted to see me after I was out of the hospital so they arranged a Saturday noontime potluck in the clubhouse next to the courts where I used to play. Dave drove me there and pushed me into the meeting room. He transferred me to a regular chair at one of the tables, and hid my wheelchair in a corner. I was a few minutes early. Everyone else was still on the courts. After a few people arrived, Dave left to do some errands. Everyone hugged me as they came in and exclaimed how glad they were to see me. "Don't you look good!" "Where's your wheelchair?" "Don't you need it anymore?" My plate was filled several times for me. Brownies and desserts appeared at my elbow. I felt like a celebrity and I enjoyed the light conversation. Although I didn't know any of these women well, as we had only been tennis buddies, yet there was a real human connection where our lives had touched. Later, as Dave rolled me back to the car, my tears kept me from seeing the tennis courts. I didn't want to remember the matches I had played there. I didn't want to remember that I would never be able to play again. I tried instead to concentrate on the genuine warmth of the luncheon.

Other invitations helped me feel part of the world. Hank, a man of Chinese heritage, invited me and some other GA people to an ethnic restaurant that served Dim Sum. Cheryl accompanied me. I had eaten Dim Sum only once, many years before in Los Angeles but Cheryl had never even heard of it. We all sat at a large round table while Hank ordered for everyone. When a dish arrived he explained the ingredients and how it was made. Cheryl tried everything, her eyes as round as saucers with amazement. I skipped some of the raw dishes, but enjoyed eating everything else. It was a jovial luncheon and I got to talk with a few people I had not seen for many months. I am sure that people felt sorry for me, but I was treated gently and no one turned their heads away from my disability. That made a huge difference to my feeling of acceptance.

Although I was embarrassed to be seen in my altered state, I decided to see my horsy friends too. The annual potluck for my old group was held at Irene's new house. She had moved there just before my car wreck. I hadn't seen her new house or horse facilities. My friend Maria, from those early days at La Jolla Farms, drove me there. Maria pushed my chair in through the garage to avoid a porch step. A chorus of cheers greeted me in the kitchen. Horse people always have something to talk about – usually horses with a capital H – and this was no exception. I found out how each person and each person's horse was doing. We chatted about riders we had known and horses in our past. I got to ask Michelle about Ameego. She told me he was his same cocky self. She was riding him regularly. I was glad to know he was in such good hands.

I wanted to see Irene's entire new house, but there were several steps up to the foyer and then a second floor. Her son volunteered to make it possible for me to get a grand tour. Ed looked like he belonged in an Aussie ad, with his sandy hair and well built physique. He was very strong and practically carried me up the steps. My feet dragged behind and occasionally I put a little weight on them and rested on the banister. Someone carried the wheelchair up, and I flopped into it, tired from the effort. From there, I was rolled through the bedrooms, and enjoyed the balcony with a view over the hills.

Afterwards, I was afraid to let Ed carry me down. It seemed too precarious. Instead, he slowly lowered me so that I was sitting on the top step. From that position, I could bump down each step. At the bottom, I was pulled up and into the wheelchair. It must not have been a pretty sight, but it worked and everyone was impressed that I made it to the second floor and back. It felt like a milestone to me. I had overcome my reluctance to be seen by friends, especially friends who knew me only as an athletic person. I had allowed myself to be put in the humiliating position of a child, who has to be helped up and down stairs. But I did it openly, and didn't care what anyone was thinking. I was taking life on, my way, whatever way that had to be.

On December 6, Dave drove me to GA and my old office. I felt like an outsider who was interrupting the daily routine. It wasn't my office anymore. My friend and coworker Bob now occupied my old space and was in charge of my group. I hadn't been away that long, 155 days, but for me everything had changed. He and I went through the bookcases and the desk drawers and gathered up my belongings. It felt very still and cold in there. My livelihood, my identity, and the place where I spent 50 or 60 hours a week for 19 years were irrelevant to me now.

The whole experience of being back there made me want to shrink into a little ball. A few people dropped by to say hello but our conversations were short. I didn't stay long. I said I was tired and didn't feel good and I retreated like a dog with my tail between my legs. That life was over. I never went back again and no one at GA even intimated that I should come back. I was no longer needed.

My past glared at me a few days later at a pizza parlor luncheon. A large group of ex-GA Fusion employees and retirees who had been in the fusion division for 15 or 20 years met annually for an old-timers Christmas luncheon. I didn't really want to go but Tammy from the Control Room talked me into it. She came to my house and escorted me, getting me and my wheelchair in and out of her car. Most of the people at the luncheon didn't even know about my accident. I felt like a freak sitting there, as they gazed past me with little or no recognition. I sat in a corner, and tried to blend into the walls. The few people who recognized me spoke softly, holding back their surprise or dismay, I couldn't tell which.

One gentleman came over, and said "Well Pam. I never expected to see you here. And like this. Tell me what happened and how can I help you?"

Manny's face was high above me and his large presence overshadowed the table. I remembered playing tennis with him my first year at GA. He had gone on to other designer jobs at other companies, purchased various houses throughout the city and by his joking description was now a 'slum landlord.' (I later found out that he was a most benevolent landlord.) He was incredibly kind to me that day. I gave him my phone number and he said he would be in touch. I was happy to talk with someone friendly for a little while but doubted I would hear from him again. I would find out in a few months that Manny was a wonderful person.

AS THE YEAR 1996 came to an end, Angie and Vivian really dug into my rehab. My time with them was to end on December 18 and they both wanted to be sure I would continue to progress until regular out-patient therapy could begin. They knew by then that I would work on whatever skills were within my capabilities, so they started me on a totally new line of activity.

Angie told me about a few of her sick, unresponsive baby patients, most less than 6 months old. They had lain lifeless with little movement in soft cribs with deep mattresses and smothering covers. When she put them on a firm surface, with no encumbrances, they started to move their legs and arms and cry. The harder surface stimulated the nerves of their body and made it easier for them to move. She told me it was time for me to get down on the floor and start from the beginning, just like the babies.

My living room floor, with a medium deep cover of carpet and padding, would be my testing ground. I needed to roll over, get up on my hands and knees and crawl. These movements are basic to the human organism and doing them would connect old nerve pathways.

At first the floor activities were very difficult for me. I couldn't just plop forward out of my chair, since I didn't have the strength or coordination to keep from falling. I was also afraid, since the floor looked so far down. Vivian held me under my arms and slowly lowered me to the floor from my wheelchair. (Vivian or Angie was always there to coach me, and to suggest ways to try and solve the immediate problem.) I finally figured out how to use my couch to lower myself. After placing my chair sideways against the back of the couch, I leaned both arms firmly across the sofa top, and then eased my legs down onto the floor. After I reached to the floor with one arm, I turned, and used both arms to lower my body the rest of the way. I ended up flat on the floor, on my stomach, face down. It was quite a contortion, but I could do it myself. Once there though, I couldn't move. I felt like I was glued to the carpet.

I needed to roll over onto my back. I learned to push with my arms, tip my upper body sideways, and roll onto my shoulder blades. My legs followed slowly. I twisted to get them over. Once on my back, I had to figure out how to roll back onto my stomach. I stretched both arms far over to my left and tried to make my hips rotate. Finally, my body just seemed to drift. I was lying on my left side, and then on my stomach. I remembered how hard this movement had been in the hospital, when I had cried out with frustration. Now I could do it!

None of this was easy. Each step took many tries, and I rested often. My movements were slow and jerky. I felt very disconnected from my body whenever I tried something new on the floor. Sometimes it was just too hard and I had to say "Enough! Let's go back to something easy that I can do."

One other movement I had to learn was to get up on my hands and knees from lying on the floor on my stomach. You might think this sounds easy, but how do you actually do it? A common way is to push up with your arms, and after your upper body is elevated, raise your butt until you are on your hands and knees. This method was beyond me. I had to invent another much more complicated way of doing it. I rolled onto my side and drew up my legs slightly. I had to push up with my arms into a semi-seated position, with my legs folded under me to one side. Then I rotated my hips over my knees, and then walked my arms around to be under my shoulders. Finally I was kneeling. My mind knew what to do, but it had been disconnected from my body. I had to think about every little movement I wanted to make. It was strange to be unable to move my body in a simple way when I had been so facile in doing new physical activities with ease – running, dressage movements, swimming strokes, skiing, and tennis. Often I needed to have someone actually move my limbs through the sequence of movements, sort of priming the nerve pathways, in order to learn.

For two weeks, both Vivian and Angie worked with me on the floor. I was often frustrated as they challenged me and asked me to do things that I could not coax from my body. Some things required more strength than I had, others more coordination than my mind could elicit from my body. I wiggled on my stomach, crawled on my hands and knees, tried to 'stand up' with my knees and lower legs on the floor and knee walk. I balanced on a large blue ball about 2 feet in diameter, tried push-ups (from the knees), did deep breathing exercises and various rolling motions. I was being asked to do a lot using a paralyzed body with atrophied muscles. I was not proficient, and usually my slowly moving arms and legs would only approximate the intended exercise. Angie and Vivian wanted me to have goals to reach for. A few times, we quit and went back to simple exercises just to end a session on a positive note but I never once collapsed in tears, although I was often disappointed in my abilities. The only thing that made the frustration easier was knowing I was being asked to do more than was realistic.

Part of their joint strategy was to keep me working for the 3 or 4 weeks before I went back to Sharp rehab. The two of them arranged to come together one afternoon for two hours, instead of their usual separate times. They were going out of their way to help me and I really appreciated it.

Don Edwards and Jeff were both invited to join us. They came to learn what I was doing so they could help me later. Both of them knew how to help me walk on the parallel bars with my gait belt. Now they learned how to help me with my awkward maneuvers on the floor.

Although the floor seems a safe place to be, it could be dangerous for me. I could easily lose my balance and tip over and I couldn't move quickly enough to catch myself. I could easily slip and land in a bad position, breaking a hand, arm, fingers, ribs or even a hip. Because I was aware of the danger, I was sometimes afraid to push myself into new territory. I had to know someone was there to cushion a mistake or slip. That afternoon, with the four of them working with me, it was actually fun. I was exhausted by the end of our session but also sorry when it was over. I knew Angie and Vivian would be out of my life when that day was over.

I did have one fall during this period, but it was not because of the physical therapy. My golden retriever Jordan, stayed very close to me all the time. He had a special rug that was spread out each night next to my bed, so that he could sleep there. Sometimes I told him "Come on up," and he sprang up next to my legs and stretched out with me on the narrow bed. I felt better when he was near. He loved to play with a tennis ball, which I unsuccessfully tried to throw for him. He also liked to tug on a knotted sock. Usually he pulled the sock right out of my weak hands. But one evening, we were playing in the long tiled hallway and I held the sock tightly enough that my wheelchair was pulled forward while he backed and shook his head playfully. Then suddenly I was on the floor. The chair had hesitated as it was pulled over a grout line while I just kept going. Darlene and Dave picked me up in about 20 seconds. There were many hushed questions: "Are you OK?" "Does anything hurt?" "Can your move your arms and legs?" and finally "What happened?" Since I couldn't sense pain or discomfort, it was several days before we were sure that I had not been hurt. Then we were able to laugh and make light of the fall.

By December, I found I didn't want to face the Christmas holidays. So many bad things were associated with the holidays for me – my mother's death, Ned walking out on Christmas Eve, and now my condition. I had no reason to feel happy, light hearted, generous, glad to be on the earth, joyous for the season or peaceful. Instead I found myself sympathizing with Scrooge. I wanted to ignore Christmas. No presents, no decorations, no wreathes or trees. Maybe if I ignored it, it would just go away.

One dark December evening there was a knock on the front door. Darlene answered it and called back to me "Come on out here. You have some visitors."

As I rounded the corner in my wheelchair, I came smack up against a small mob of people, with a Christmas tree.

"We wanted to be sure you didn't miss Christmas this year, so we brought it to you," said Ken. "We have decorations, sandwiches and drinks for everyone. We can all get into the spirit and help."

How could I not get into the spirit that evening? Everyone was enthusiastic and bubbling over with their own infectious happiness. After rummaging around in the garage, someone found the Christmas tree stand and a few strands of blinking lights. We picked out a place for the tree where I could see it from my bed, without blocking my wheelchair route. I hung some of the balls on the lower limbs and watched as a star was placed on the top. My friends had even brought me presents. When the tree was complete I was practically speechless. What had I done to deserve such love and affection?

I simply can't answer that question. Every person who knew me would likely have a different slant on the answer. I think people rallied around me because I really needed their help. They knew I was struggling against tremendous obstacles.

They also knew I didn't complain, bemoan my situation, or make them feel bad because they were whole and I was not. I was so glad to be treated as a member of the human race and not forgotten as a useless cripple. I also knew I was different in my new state. I was easier to approach, softer and more accepting of people. That night I tried to show my very real appreciation to everyone.

Several large submarine sandwiches were parceled out. I was able to hold mine and eat it like everyone else. I could even lift and drink from my own can of pop. The mess was quickly cleaned up and everyone headed out the door. "Merry Christmas, Pam." "Good to see you." "Have a happy holiday." "Happy New Year," they called as the door closed behind them.

A small whirlwind had come and gone in my front hallway, leaving the shining tree with its presents behind. I was numb with the surprise and wonder of it all. I fell asleep that night with the Christmas lights reflecting off the tree ornaments.

By the end of that year I could walk from one end of my parallel bars down to the other end and back. I did this haltingly, always using my arms for balance, and sometimes leaning on them to keep going. I shuffled and couldn't stand up straight. I was hunched over with my butt sticking out behind me, but it didn't matter. It took me almost two minutes for the round trip on my parallel bars but I was making progress. It was the beginning of walking on my own two legs.

Don Edwards helped me move into the New Year of 1997, with a glass of champagne and a kiss on the cheek at midnight. 'My life is pretty bad,' I thought, 'but some of the little pieces are simply wonderful.'

Chapter Seven

Pam Before - California, Flying for the
Wrong Reasons and a Career

MY HUSBAND QUICKLY settled into his new job in California. My search for a job in the Los Angeles area was disheartening. The early 1976 economy was slow. If I even got to see someone or talk on the phone, the only remark was 'There aren't any jobs. We'll call you.' Then I spoke to my next door neighbor. He was an electrical engineer and worked for Litton Industries in Woodland Hills. I asked him for the names of anyone in the company who knew about computing. I knew that personal contacts were much more likely to land me a job than blind resumes and letters. He gave me the name of a manager of a computing department where he worked.

I showed up at the employment department of Litton and was given the usual line: 'We really don't have any jobs, but please fill out the application form. The employment manager is not here today, so you'll have to return on Thursday if you wish to talk with him.' I did as directed, and just before leaving, asked if I could call someone in the building.

I was lucky enough to reach the computer department manager. I gave him a brief description of my background over the phone. Someone came to get me right away. I was escorted to the manager's office where I met him and another manager. We all went to lunch. At Argonne, I had worked on the new real-time terminals and on an IBM 360/195 central computer. I was familiar with the control language and the terminal commands. As it turned out the department at Litton had a position open for someone with exactly my experience. I was told I probably would be hired, but nothing could be done until the employment manager was available.

On Thursday, I duly returned. My application could not be found. I then spent tedious time filling out another, and waiting to talk with the employment manager. He finally appeared in the waiting room, and hovered over me in a very superior manner. He said, "I see hundreds of resumes just like yours every week. We are not interested in your qualifications."

I knew this couldn't be true – how many women with master's degrees were experienced in computers and sending him resumes every week? I told him "Well I talked with Mr. Stone, the department manager, when I was here Tuesday, and he seemed very interested. I think you should check with him."

A short time later, the same man returned, and seemed to have been transformed. "Ms. Henline, please come into my office. Mr. Stone would like to hire you." My lost application was also found. The employment manager reminded me of my physics teacher who thought women belonged at home.

I started work immediately. This Litton division made inertial navigation systems for military aircraft including the F14. These systems operated inside an aircraft, telling the plane its exact location with no outside input or radio-type contact. I enjoyed learning about the technical aspects of inertial navigation, gyroscopes and associated equipment. I was an expert at my job on the first day, since my previous computer experience was so similar. I received a Department of Defense Secret Clearance, as the accuracy of the systems was a guarded secret. These systems are archaic now, having been replaced by satellites and global positioning systems, but they were very advanced at the time and a hot weapon in the Cold War.

My job was to write and maintain a set of procedures used interactively by the engineers. Whenever the Litton computer systems were being upgraded, I had to be sure the procedures continued to operate smoothly. I worked weekends and evenings, when a new system was switched in for testing. I was using an antiquated, undependable terminal and frequently backed up all my files and made printouts of the changes I was making.

Nevertheless one afternoon the terminal failed and I lost most of the work I had done that day.

I was so frustrated, I headed up the hallway to the office of my immediate supervisor. He was not in but I could see Mr. Stone in his office. I stuck my head in his door and asked if he had a minute. When he nodded yes, I exploded. "I've been working for weeks to get this new stuff ready. Today I worked and saved all my files, but the terminal screwed up again and everything I did was lost. I can't keep working like this. I need a new terminal. I'm so frustrated today I'm going home now."

Within two days I had a new terminal. This incident turned my view of myself around. I deserved recognition as an individual and for my work contributions. I gained a whole new sense of self worth.

I still resented that my Litton starting salary was the same amount I had been paid at my previous job with Argonne. My work was good and I deserved better. I continued to read advertisements and applied for several jobs. I finally found a job that looked good, with a division of Hughes Aircraft. Hughes offered me a twenty-percent salary increase. I was very tempted by the job, the company and the company location.

In an unusual move, Litton offered me a twenty percent salary increase. I was torn. I made up a list of positives and negatives about each job. In my typical analytical manner, I assigned numbers and weights to each item. Still the two jobs seemed equal. My Litton boss asked me what it would take to get me to stay. I quickly answered "More money!" Litton then countered the Hughes offer with a twenty-five percent raise. It was another giant step upward in my confidence. I stayed at Litton.

Ned, my husband, was soon established at Rockwell with his new job. He spent his spare time in our garage, building his new Pitts airplane. I sewed the nylon fabric for each wing on my sewing machine. I'm still amazed that my simple stitching was enough to hold an airplane together! I used the leftover nylon thread to repair horse blankets. It is the strongest thread I have ever encountered! As the plane's pieces were finished they were taken to the Santa Paula airport for assembly and painting. Once the plane was moved to Santa Paula, Ned was gone much of the time.

I worked full time, rode Salty, my horse, four or five times a week, and took care of the house and yard. Ned and I still did some things together – he attended a few horse shows and I visited him at the airport several times. We had one skiing trip together during this period. But our lives had become very busy with different professional careers and separate leisure activities.

It was a momentous occasion when the airplane was first flown. Planes have been known to crash after assembly by amateurs but this one worked. It received its Experimental Status from the FAA.

But Ned was not satisfied with his job and neither Ned nor I was happy with how crowded Los Angeles was becoming. He started looking for a new job. Somehow it seemed he was always unhappy with his jobs while I was the one with a fulfilling job where I was respected.

Around this time it became apparent to me that Ned was having an affair with a teenager who had been hanging around the airplane hanger. I was shocked and couldn't understand why this was happening. I felt betrayed.

Ned said he didn't want to break up our marriage, but he was infatuated with this girl, Jacee. But he found a job in San Diego, and said he hoped he could leave the affair behind him. In March of 1977 Ned accepted the new job. Again, I would have to give up my job, move to a new area, find another job and make a new career for myself. Believing and hoping that everything would be better for both of us if I was supportive and enthusiastic about the move, I consented. We made an offer on a house in San Diego and he started work there in April.

I joined him in San Diego in June. My first days there were unhappy. I was depressed because of my marital situation and I had looked for a job and applied at numerous locations but had no luck. I felt very abandoned.

It was becoming clear that neither Ned nor I felt comfortable living together anymore. We unpacked the essentials but left everything else in boxes. I didn't hang pictures or do anything else to make the house feel like home. It was an uneasy time.

I did have Salty though and every morning, after Ned left for work, I drove over the top of Mount Soledad to La Jolla Farms where he was stabled. The bright blue of the Pacific greeted me as I reached the top of the hill. This was the best part of my day. At that time of the morning, there were few other riders. I had all the time I needed to groom Salty, work him on the longe line and ride. He had a nice outdoor corral and I could ride in several rings and on a small track.

I met another woman at the barn whose marriage was also in trouble. We quickly became friends. Maria's horse had become a refuge from the unpleasantness of her life, just as mine was for me. We found we were both interested in dressage. She introduced me to other people who were doing dressage and helped me locate a good farrier, several attending veterinarians, feed stores and saddlery shops. Maria also loved dogs and had several Afghan Hounds. We visited each other and took our dogs for walks together. Our friendship helped support one another through the bad days.

Then I made an unusual decision to try to save my marriage. If a skinny teenager could attract my husband by her interest in airplanes, I could certainly do better. On June 24, without telling Ned, I started taking private pilot lessons. I flew a Cessna 150 out of a nearby small airport. I soloed in the early morning of July 25, 1977 after 10 lessons and 12.2 hours in the airplane,

I still remember the thrill of that day. The adrenaline was racing through my veins. I was comfortable using the radios and making basic turns in the air. Take offs were fairly easy and I knew all the required speeds, airplane configurations and procedures. Getting the plane on the ground however was not so easy. I tended to fly into the ground, hitting with a hard bump, rather than letting the plane settle down onto the concrete. That morning my instructor and I started out flying around in the airport pattern, doing a few landings and takeoffs. Then we taxied off the runway and came to a stop. My mouth dropped open when my instructor opened the door and got out of the plane. He told me to do three more takeoff-landing combinations, called touch-and-goes. He felt I was ready but I was not so sure. I taxied out and took off confidently, but I had butterflies in my stomach as I turned the final leg and descended toward the runway. With my heart in my mouth, I managed to bump up and down during the three touch-and-goes. I bounced around each time I hit the runway, but I tried to force all emotion from my body and focus clearly on the numbers and parameters I had been taught. When I finished and taxied off the runway, I let out a sigh of relief and suddenly felt all the emotions I had pushed out of the way. I felt totally high, sitting there on the ground. With my minimal flying skills I had defied death by getting the plane on the ground in one undamaged piece.

Afterwards, I felt like I was flying without wings. I was full of pent up energy and longed to share my accomplishment with someone. A few weeks later I told Ned about my flying and my first solo. He had no interest in what I was doing or in me. If anything, he seemed to resent my foray into his territory. At that point I didn't think anything could reunite us. I found a lawyer and had the terms of divorce drawn up. We quickly agreed on splitting up assets and terms of the divorce. In our eleven years of marriage, we had each earned about the same total income and the settlement pretty much divided everything equally in a way that made sense. On September 1, he moved out of the house and shortly thereafter, he moved in with Jacee in a nearby community.

I was amazed at how hard I was hit as he drove away. As much as I had tried I could not overcome our problems and this was a bitter lesson for me. In spite of all my hard work, my marriage was over.

Not long after Ned moved out, I started to date Tim, who also owned a Pitts airplane and was a commercial pilot. I was amazed at the new feelings of warmth that could exist between two people. My whole attitude towards living became more positive and joyful.

However, Ned and I were still in touch. We hadn't given up on each other, and decided we would try living together again. In December 1977, just before Christmas, Ned moved back in, but the relationship was very cold. He became more and more agitated, and decided on Christmas Eve, that he had to be with Jacee. He loaded up his car and left.

Christmases were difficult for me because of the association with my mother's death. Now there was Ned's desertion on Christmas Eve. I couldn't imagine anything worse as he drove away. I called my one friend Maria, hoping she would be home. Fortunately, she was, and was just going to visit two friends for the rest of the day. She asked me if I wanted to come along. I arrived at her house in record time. In the company of new friends, I was able to forget my feelings of total rejection. The four of us spent the evening drinking eggnog and singing carols around a grand piano. I must have belted out many off-key but enthusiastic choruses.

I slowly started to make friends, especially after I started working. My co-workers had diverse interests. I went on rock climbing expeditions, did some flying as several of the men were pilots, and went sailing on San Diego Bay. The dating that I had missed when I was 17 and 21 years old was now happening to me at age 34.

But I still felt very vulnerable. I distrusted men and their willingness to keep a commitment in a relationship. When my father died, he was having an affair with a neighbor woman, and at the age of 16 even I was aware of those escapades. And then my husband followed the same cheating and lying route. So I enjoyed the company of new boyfriends, but I didn't let myself get too involved. I had plenty to keep me occupied – a job and my best friend Salty.

I did discover how much I liked flying though and so I continued taking lessons even after Ned was gone. By this time I was working and took flying lessons on weekends. On December 17, 1977 I passed the FAA written examination and took a check ride to receive my Private Pilot's license for Single Engine, Land airplanes.

By that time I had friends who flew. They encouraged me to continue. In early 1979, I flew a Cessna 172 several times and was checked out just prior to a trip to the Grand Canyon, accompanied by a fusion physicist I'd begun dating. Landings still were not my forte, and I made a horrible one on the way to Arizona, with the plane skipping up and down on the runway like a bouncing ball. We slept under the wing by the side of the runway on a warm desert night and continued on to the Grand Canyon airport. We joined another couple and hiked in the Grand Canyon for 4 days. It was a fabulous experience and we even heard the braying of the wild donkeys as we walked in remote side canyons.

Around this time, United Air Lines was actively recruiting female pilots. Minimum requirements were 500 flight hours, a commercial rating and passing the 727-jet flight navigator written exam. I continued to fly and received my Instrument rating. I decided that I would like to acquire the necessary credentials to become a commercial pilot. I calmly marched in to my supervisor and said I would like to reduce my workweek to 30 hours for a while, would that be all right? The necessary arrangements were made with personnel.

I started working on skills for a commercial rating and received my commercial certification on November 12, 1979.

All was not smooth sailing though. I had an emergency when I was flying alone in a Cessna 150. The plane had been using large amounts of oil, but had been examined by mechanics and found to be in good running order. I added a quart of oil, filling it up, before taking off. I was headed north and slightly inland from the coast. The engine temperature was fine but then all of a sudden the gauge started rapidly moving up toward the redline where it was no longer safe to operate the engine. I backed off the throttle, setting the engine rpm at a low level and lowered the nose of the plane so that air would more easily flow into the cowling and over the engine. But the temperature gauge kept creeping up until it entered the redline area. I had been scanning my air chart, looking for nearby airports and at this point was over Lake Elsinore. Lake Elsinore airport was closed to general aviation and was used primarily by planes that took out parachute jumpers. I didn't hesitate. I broadcast my intentions to land and set the plane down. My heart was beating rapidly until the runway was under the wheels.

There was no visible activity on the field so I taxied to a hanger that was open. When I checked the engine, the oil dipstick came up two quarts short. I left the plane sitting with the cowlings open and went in search of help. I finally found two people who scrounged around for two quarts of oil. After adding the oil, I nervously drank a can of Coke, waiting for the engine to cool some more. Then I taxied out and took off again, watching the engine temperature gauge like a hawk. I hoped it would remain in the safe zone. If not, I would re-land at Lake Elsinore and be stuck there. I knew it would be difficult to make arrangements to get back to San Diego. Fortunately the engine temperature hovered at the high end of its normal range on the trip home. When flight control asked me to climb several thousand feet in altitude on the way home, I told them I'd rather not and explained the situation. The flight control guys understood and kept track of me until I was safely on the ground at Montgomery Field. I was happy to be back, but upset that the plane was not airworthy, even after it had been cleared by the mechanics. Still, I was pleased with my reactions to the emergency

I continued to fly and accumulated over 500 hours. I flew a Mooney 231 and got my Commercial rating. The last step to complete the requirements for United Airlines was to pass the written test for a 727 flight engineer. I signed up for a three-day cram course in Los Angeles where I was pummeled with terms and information. I took the FAA test the next day and received a passing score. Unfortunately, at that point, the economy had slowed. United was furloughing many of its pilots. I could still be hired, but would not be able to sign on until all the furloughed pilots were recalled. By the time the recall was completed, I had managed to end up on the wrong side of the 35-year old age limit.

I enjoyed all the time and effort associated with flying. In a period of four years, I had evolved from someone who hated the noise and mechanical nature of airplanes, to a competent pilot. I flew for the last time in October of 1981.

TEN YEARS EARLIER, when I was working in Pittsburgh, I thought that a job at General Atomics (GA), in San Diego, would be a dream job in a dream place. Now I had that job in a division that was building a new tokamak, a device to study fusion reactions similar to those occurring on the sun. After submitting a resume, I quickly interviewed for two positions at GA. I had the luxury of choosing between the jobs and I started work in August 1977.

The DIII tokamak (pronounced Dee Three) would begin operation in nine months and I needed to come up to speed quickly. My first task was to write programs to collect and display tokamak data.

The experimental building was vacuous, waiting for all the equipment which was planned for the coming years. The main control room, where I did most of my programming, was also largely empty and colorless, with just a few people working there. Some days I sat at a computer terminal, with silent tears rolling down my cheeks, but no one seemed to notice. I felt alone and isolated and was glad that I had something else to think about. My personal life seemed empty, especially with a failing marriage.

I was very much defined by my work. I needed to be self-sufficient and dependent on no one. I spent many hours at work, and always gave my best. I can't think about myself without thinking of my long employment at GA. Nineteen years encompasses a long time and I was richly rewarded during my time at GA. Many hours of hard work resulted in new opportunities. I grew as my job changed and as I took on new responsibilities. Sometimes now that era seems like an irrelevant memory, but it was a long and important time for me.

I was comfortable working with highly individualistic men with strong opinions and Ph.D. degrees. The tokamak environment was totally new, and my group had to develop ideas, algorithms and operating scenarios entirely from scratch. It was stimulating work, and I liked the fact that the project would ultimately be good for the environment, as fusion promised to generate 'clean energy.'

After a few months of work I felt much more like my old self – the job helped me revive my self-esteem and get through the divorce. February 25, 1978 was an exciting night at work. Everyone in the control room held their breath as the countdown proceeded, ten, nine, eight,...,two, one, fire. This was the first plasma shot[3] of DIII. We waited as traces appeared on the analog equipment, showing what had happened behind the thick cement wall. It was even more heartening to see computer plots of data a few minutes later. I was a part of the project and the place.

---

[3] A plasma shot is a short burst of energy that lasts for a few milliseconds or a few minutes. The inside of the tokamak is heated enough to produce a plasma for a short time.

After being on the job for about six months, I was asked to write a technical paper for the MODCOMP users group (MUSE) meeting. Many of our computers were MODCOMPs. I had never been to a technical meeting nor had I ever been lead author on a technical paper for presentation at a meeting. In fact, I hadn't traveled on business at all. I'd never been to Florida before either, but I attended the meeting in Fort Lauderdale, Florida in December 1978.

There were about 150 people at the meeting. I stuck out like a sore thumb because I was one of three women attending. Although I was nervous, my speech went well. I was relieved when it was over, and I could relax and enjoy the rest of the meeting.

Six men attendees were employed by Alcoa. When they discovered that I had briefly worked for the company, they included me in their social gatherings. One of these men was Jim Newman. I couldn't guess how important Jim would become in my life, when I was totally incapable of caring for myself. At that time, Jim was working in Tennessee. I called him many times throughout the following years, for advice or to get his help with technical problems. I would see him almost every year at the MODCOMP annual meeting.

When Jim took a job in Australia, he recommended me to fill his position on the MUSE board. There I learned about running a small business, with the complexities of members all over the world. The time zone and currency differences were always an issue. In 1982 I was chairman of the board. I had to be a spokesperson at meetings and I became much more secure about talking in front of a group.

Besides gaining recognition among peer groups outside GA, I also was gaining additional respect within the company. My work was always well done, helping achieve the overall goal of the fusion division. I had little avenue for technical advancement, but I didn't mind because the job was always changing.

In the early 1980's, the Federal government awarded a contract to GA to construct and operate a center. When the proposal was funded, my boss left his job in the fusion division to be head of engineering at the supercomputer center.

In March 1985, when he resigned, I was practically bowled over when I was asked to be the acting manager of the Control & Data Acquisition group. I may have hesitated for a split second before accepting the position but it seemed like an opportunity I couldn't pass up, even though I felt unqualified in many areas encompassed by the job.

Others in my group felt they had been slighted and deserved the job and upper management made the decision to name me as ACTING manager. The job was posted internally so that other GA personnel could apply for the position. This felt like a great slap at me, since I had never seen a managerial job posted for open bids. About 10 people bid on the position. However, on June 29, 1985 I became the uncontested permanent manager of the computer systems group.

My work changed from details of my own projects to overseeing 8 people. I started from scratch, developing my own style as a manager, dealing with records, contracts, budgets and personnel. I had several bosses over the years. I had to learn how to work with each effectively. Moreover, I learned how to behave in a technical man's world in order to be heard. I learned to present solutions, rather than just enumerate problems. It was essential that I conduct myself as a man in a man's world. I stumbled many times but I learned.

In 1987 the company appointed me as their representative to the San Diego's YWCA Tribute to Women and Industry. I was happy I had received the support of my division and of the whole company. I appreciated their vote of confidence.

In 1990 I was nominated by GA to attend a semester long course given at San Diego State University. The course was called Executive Challenge and taught business management. The course emphasis was to empower the groups and individuals at a company to do their best. Many of the principles I learned pertained directly to the computer group and helped me to do a better job.

In 1991, a new national group was formed, made up of all the departments and laboratories who were doing fusion research with government funding. We named ourselves the Fusion Computing Council (FCC), and our function was to provide information relevant to computer usage and purchases to the Department of Energy.

The best part of our new organization was the cooperation and camaraderie created in its members, who were scattered across the United States. I was a founding member and acted as chairman for one year.

At GA, another computer center existed in the Fusion Division, with different management. The group had originally been a general-purpose user facility. Now this center was essential to experimental operation. In 1991, the two centers were combined under me. I now was responsible for 14 people, $3 million dollars worth of computer equipment, about 10 large computers, many workstations, hundreds of desktop computers, and a $2.4 million dollar annual operating budget.

I was pleased by the confidence that was placed in me. I had assumed a great deal more responsibility, and I would be at the front of the firing line. But I still reported to the same boss and received the same salary. If someone had been brought in from the outside, the salary to entice him or her would have been far greater than mine.

I had to keep up with the fast changing computer technology. This was difficult to do with so many interruptions during the day, as was completing some of my written reports. I usually stayed at work until 6:30 p.m. or later, and took magazines and reading material home. My dogs always greeted me enthusiastically, and their companionship took my mind off the job. My horse riding was safe from the strain, as I still rode before going to work.

By 1993, the amount of data collected had grown enormously. New computers with new operating systems were needed. There was much debate about the best choice. One particular physicist tried to browbeat everyone with his personal favorite model. He spread miss-information and harangued me everyday, sometimes for hours. One night he confronted me in an empty hallway. He ranted and raved about the upcoming decision. He yelled, "I'm going to show everyone that you don't know anything about your job and ruin your career." I was afraid he might get violent so I backed away from him and said nothing. Fortunately, after his tirade, he stalked away. The rest of the division supported my choice for new equipment, which was purchased and installed, and made everyday operations better for everyone.

The collaboration with other facilities increased during the 1990's. The government awarded a $1 million contract to GA with Princeton Plasma Physics Laboratory, Oak Ridge National Laboratory, and Lawrence Livermore National Laboratory as partners. We were to develop a collaboratory, which would allow remote operation of our tokamak, even from across the country.

I was glad to be doing this new work. We installed cameras, displayed results at remote locations, broadcast audio messages and set up meeting rooms for remote conferencing. Physicists in their offices on their desktop computers could view planning and status meetings. Eventually, our large physical space, complex hardware, with many participating scientists and engineers could be operated remotely.

Early in 1996, I dusted off my old resume, and brought it up to date. I wanted to enlarge my area of experience, to use computers in new environments, and to keep exploring the collaborative efforts. I had talked with some local companies about possible positions, and felt that my skills could be used effectively in several places. I would never get to explore those possibilities.

Chapter Eight

Pam Before - My Passion for a Few Good Horses

SALTY WAS A very large part of my life. I rode four or five days a week. I took lessons. I paid vet bills and farriers, bought extra feed and lugged 50 pound sacks of grain. I entered horse shows. I hung around the stable. I breathed horses every chance I could.

I loved that horse. It didn't matter that he wasn't the dark brown or black horse I had originally pictured in my mind. Each year his soft coat became whiter and even in the winter he kept his sleek appearance. The white blaze down his head became less distinguishable each year. It also was difficult to find his three white socks, as he looked more and more like a white horse (technically he was a gray horse because his skin was gray). His velvety muzzle was a slate gray that contrasted elegantly with his white head. The pink portion of his nose occasionally sun burned and peeled. He had large soft expressive brown eyes, yet inquisitive and playful. He always whinnied when he saw me and nuzzled me gently for treats. When I said, "Salty, want some carrots?" as I briefly showed him a piece, he nickered in his throaty way, calling to me 'Hurry up, Mom, I'm hungry.'

In Los Angeles, I was easily drawn into the world of dressage. Hilda Gurney, on her horse Keen, received national attention. Although she was still teaching special education, she worked with pony club members and had students of her own. She was an enthusiastic presence and helped me out on many occasions.

The sport of dressage seemed to be made for me. Each day of riding was entirely different from any other, and I had to be mentally acute to keep up with my horse! The training took several years. It was technically challenging. A horse had to learn many movements as he advanced. There were a million little points involved in doing each movement correctly. Each time I rode Salty, there were at least 10 or 15 things to work on and improve, and 20 new things to learn. And I always had to take into account that Salty was an individual, with his own moods and preferences. I wasn't in a hurry. I knew that the most experienced riders took years to train their best horses.

It didn't matter that I was a neophyte, and Salty a young inexperienced thoroughbred who had the breeding, disposition and confirmation to race. Many horses who had been bred to do dressage (European warmblood breeds) failed to reach the upper levels because of confirmation or disposition issues. An extremely athletic horse, with a pliable disposition, trained by an experienced horseman was required to succeed in dressage. I was undaunted by this equation, feeling that I had the physical ability to be an expert rider, and the skills needed to train my own inexperienced horse. I didn't know a proper collected canter when I saw one, but I could teach it to Salty. My love and close connection to Salty would surmount all difficulties.

Dressage competitions consist of riding a specified pattern in a 60 meter by 20 meter ring, with letters marking fixed positions around the ring. These patterns, called tests, in the U.S. consist of five levels, Training Level and First through Fourth level. There are several tests within each level. As one advances, the tests become increasingly difficult, more challenging in athletic ability and skill for both horse and rider. Each test consists of prescribed maneuvers to be done at a specific pace, proceeding from 'Trot rising on a 20 Meter circle,' 'Sitting trot circle 10 meters,' 'Collected trot, half-pass,' 'Working canter 20 meter circle,' to more advanced moves such as 'Collected canter 10 meter circle' and 'Collected canter half pirouette.' Every few years a new series of tests are issued which vary the patterns and usually adjust the difficulty level.

The highest level tests are called international tests and have been designed by an international committee made up of experienced equestrians. The same tests are ridden all over the world, and they are used at international competitions such as the Olympics, Pan American Games, and European Championships. The tests have a variety of names (including Prix St. George, Intermediare I, Intermediare II, and Grand Prix) and increase in difficulty. At the highest of these levels, horses perform piaffe (trot in place) and passage (a floating trot where the horse seems to be suspended in air between each step).

I had watched a few horses perform these international tests. I always got goose bumps as the horse and rider moved around the ring effortlessly. They appeared to be a single unit, floating on air, like dancers performing to soundless music. I wanted to melt into my horse and feel the magic of two species moving as one entity.

I loved Salty, the discipline of training and the outdoors. Dressage made it fit together. As a rider, I needed to train my body to become one with the horse, and to sense when I was riding correctly and the horse was executing the movements correctly. I was starting from ground zero and so was Salty.

When I rode well, my horse was also having a good day. We reflected each other's moods. Ideally, I was always conscious of how I was riding, and how the horse was reacting. I had no time for stray thoughts or worries when I was aboard Salty. Our partnership grew stronger and stronger over time, as he learned to respond to light cues from my legs and seat. Sometimes it seemed he responded to my thoughts and we moved in complete harmony. The intense training created a unique bond between us, especially as the level of difficulty increased. Both Salty and I expanded our mental and physical limits.

Not long before leaving Los Angeles, I knew I wanted to show Salty in nearby competitions. I needed reliable transportation to the far-flung show grounds. I purchased a three-quarter ton Chevy van, equipped for hauling. I purchased a no-frills used 2-horse trailer with a ramp for loading. Salty had been nervous getting into a step-up trailer, but went quietly up a ramp. My first big driving experience with the horse and trailer was hauling Salty from Los Angeles to La Jolla Farms in San Diego.

Now I could go to competitions when and where I pleased. Driving my heavy truck and trailer gave me a feeling of independence. But I was always on edge when I hauled Salty, worrying about all the other drivers, hoping to avoid any sort of wreck.

Only by chance, when I moved Salty to La Jolla Farms, I ended up in the perfect place to further my dressage training. A local couple were breeding dressage prospects and were showing a horse at the International Level. Several other boarders were learning dressage. Clinics and shows took place on the grounds. I signed up for everything.

Well, almost everything. A strange reminder of Mafia activity cropped up in La Jolla. One of my new friends told me that she often rode in the morning with a lady named Ann. I never did meet Ann, but saw her several times from a distance. Ann lamented about the horse she had lost back in Chicago. A gray horse, young, who was going to be her mount. A horse who had been stolen.

It didn't take long for me to realize she meant Salty. I couldn't believe that I had ended up at the same barn. I now remembered that the letter in the mail asking to give Hightop Grey back had a second address of La Jolla, crossed through in pen. I tried to lay low and avoid Ann. She was not a good rider and would not have been able to handle Salty. I had changed Salty's show name to Windfall, but still used Salty around the barn. Fortunately, Ann never talked to me and nothing was ever said directly to me about Salty's origins.

The local couple bought land and built a facility in nearby Carmel Valley. They took on a few boarders, including Salty. I was happy to leave La Jolla farms for a new stable where I wouldn't have to worry about Salty's past.

Fortunately, I had enough money to pay the mortgage and keep Salty. In California, horses were kept outside and the hay was grown nearby, which kept costs low. I paid only $125 a month for a corral, twice-daily alfalfa hay feedings, and water. A young successful student of Hilda Gurney kept her horse at my new stable, and I took a weekly lesson from her, at a cost of $25 per lesson. Vet costs were low (fortunately Salty was pretty healthy), and shoes cost about $45 every 6 weeks. Any extra money that I had went to the cost of horse shows.

When it came to Salty, I was extremely lucky to have my job at General Atomics. The DIII site was located in Sorrento Valley, not far from the stable. No one punched a time clock; our schedules were fairly flexible as long as we got the work done.

At home, I gathered my working clothes in the evening, and placed them in a large drawstring bag. I arose at 5:30 a.m., summer and winter, and rode Salty three days a week before going to work. I left my Pacific Beach house around 6 a.m., drove 10 miles to the stable, and was ready to start riding shortly before 7 a.m. In the wintertime, the sky was just getting light when I started brushing Salty, and many winter mornings it was so cold that his water was frozen. One morning each week, I took a lesson at 7 a.m. By the time I finished riding and putting Salty up, it was 8 a.m.

I drove to work and quickly changed into presentable clothes in the rest room. Fortunately, no one ever complained that I smelled like a horse. A few days I forgot my work clothes, and had to go home before making it to work. After that, I kept an acceptable change of clothes in the car, permanently. My car looked like a gym locker anyway, as I was always prepared for some physical event: running clothes and shoes, a sweat suit, tennis skirt and shoes, a tennis racket stacked somewhere in the back, along with any special horse equipment, riding clothes and of course horse treats.

On riding mornings I was at work and sitting at a computer terminal with a cup of tea and a bagel by 8:30 a.m. I always made it to 8 a.m. meetings by switching around my riding days. The physicists almost never got to work early, so this schedule worked out well. My horse passion was well known at GA, and my colleagues rooted for my success.

During 1977, my real horse showing career started. Most of the shows were in the LA area, a two to four hours drive from San Diego. I usually traveled alone. I felt very powerful, handling the hitching up, loading, and driving on my own. Fortunately Salty was comfortable in my trailer, practically leaping in when he saw the hay in the manger. Once moving, he was steady and quiet in the trailer, but he stomped his feet at gas stations or during long traffic lights. And sometimes at gas stations, pee dripped down between the floorboards. I tried to pretend it wasn't happening as I made a quick get away. Hauling a large trailer with a 1200 pound horse never became easy or routine.

I quickly graduated from the preliminary classes of Training Level and started to show in First Level. The movements at this early stage are not difficult. They require some precision and a cooperative horse. Most horses have the ability to do these movements, and get acceptable scores. (Scores are displayed in percentage points. Above 50% is just barely acceptable, and 60% or higher is respectable.)

Salty had the ability to get good scores, but he liked to act up at show sites. Before mounting, when I let him go around me in a circle, attached to a long longe line, he would run, buck, and leap, while I struggled to keep hold of the longe. Viewers often remarked "You're going to ride this horse?" It was difficult keeping his attention on me when I was in the saddle, much less performing in a smooth pleasing way. No doubt there was a brilliant performance in there somewhere, but arranging to have a very good day for both of us did not come easily.

Each section of the dressage test gets a separate mark ranging from 0 to 10. Salty usually scored between 3 and 7. The scores which rated his obedience and his forward movement were often low, because he was trying to do his own test. I just tried to slow him down so that we would stay in the ring. I didn't get discouraged, because I knew eventually he would calm down.

In fact, I was sure that he would be able to progress to higher levels and do movements that most horses could never do. In 1977, I had one score of 58.6%, from an experienced judge who I respected for her judging and teaching ability. Over the years, I participated in several of her clinics. She knew Salty, and encouraged me to keep at it, even though I often had low scores. During this beginning era of dressage in the U.S. scores were generally very low, usually below 55%.

We also hoped that his habit of sticking his tongue out on the right side of his mouth would disappear. Salty was a very oral horse. He liked to put things in his mouth, to play with his tongue (with or without a bit in his mouth). Most judges and riders felt that sticking out the tongue was a sign of disobedience and a lack of submission. With Salty, it was more like a sign of concentration or perhaps concern about what was going on around him. I read every training book and tried every humane way to break him of this habit. But I could not convince Salty to listen. When he was calm or tired, the habit sometimes disappeared. Sometimes at shows he was a perfect mount.

He also had a mild cribbing habit, where he held the edge of a fence with his teeth, arched his neck, and sucked air into his lungs. However, the cribbing problem, or wind sucking, could be controlled. It is thought that horses indulge in this activity because it elevates their endorphins. Sometimes a special strap around a horse's neck makes cribbing uncomfortable. The strap didn't work with Salty and I didn't want to strangle him! But I could place electric wire just on top of the fence rail, so that he could not grab the fence without getting shocked.

I spent a whole day, setting up his corral the first time. I placed a battery in my tack shed with the wire slipping through a large hole to his nearby fence. I hammered insulators along the tops of the fence rails and arranged an insulating handle across the gate. I was quite satisfied to have planned and done it all without help. I wanted to see how Salty reacted to the live wire, since I didn't know if he had ever been exposed to an electrified fence. Apparently not! Almost as soon as I turned on the juice, he approached the fence. The feelers on his nose should have alerted him to something happening in the wire, but he didn't know what to expect. He felt the shock, reeled backwards, and looked very surprised. I wanted to be there, watching to be sure he didn't hurt himself or get too upset. I had been shocked several times while setting up the fence, and it wasn't so bad, more like a powerful surprise. He touched the fence two additional times, more carefully each time, and convinced himself that the wire was not something he wanted to mess with. I left that evening feeling like the arrangement was a success.

I was back early the next morning, mostly to check and see that everything had been OK with the fence overnight. I ended up feeling like a heel, like a good for nothing jerk. All of the hay was still in Salty's feeder. When I touched the hay, I got a shock. Poor Salty had been taunted by his dinner all night, but had not been able to eat it. The electric wire ran behind the metal hay feeder, and in the moist air, the feeder had picked up the charge and passed it on to the hay. I rerouted the wires and the problem was fixed. Fortunately, it took only a little encouragement to convince Salty that his hay was safe to eat. Wherever I kept Salty, I wired his enclosure to prevent cribbing. It was usually a hassle to maintain, but I felt he was safer and healthier.

The next year, 1978, I began to have some success at shows. I was taking weekly lessons, occasionally participating in clinics, and showing Salty extensively. I had advanced to Second Level. The movements were a little more difficult and Salty could do well because of his athletic abilities. The statewide dressage organization held an annual competition at each dressage level, with members riding for qualifying scores during the year.

As usual, Salty's scores were erratic; some were respectable scores, and some were dismal. I usually rode in at least two classes at each show. By the second class, Salty had less energy, and was more familiar with the show environment. Then he sometimes behaved like a dressage horse, receiving better scores.

I was awarded scores of 6 for Ability of Rider, often with comments of 'a very tactful ride' or similar allusions to my struggle to maintain control of Salty while appearing to do nothing.

During this year, I qualified for the state finals at second level. Salty also got his first 8 (out of 10) on a dressage movement. His performances were occasionally surprising, including one show where he neatly stepped over the rail and out of the dressage ring when a sprinkler was turned on nearby. He was automatically eliminated for that maneuver. I had learned to be relaxed with Salty's unexpected actions. Another day, another class.

At many of these shows, I competed against Hilda Gurney. Her presence actually inspired us all to do our best. The competitors and spectators gathered to watched Hilda show Keen at the Olympic level tests.

That year I attend a five day workshop/clinic held at the Malibu Tennis and Riding Club. I traveled there with a friend and her mustang, who lived in a corral near Salty. For five days, all day long, we worked under the tutelage of Hilda Gurney and an assistant. We took lessons on our own horse twice a day. We also rode a school horse being longed so that we could concentrate on our own riding form. There were 8 participants. We watched each other and learned something new almost every minute. We stayed in rooms near each other, and we talked, slept, dreamed, ate, drank and breathed horses for the duration - about 100 hours. It was a heady experience, back in the early days of dressage. I feel so fortunate, looking back, that I had these times to enjoy. I was proud to have trained my own horse and been invited to participate. We all owed a huge debt to Hilda. She was helping the sport of dressage by her strong personal performances on several horses. She was also teaching many students, judging at shows and working to help dressage grow as a sport.

IT WAS SEPTEMBER 23, 1978, my birthday, and I was competing at the annual California Dressage Society show, having qualified for the Second Level finals. It was a little over a year since my first breakup with Ned, and I was happy to be taking care of myself, showing my horse, and moving on with my life. I had arrived at the show grounds a day before competition began, and Salty was starting to calm down a bit. When I rode my tests that weekend, I kept asking myself 'Why is Salty being so good? He feels just great and I can't believe he is performing so well.' The judges liked him too. We received some very good scores, with an average from four judges watching two Second Level tests of 63.38%. We placed seventh out of 25 or 30 riders. I noted with some satisfaction that Hilda Gurney had placed fourth on one of her younger horses, with a close score of 63.92%. Salty and I were hanging in there, doing OK!

I kept at it, training and taking lessons. It helped that riding was easy to do year round because of the good weather in San Diego. In 1979, I moved up to Third Level. The movements were more difficult, but Salty was a very athletic horse, and had no trouble doing the tests. He was still a handful to control.

One of the highlights of that year was riding a Pas de Deux test with my friend Samie Brown. She kept her black thoroughbred horse, named Green, at a nearby stable, and we occasionally rode together on the trail. Our horses excited each other, and several times they had spontaneously taken off, racing across the hills. Samie and I carefully choreographed our performance. We chose movements to do side-by-side at the walk and trot. But at the canter, the two thoroughbreds could not contain themselves. They jumped, pulled at the bit, and raced with each other, even in the 20-meter by 60-meter dressage ring. For the canter part of our ride, we designed mirror image movements, at opposite ends of the ring, in order to keep the horses under control. Since Green was black, and Salty now nearly white, this contrast was effective. Samie's husband taped music from different songs that matched the horses' footfall of walk, trot and canter. It was a lot of work and a lot of practice for a five-minute ride, but we came up with a memorable performance. Both horses went well and the judge didn't notice that our canter patterns seemed unusual. I still have the framed photo of Green and Salty, side by side, doing a shoulder-in along the rail.

Towards the end of the year, I moved up to Fourth Level. The gas shortage was felt throughout California, so in order to keep showing, I had to modify my truck. On one trip, I had been low on gas, and could not find a station that had regular gas in their pumps. I was panicked that I might get stuck in some bad place with Salty, no gas and no way out. I had a second gas tank added, and could carry 40 gallons with me. Even though I was getting just 12 miles per gallon, I could now drive to a show in Los Angeles and back to San Diego without buying gas along the way. A gas shortage was not going to stop me from showing Salty, even if it did take 20 minutes at the pumps to fill up both tanks!

The next year, 1980, I again rode Salty at Fourth level. At this level, judges were not likely to be lenient. Well-known and more experienced people judged the higher level tests. My scores were mid-50's, but one 60 and a few high 50 scores were enough to keep me going. I was being encouraged to proceed during my lessons and clinics. Even though the imported warmblood horses were now dominating the competitions, especially at the higher levels, Salty was not totally out of place. The warmblood breeds have better natural gaits for dressage and a better body carriage. Thus it was becoming harder for Salty to get good scores, relative to the competition, but with his athleticism he could perform the difficult movements. I wasn't so confident in the difficult competition. Even though our scores weren't the highest, I loved the feeling I got when Salty and I teamed up to do a difficult movement well.

In 1981, I made my first tentative appearance at the international level of competition, performing the Prix St. George test twice. This was a big step up. The rider performed 45 or 50 distinct movements from memory. The horse wore a double bridle. One pair of reins was attached to a snaffle bit and another to a curb bit, and each pair was used independently. The horse ended up with a lot of hardware in his mouth, and the full bridle was pretty heavy to hang on his head. The rider wore a riding coat with full tails, white gloves, and a top hat. The outfit sounds silly, but it gave the mounted competitor a very elegant air.

Most of my budget was used to pay for horse show fees, so I decided to make my own tailcoat. I made a pattern from some borrowed jackets, and then sewed my own jacket. I chose a blue gabardine, just slightly brighter and lighter than navy blue. It looked smashing against Salty's white coat especially when paired with a blue edged saddle pad. I was extremely nervous during these rides. 'What am I doing out here – just a dumb amateur on a race horse,' I thought. 'Suppose I forget a pattern in the test, and end up going the wrong way? I'll really show how much I am out of place.' But I remembered the movements and got through the tests. Our two scores were low, but at least one was above 50%. I was a little uncertain about continuing, but I wanted to prove to myself that I could do a good job.

In 1982 and 1983, I continued up the ladder, showing in Prix St. George, Intermediare I and Intermediare II. It was obvious that Salty was good at some of the required movements. At one show he received a score of 8 from Hilda Gurney for 7 flying lead changes at the canter, executed every other stride. Salty had been doing flying lead changes since he was four, when I was just barely cantering him. Doing the collected piaffe, or trot in place, he usually received a grade of 6 and sometimes higher. Piaffe was also a natural gait for Salty. I remembered a time when Salty was four and my husband sat on him bareback, with me standing alongside. Salty had taken a misstep, alarming Ned, who instinctively tightened his long legs around Salty and pulled up tight on the bridle and bit. At this point Salty started to piaffe in place. I had to persuade Ned to loosen up so that Salty would leave all four feet on the ground. My job was to get Salty to do these movements in a relaxed effortless way, at my command.

In 1983, horses were being observed for possible inclusion in the Olympics the following year. I rode in several of the competitions during 1983, although by that time, professional riders and warmblood horses dominated the scene. The Los Angeles Times was doing features on local people who were thinking about Olympic competition. One day a photographer came to the stable at 7 a.m. to take pictures. I hoped that a wonderful picture of Salty doing piaffe, elegantly collected and trotting in place, would be used. Later on, I talked with a reporter over lunch about my riding history. A long article with a picture appeared on the front page of the Sunday LA Times Sports section, San Diego edition, on June 26, 1983. Most of the information in "Dressage: It Is a Beast's Ballet" was correct, but the picture was not so elegant, showing me wearing a babushka, whispering in Salty's ear.

In 1984, all of my test scores on Salty were above 50%. I knew he wasn't ready for the ultimate test, the Grand Prix, but we were getting close. I decided to push the envelope a little, and am now so glad that I did. Some moments in life can be savored forever, even if they are not perfect. Our two Grand Prix tests received scores of 53.8% and 54%. During the second test, Salty effortlessly performed all 15 one-time tempi changes of stride at the canter, a movement where many better horses made mistakes. I also rode my only free style program, with Grand Prix movements, to the music of Jean-Michel Jarre and Equinoxe. The ride was in a covered arena, and the music and movement seemed to excite the very air.

Salty was injured a few times during his career, but nothing serious. I remember a few abscesses in one or another of his feet (a usual hazard for horses wearing shoes) and once he pulled a shoulder slipping in some mud. A few times during 1984, he seemed a little off in his movement, uneven or irregular. The problem was fleeting; sometimes I felt it only a minute or two when I rode him. In March 1985, I went skiing for a week and had someone look after Salty, making sure he was not only safe but getting his little extra grain treats. I had longed him just before leaving, and his left shoulder seemed to be bothering him. He actually fell once when he was jumping around and seemed to come down on that shoulder. When I returned I planned to take him to a vet for in-depth x-rays and evaluation.

I looked forward to seeing him as I approached his corral, and Salty nickered when he saw me. The corral was located in the center of a small pasture, where Salty had other horse companions around him, but not close enough to get hurt in any horse contests. His nickering became almost a plaintive cry, and as I got next to him, I could see he was moving like he was drunk on his feet. I haltered him, and we carefully walked down to the barn area. I had to go very slowly so that Salty would not get his feet tangled up and fall. I had trouble walking too, as tears clouded my eyes.

I knew about a disease called wobbles, where horses are unsteady on their feet. The disease usually affects young horses and is caused by neurological problems associated with growth. But Salty was 13. The local vet came right away, and watched Salty move. His diagnosis of wobbles described the symptoms he saw, but he didn't have a clue about the cause. I was heart broken, seeing Salty like this. A blood test gave no helpful information. I went to see Salty each day, and his condition was worse each time. He whinnied forlornly to me. It sounded like he wanted me to make him better, to help him. I cried when I saw him, feeling helpless as he lost about 100 pounds during that week. It was hard to concentrate on work, and I was glad when Saturday came.

I loaded him up in my trailer, and drove two hours to an excellent equine clinic and veterinarian hospital, specifically for horses. I was afraid he might fall during the trip, and die in the back of my trailer. I drove very slowly and carefully. We made it to the clinic, and I backed him down the ramp onto a grassy area, hoping that he would not fall. He was shivering and upset, and followed me closely into the clinic. It was all I could do to keep from crying, as I told the staff about Salty's symptoms.

The vets evaluated his movement, poked and prodded him. Blood was taken for analysis. I watched as they placed him in a squeeze shoot, and did a spinal tap. Even though he had only local anesthetic, he barely moved. The spinal fluid was also sent out for analysis. There was no more for me to do, so I led Salty to a large box stall. I waited there with him until a warm blanket was placed over him. He settled down a bit. I tried to comfort and reassure him, as I stood by, waiting for him to stop shivering. I had to leave him there, alone, with no friend or companion, in a strange place. It would take a few days for test results to be returned. I felt terrible when I left, like I was deserting him. It was hard to walk away – I didn't know if I would see him again. I could barely see through my tears as I drove back to San Diego.

Nothing definitive was found out from the tests. No bacteria were in his blood or spinal fluid. The spinal fluid was clear, ruling out injury. I felt like I had only one option, especially in light of Salty's suffering and the recommendations of the veternarians. One afternoon the following week, Salty was euthanized at the clinic. For some reason I had a desperate need to know exactly when his death occurred, and talked to the clinic shortly thereafter. I felt totally helpless and cried and cried. I felt like I had let Salty down, my friend of 10 years who was only 13 years old. 'We should have had many more good years together,' I thought. Even now, many years later, I still weep when I think of Salty's untimely end. We had a bond and an understanding that I will probably never have with another animal.

About five years later, the disease equine protozoal myeloencephalitis (EPM) was being diagnosed among horses. EPM is a disease that affects the horse's spinal cord and brain. Opossums are the normal host animals and opossums certainly had easy access to Salty's corral in the middle of the pasture. Although diagnosis is made from blood and spinal fluid, vets and laboratories were not routinely testing for this disease in 1985. The treatment for EPM takes about a year, is costly and most horses do not return to their previous state of health.

I suspect that Salty may have contracted EPM. If only I had known then what I know now, he could have been treated and then retired to a life of ease. I still have tears of gratitude for that wonderful beast, and sorrow because our time was cut short.

I KNEW I didn't want to buy another horse immediately. I needed to live with the emptiness Salty left. And this same month, I was promoted at work and feeling the pressure of a new job. I just needed to lay low for a while, and I concentrated on things at GA.

A large part of my life was gone. I suddenly had many extra hours, both on weekdays and weekends, which had previously been devoted to Salty. The hole seemed enormous. I realized how much enjoyment I got from contact with my horse, and how much I was able to get away from everyday problems and worries when I was at the stable. Especially with the new work position, I realized that I needed a horse to distract my mind and relax my body.

I didn't want the strain of competition, only to have a relationship with a horse. I wanted to continue with dressage training on my new horse, but just for my own pleasure. I set out looking for a nice horse with a good disposition. I made calls to a few dealers, and talked to people who had advertised their horses in the paper. I went to look at 4 or 5 animals, and rode 2 or 3 of them, but none interested me. I heard about a woman who had bred a horse for dressage, but had not done much with him because of her divorce. I knew her reputation as a fine dressage rider.

On the telephone, she said she would consider selling the gelding. He was in a pasture, and I went with a friend to see him. We found him behind the barn (no one else was around), haltered him, and led him around and looked him over. He circled us on the longe line, and we watched him trot and canter, so we could evaluate his gaits, attention and manners. He was quite handsome. A good height, 16 hands, dark bay in color with no white, round and in good condition. He did not have the athleticism of Salty, but he was well built and sound. He was almost five, and had never had a person on his back, so I couldn't ride him. But I put a saddle on his back, and a bit in his mouth, and walked him around to see how he reacted to the gear. He was quiet and accepting.

I hadn't ridden a young, green horse for many years, but I was ready for the change. I purchased Ameego shortly after seeing him, and moved him to his new home at Rancho Ballad, a different ranch from where Salty had last been stabled. The new stable had large corrals (about 45 feet by 90 feet). I wouldn't have to go every day to see him. Ameego would have plenty of room to move around, even run and kick. Here, I wasn't reminded of Salty at every corner.

It wasn't love at first sight. I knew it would take time to really like Ameego. Salty was a hard act to follow. I liked Ameego's personality – he was more inquisitive and more sensible than Salty had been. His rich bay color, with a hint of red, and his black legs, and long black mane and tail were very striking. He had a way of looking me in the eye, like he was saying 'I'm a handsome fellow. Pay some attention to me.' His slightly dished Arab face and deep brown expressive eyes always impressed me. In the winter, his fur grew thick and he looked and felt like velvet.

His name when I got him was Ameego, and I didn't change it. Most people thought I was using the Spanish word for friend, but his name actually came from his parents. His father,

Amer Ramon, was an Arabian stallion, and his mother, a racehorse brood mare, was named Go Go Cahon.

I had a young lady, who was more experienced with young horses, sit astride Ameego for the first time. He acted like nothing unusual was happening, and walked around the sheltered pen like a pro. He was calm and well behaved with a rider.

But at 7 a.m. in the morning, I was usually alone at my new stable. I spent a week leading Ameego around, with saddle and bridle, standing at his shoulder and leaning on his side and back. I guided him, as I would do mounted, with my hands just above his withers. I longed him and let the saddle slap around a little, so that he got used to noises coming from his back. He was so good, that I just couldn't wait for someone to be around and help. One nice morning, I got on him in the fenced lower ring, and started to walk around. My only fear was that some external event would scare Ameego. I always rode wearing a helmet, just to be safe. Fortunately, nothing scary happened that early in the morning.

The first weeks, I let Ameego take a few trotting steps, guiding him around the fenced ring. I started to teach him my commands. One day, he broke naturally into a canter, but there was no hurry or mistrust. Later I took him outside the ring, when he seemed calm, and began to ride around different parts of the property. From then on, it was sheer pleasure. I started to teach him the basic maneuvers of dressage, to go on the bit, and respond to the pressure of my leg. I went on leisurely trail rides, always in the company of another quiet horse.

I realized how much I enjoyed teaching a young horse who knew absolutely nothing. All my previous riding made it easier for me to work through the everyday problems that arose. My patience and skill were rewarded each time I rode. Every new step and movement that I taught Ameego was a thrill to me, every small increment of accomplishment a rewarding achievement. I started to like Ameego as an individual. The pain of losing Salty lessened.

Work was very busy, demanding, sometimes difficult and upsetting but I found I could lose all those tensions when riding. I was glad to have Ameego in my life.

For the next ten years, I rode Ameego at least four times a week. He wasn't always easy. With his thick strong neck, he occasionally would bolt and take off with me on the trail. I switched to a stronger bit for trail riding, which made him easier to control. I felt considerably safer then. He learned more and more dressage. Occasionally I taught friends on him when they wanted to learn the feel of a certain movement. He didn't have the free movement or grace of Salty, but that didn't matter. I still enjoyed each ride. I taught Ameego to do as much as he could, given his physical limitations. I showed him a few times at training and first level, but my heart wasn't in it.

But my heart was wonderfully filled by my love of horses. I pretty much thought like a horse, and had a deep sense of togetherness with my horses. The understanding and respect that I have had with all my horse companions is unique. It's a partnership, which absorbs my body and soul when I am physically in contact with a horse.

I schooled more and more dressage movements on Ameego. He finally learned to do flying lead changes after a whole year of patient teaching. Salty had known and responded instinctively the first try. Ameego learned to do a reasonable half-pass at the trot and canter. He never managed a very good canter half pirouette, but he tried. He was very difficult to collect, and I was just starting to have some success. I managed to get some half steps in preparation for piaffe, that last Monday morning. Eventually he may have learned to do a lovely piaffe for me.

I am glad Ameego shared the best part of Monday, July 8, 1996 with me. It was a nicer than usual day, getting away from my hectic world by spending the morning with Ameego. I am sorry I was never to ride him again.

CHAPTER APPENDIX – a short history of dressage

Horseback riding goes back to the time when man first domesticated the horse. The Greek Xenophon, born about 430 BC, wrote the earliest known work on training horses. As a military leader, he needed strong obedient stallions for battle, where the horses pirouette, turn and leap on command. Hannibal's mounted armies, and the Carthaginians on Iberian horses were successful against the Roman foot soldiers, and thus riding astride again became prevalent.

Mounted soldiers came back into recognition during the Renaissance. Light arms were carried, and the movements of the horse could now help a warrior win at battle. The piaffe (trot in place), levade (suspended jump into the air), pirouette (abrupt change of direction), courbette (where horse jumps into the air and slashes out with hind feet) were effective movements to injure or escape the enemy.

As early as 1580, Lippizan stock (these are the famous White Stallions of the Spanish Riding School in Vienna) was brought from Spain to Austria specifically to do dressage. During the nineteenth century, dressage schools were established around Europe, including France, Germany, and Austria.

In 1912, dressage first appeared in the Olympics, held in Stockholm, Sweden, with teams made up of commissioned military officers. Civilians did not compete until 1952. Since then, Germany has dominated the competitions and women have become important competitors. In 1972 at Munich, Germany's Liselott Linsenhoff became the first female gold medalist. Since 1972, a woman has won a medal in individual dressage in every Olympic Games. And in Seoul in 1988, for the first time, all three medalists were women. Since 2000, each rider must perform an individual ride, set to music, which shows grace, art, and beauty, along with the required figures and paces. This free style test is wonderful to watch and exhibits the art of dressage as a type of human-horse ballet.

Chapter Nine

Setbacks and Progress

1997 WAS PROBABLY the second worst year of my life. I was home and trying to get better, but my body was not always cooperating.

I started to have problems with old hemorrhoids from my teenage horse riding. There was an insidious burning but since I couldn't sense pain, what was it?

I had an appointment with a surgeon in January. The bus to the doctor's office was so shaky it did a thorough job on my insides. I needed a complete cleanup once I got there. It was very embarrassing.

Dr. Lander assured me when I got out of my wheelchair and moved clumsily to the exam table, "Don't worry, with all your movement, you should be able to get control of your bowels."

After the exam he said he could find no real problem but on the way back home, I was extremely uncomfortable. I went directly to bed. By afternoon I was crying because of the pain. I curled up in a ball on my side and wouldn't talk to anyone. Darlene became quite concerned.

"He was awfully rough and really hurt you, didn't he?" she asked.

She arranged to get a prescription for Vicodin but it didn't help the pain much. The only way I could get any relief was to stay in bed. I couldn't stop crying.

It was then I realized that I lose the ability to cope when my body is experiencing physical problems. It's simply too hard to face the physical predicaments on top of the stress of just getting by day to day.

My caregivers had their own coping problems. Cheryl's body had recovered from her car accident, but her psyche had not healed from the many troubles she had had over her lifetime.

She had lived a hard life, on welfare, with 5 stepfathers. She had missed her mother since her death in 1992 and in January 1997, when her biological father died, she had a heavy load to handle. With the accumulated burdens Cheryl felt she would rather be in heaven with her dead relatives.

Darlene had been through some hard times as well. She had been very in love with her husband and had lived in a beautiful house on the Pacific Ocean in Malibu. Then about the time her marriage began to fail, the lovely house caught on fire and burned to the ground. Darlene and the dog were both scorched during their escape. She felt as if her life had turned to ashes and that she had merely wandered aimlessly through the months and years since the fire. She had drifted into my life, apathetic and unwilling to deal with her physical problems. It turned out she was hypoglycemic, and could control the symptoms, including collapse and seizures, with diet but she seemed to lack the mental fortitude to do so.

Our common bond of physical and mental pain made it easy for the three of us to get along. When one of us was down, the others respected the feelings and the need to be tolerated. No clumsy attempts were made to say "It isn't so bad," or "It'll be OK."

When I woke up each morning, I could tell, just lying in bed, whether it would be a Pain Day or an OK Day. I gulped Ibuprofen, Tylenol and Vicodin but nothing seemed to help. The burning pain was an unremitting companion.

I wanted to be independent. I tried to do just a little more each day, each week but I couldn't sit down and set exact goals because I was afraid dates would be too difficult to negotiate. I was not ready to handle any more disappointments. Although my friends and caregivers were always ready to help, one of my major tasks was to train them to be patient.

"Let me struggle a little. If I can't do it, or have tried for a while, I'll ask you to help," I'd say.

Everyone was agreeable.

In the meantime, I was learning more about my foley catheter and so were my caregivers. Darlene was a good teacher. This was especially important one evening when it fell out. Darlene had ordered spare supplies and Dave was able to remedy the situation. I avoided a trip to the emergency room that night because my staff was so competent.

With the foley catheter, I had a degree of independence. By the end of January 1997, I could empty the bag strapped to my ankle myself. From the wheelchair, I was able to lift my foot to the edge of a low toilet with my arms, open the clip and drain the bag.

But a foley catheter is a hazardous piece of equipment. It became a dangerous highway for bacteria to climb into my bladder. Soon my bacteria counts became high and I began to run a fever. Although I was resistant to the first antibiotic Dr. Newman put me on, the next one cleared up the immediate problem. He talked me into switching to intermittent cathing, to help eliminate some of the infections. This change meant I would be 100% dependent on my caregivers to cath me regularly.

I had no choice. The foley came out as I was switched to intermittent cathing. Almost immediately the bacteria took hold and flourished. Two days later, my temperature spiked, my body contracted, spasmed and jerked and my bladder leaked constantly into large absorbent pads. Darlene rushed to put in a new foley and I tried to drink fluid and flush out the enemy. But it was too late. I was admitted to the hospital.

I was shocked at how quickly my body could fall apart. The antibiotics and fluids helped and once I began to improve I talked my physician into releasing me from the hospital after 3 days. I wanted to be home. I was back on a foley. Intermittent cathing would have to wait.

Don drove me home. As we approached my street, I saw Darlene's beat up 280Z parked against the curb with the front end mashed in.

"Oh no," I said to Don. "I bet Darlene had a spell while she was driving."

She and I had talked about this, but she kept insisting she could tell how she felt. I was afraid for her and other drivers.

After Don got me settled into the house, we tried to find out what had happened. Mission Bay Hospital had called the house and talked to Dave telling him that Darlene had hit a parked car, was groggy and unresponsive, and that an ambulance crew had taken her to the hospital.

Don drove to the hospital and found her recovering in the ER. Don and Darlene convinced the doctors that it was OK to release her. The next day her incapacitated car was towed to my driveway. I was secretly glad that she didn't have the money for repairs. Everyone was safer with her off the road. She continued to have seizures and fainting spells over the next few days. My life was much more complicated than I felt I could handle. I felt overwhelmed.

Then another caretaker problem cropped up. Dave suddenly decided that the ex-spouse of a friend needed him more than I did. He quit abruptly, leaving me with a temporary worker for the coming weekend. Suddenly, everything was up in the air. I felt panicky, but I had to deal with it.

This time, I was blessed. When Cheryl heard about Dave's sudden decision, she said, "I was thinking about quitting my job at Eddie Bauer anyway. I can work for you full time, 7 days a week, 24 hours a day."

Darlene was there for relief and I placed an ad to find help for the weekends.

Some days all the lack of stability made me just want to disappear.

One morning I said "I'm going out and walk on the parallel bars until I collapse. Just leave me alone."

By now I could safely get my wheelchair down the low ramp to my patio and over to the parallel bars. But safety wasn't on my mind. I hoped exhaustion would numb me but it didn't work. I walked 12 lengths on the bars, about 230 feet, the longest distance so far. I was tired but I didn't collapse.

Within a few days, I didn't even have the mental energy to get up. Almost every day was painful, mostly from the burning pain in my butt. Staying in bed provided the only relief. One day when it was cold, I retracted my head into my fleece sweatshirt and refused to come out.

"Leave me alone. I don't care any more. I don't want to know anything. Just go away."

After a few hours of self-enforced solitude, I returned to normal and rejoined the household.

I started back on intermittent cathing. This changed everything about my body. My bladder had shrunk while using the foley and I couldn't drink much. A uro-dynamics test indicated that my capacity was about 100 cc's (half a cup). More than that and my bladder leaked and/or spasmed. The diapers I had to wear became wet and my skin irritated. The sensations from my bladder were irritating and uncomfortable and with my butt hurting as well, I became very introspective about my body.

Then just as suddenly, Cheryl told me she was leaving, in about 4 weeks. She and her old boyfriend, Mark, had decided to marry. I was happy for Cheryl but concerned about finding help again.

Cheryl and I had become very close by then and she felt to me like the daughter I never had. I knew Mark would care for her, deal with her ups and downs, and her wanderlust. I wanted to help them get a good start and I volunteered my house for a small reception and buffet. The wedding morning Cheryl banged around my house, her emotions traveling through the gamut of 'I can't wait to get married' to 'I don't want to go through with this.' She wore a beautiful lacy pure white wedding dress that she had purchased several years earlier. Her blond hair was arranged in curls at the back of her head with tendrils escaping and caressing her cheeks. After much searching, we found my wedding veil and tiara. It fit nicely on her and completed the picture.

The wedding took place nearby, atop Mt. Soledad, in the shadow of its large white cross. The breeze was light, the storm clouds cleared and the sun blessed us all. Later, everyone was in good spirits when we dined at my home. Once everyone packed up and left, the house felt lifeless.

I knew how much I would miss Cheryl. She had become a special person in my life. We were equals when we talked about sports, exercising, and pizza with mushrooms and pepperoni. We were more like mother and daughter when it came to caring and contemplating life. In fact, I was born the same year as her mother, so the comparison was even more relevant.

I became depressed when I thought about losing her. It felt as if life was leaving me behind. She had recovered from her accident, but I was still stranded in a wheelchair.

The one unexpected development in my life was Don Edwards. He had been a good boss when I was working for him, back in 1977. He watched out for his people, and gave us all opportunities to grow, develop expertise and attend professional meetings. At that time he was married, with two young boys. After he joined the San Diego Super Computer startup core of employees in 1985, we had occasional professional contacts. Later, I had heard he was divorced and was living alone in La Jolla.

After my accident Don became very generous with his time. Once I was home he was especially helpful. He saw me through the crisis with Darlene's collapse and at the end of 1996, he assisted me with my floor exercises, after the therapists had finished their month of service. He was tall, with dark eyes and a healthy head of hair. Don was the opposite of the athletic, active men I had admired in the past but I thought he was in good condition for someone in his late fifties.

He made me feel so cared for that I began to look forward to his every visit. He cooked well and helped me get through some miserable days. He liked to touch my shoulders and arms and hold my hands. I could see that his visits were expressions of his devotion and concern.

Caregivers came and went. Some were competent but some were so peculiar and unstable that I had to let them go. The merry-go-round of finding good help was a tremendous strain on my already over-burdened system. I knew I could depend on Don as my life changed that horrible year. Over the months, he had become my stability.

I STARTED OUT-PATIENT rehab at Sharp, three times a week in January 1997. My body was ready to do whatever I could coax, cajole or force it to do. The therapists at Sharp were amazed at how much progress I had made since I had left the hospital as an inpatient.

"I have secret weapons," I told them. "Parallel bars and friends who help me."

At this time, I could shuffle 60 feet using my bars and my arms were strong enough so that I could catch myself before falling if my legs gave out.

On my first try on the weight machines at Sharp I was amazed at how much I could do. I could push down 60 pounds – the very amount Lisa, my role model, was doing when we were both patients working out together.

My reward was a walker just two weeks after I started out-patient PT. At first I was afraid it might slip away from me or let me fall if my legs collapsed but my therapist held me firmly with my gait belt and soon I could walk from one mat table to another.

It was hard work. I had to watch both my legs and my feet in order to move them. Watching helped me direct the nerves to action. If I concentrated on every part of the sequence I was about to do, mentally telling my body to respond, my legs obeyed. The list in my head went something like this:

> Pick up left foot
> Contract quadriceps muscle

Bend knee
Swing leg forward from hip
Keep ankle flexed
Don't drag foot
Stand up straight
Keep shoulders back

I was figuring out how to move again.

My physical therapist said as she watched me, "Pam you always look so serious."

"I am serious!" I told her. "I have to concentrate this hard to make anything happen."

After a few sessions, I was allowed to bring the walker home. I grabbed any opportunity to use it around the house. Whenever someone was around to support me, I found excuses to walk from one part of the house to another. In the morning I used the walker to go from the bed to the kitchen. I had my helpers place chairs throughout the rooms of the house and along the hallway, each about 20 feet apart. Then I'd use my walker to go from one chair-island to another.

My energy began returning. I wasn't getting as tired as I had been before. Many days I was able to stay up, using the wheelchair and the walker, without needing to retreat to bed to rest or nap.

One afternoon at rehab, Dr. Newman saw me walking on the parallel bars and doing tiny knee lifts during my PT session. He came over and watched me for a while.

"You are amazing!" he finally said. "I'm going to have to put a curtain around you when you come in here and walk, because all the other patients are getting jealous. I never thought you'd get enough support from your hands to be able to use parallel bars or a walker like this."

"Now that you are starting to walk, Pam," Dr. Williams, my surgeon, said when she examined the final x-ray taken of my neck. "I can tell you this. The two neurosurgeons in the ER who examined you gave you only a one percent chance of ever walking."

"Those people just didn't know how hard a real athlete would work," I thought. I chalked it up to my determination, a good surgeon and some luck.

Only my bladder infections retarded my progress. Another infection reared up at the beginning of April 1997. My Sharp doctor prescribed Macrodantin even though he knew I was slightly allergic to it. I started taking it with Pepsid to settle my stomach, but it didn't work. I started to throw up, became dehydrated, developed a fever and could barely move. At 4 a.m., Don carted me to Sharp where I again entered the hospital through the ER. I was started on an IV antibiotic. In twelve hours, my fever dropped and I felt much better.

Although I went home two days later, I felt defeated. I would gain some strength and then the bladder infections would take it all away. My body seemed to be my enemy with a will all its own. My moods were frequently black and somber. Why should I want to live in this condition? Sometimes I was ready to give up.

Nevertheless, my life went on. Jill, my latest caregiver, was trained by the nurse at Sharp rehab to do my bladder catheterizations. She was a quick learner and soon after my April hospital visit, I started on intermittent caths again. I hoped by doing this to break the vicious cycle of infections.

After a few weeks, I was again acutely aware of how poorly my bladder was working. I decided to abandon the intermittent cathing, and return to the indwelling foley catheter for a while longer.

My primary care physician was a savior to me. Dr. Joe had a round face, jet back hair and listened intently to whatever I told him. He admitted he knew nothing about spinal cord injuries, but said he would help me get to appropriate doctors for my various problems, one of which was constant butt pain. It was interfering with my ability to do rehab and to just get through a day. I was afraid to see another surgeon after my last painful experience. Dr. Joe referred me to a proctologist he knew and trusted.

I dreaded another painful exam as I waited to see the new doctor. I wasn't sure what I wanted to hear but I had been miserable for 8 months and just wanted to get better.

"Please be gentle," I implored, after I gave him my history. He was very kind and his news was good. He said that there really wasn't anything physical that needed to be fixed. What I needed was to look to other avenues for pain management.

My spinal cord doctor felt that my entire neurological system was changing and one of those changes was resulting in nerve pain. I was sensing pain from my butt through misdirected nerve impulses. He prescribed amitriptylin, an antidepressant with the side affect of controlling nerve pain. As much as I had previously resisted antidepressants, I rapidly consented to try this one. I still had some bad days and nights but gradually the medication helped.

Looking back, the rough handling by the first surgeon who had examined me actually sent some real pain signals to my brain. This rough handling had activated nerves which then became supersensitive, causing me more pain. I would have to control the nerves with medication and hope that gradually I could lull them back to a quieter state.

Then came the Fourth of July, which I associated with the accident. I found myself becoming distressed as the holiday approached. I didn't want to be reminded of that day. I tried to remember the good times I had enjoyed, especially riding Ameego and running but those memories taunted me. They made me feel like my life was gone. I knew the sound of fireworks would be especially upsetting. My house was close enough to Sea World in San Diego for their fireworks display to be loud and clear at my house. I couldn't bear to think about a barbecue or other festive gathering. Don and I spent a quiet day on July 4th and after dinner we went to a movie. Still I cried because everyone else was off having fun and celebrating while I was stuck in a wheelchair.

"Let's go in. The movie will be good," Don said when we got to the parking lot.

He knew how to deal with my mood swings and emotional outbursts. He didn't tell me how lucky I was to be alive, or how much better off I was than I had been just 6 months ago. He knew I couldn't be cajoled into a better mood. He also knew to leave me alone and just stay nearby in case I needed him. Slowly I would emerge and pick up where I had left off.

The actual one-year anniversary of the accident wasn't too bad. I had therapy sessions at Sharp that day and I made it my business not to think about the car crash.

Finally things seemed to settle down. Cheryl stopped by to say she would occasionally be available for relief work if I needed it. I was glad we could be together again and we agreed to arrange something in the future.

I decided to try intermittent cathing again, during the week, and use the foley all weekend. I was overly optimistic. On August 26 I went back to the ER and was admitted to the hospital with a high fever, feeling like a steamy wet rag. I couldn't escape the bladder infections. I wanted to curl into a ball, turn my back on the world and cease to exist. For a while, I again lost my will to live. My temperature rose over 104 before the lab found an effective antibiotic (Rocephin), which worked wonders.

I went home on August 31 with an IV access line in my left arm. A nurse came to see me for the next ten days, administering the Rocephin over an hour's period each day. None of the women I knew, who either intermittently cathed or used a foley, had these stubborn and frequent bladder infections. Tests showed no abnormalities in my bladder or kidneys. It was a puzzle.

'Just my luck,' I thought. 'Here I am, actually getting better and bacteria in my bladder are going to kill me.' I later learned that my doctors thought that these bladder infections would kill me in less than ten years.

I didn't see any way to cope with the situation.

I didn't need another birthday either. I didn't want to celebrate being alive. Nevertheless my old helpers, Darlene and Cheryl, took me for a 'surprise' lunch at T.G.I.FRiDAY'S. We talked about inconsequential things and skipped our past and present problems. I enjoyed their company and a short respite from my troublesome life.

By the end of the year, my caregiver was working Monday night through Friday morning. This was enough to get me to my exercise sessions and put food in the refrigerator. Don came on weekends and stayed overnight on Fridays and Saturdays. Sunday night I stayed alone. Once I tallied things up, I was amazed to be this independent.

My nerve pain was indeed receding so I started to slowly lower my medication dosage. I also managed to stay out of the hospital during the last 4 months of the year. Still it had been a very difficult year and I was glad when 1997 was over.

MUCH TO MY surprise early in 1997, Manny, from the GA Old Timers Reunion, called me.

"How can I help, Hon?" he asked.

"Could you pick me up from rehab sometimes? That way I can give my aid a few hours off for errands."

Manny showed up an old 1987 Oldsmobile and I felt lucky we'd renewed our acquaintance at the pizza luncheon because he was a delight. The car had a long bench seat for the front passengers. After Manny helped me in, he folded the wheelchair into the trunk, buckled my seat belt and off we went. He knew my abdominal muscles could not yet support me so he was very conscientious. Whenever he made right turns and I tipped to the left, he'd put his hand on my left shoulder to keep me from ending up in his lap. Riding in his car was fun!

Manny had purchased several small apartment buildings over the years and he was like a father to his tenants. He'd cart them to doctor's appointments and even wait during their visits to nursing homes. His description of himself as a "slum landlord" was mere hyperbole. Manny was kind, warm and extremely generous. We became extraordinary friends.

Once my hands were better and I was stronger, I pushed myself to keep improving. I took a shower on days when I did not have PT and OT. Once I was undressed, I could now get onto the shower chair and over the edge of the tub, picking up my legs with my hands. I could manage the flexible showerhead and do my own scrubbing and rinsing. I was able to pull my large terry cloth robe around myself. All this took over an hour, but I could do it and it made me feel good. I couldn't shower and do PT/OT on the same day because I just didn't have enough energy for both, but I was getting there.

My therapist was surprised when I told her I could get from the floor back into my wheelchair by myself. She spread a mat on the floor for me to demonstrate. I told her it had taken me several days at home to figure out what worked. I promptly pulled myself up off the floor and into the wheelchair.

"That's such an important skill," she said. "If you are out somewhere alone, pushing yourself and somehow fall out, it will be crucial to be able to get back in the chair. It sure would beat being stuck on the ground." (I had to agree.) "I wish all our patients were so motivated," she told me.

Her remarks made me feel good. I was still an athlete after all. I wanted to try harder, be a little stronger, figure out new things just to make progress and my efforts were paying off. My world was expanding.

Yet in spite of my accomplishments, seeing myself in the mirror was awful.

"Cheryl," I complained. "Just look at me. I hate my body. I have fat thighs, my stomach sticks out and my shoulders are bony."

"I can help you," she said. "I'll stand in front of the mirror so you won't have to see yourself." We laughed at her solution!

But she understood. She didn't like to see her body either. The ugly scars from her auto accident, on her back, shoulders and arms, were just starting to lighten up and lose their angry red look. Her sympathy always made me feel better.

Now that my legs were beginning to work, even in a limited way, my next big job was working on my hands. During occupational therapy we started to concentrate on them. I couldn't fully close my fingers on either hand, and in spite of my arm strength, I had a very weak grip. My little fingers stuck out on either hand as if they were attending a British tea party. The sensitivity of both hands was impaired, with the right one worse than the left. The thumb and forefinger did not meet which meant I couldn't pick up small things from a table. On one occasion, the therapist tested my hand sensitivity by placing various objects – safety pin, dime, a marble and a screw – in my hand when my eyes were shut. I had to guess which object I was holding. I found I couldn't distinguish between them. The dime and the screw seemed so strange that I couldn't even hazard a guess as to what they were.

During OT, we started to use an electronic muscle stimulator (e-stim machine). When the current was pulsing through the appropriate arm muscles, I could clench and release my fist. Constant repetition strengthened my muscles. Eventually I could make a pinch with my right thumb and index finger but although I've worked hard at it, the pinch is still very weak. (I often have to substitute my middle finger or use my left hand.)

I could do some new things though. At home, I had begun to stand up by myself in my bathroom to brush my teeth. I still put the toothpaste directly into my mouth from a capless tube, but I could turn the lever-type faucet on and off, fill my own water cup and rinse out the sink when I was done. It took me longer than most people, but I could do it myself. One morning, I leaned against the sink cabinet, which took a little weight off of my legs. I leaned too much, pressing against the cabinet with my knees. Suddenly my knees spasmed away from the pressure and I collapsed. Fortunately, my wheelchair was directly behind me and I landed in it. I learned I could never lean on my knees that way and anytime I did something new, I had to anticipate that my body might react unexpectedly. Each new movement and activity is an experiment. I have to remember that for my body there are sudden, lurking dangers.

The first time I stood and looked around the kitchen, my five foot three and a half inches felt like six feet! I'd been seeing everything from wheelchair level. Suddenly I was as big as everyone. Moments like that made me appreciate how far I had come.

I kept trying to do more things at home. I stood next to my kitchen counter and folded towels. My hands were slow-moving and awkward and I fumbled and dropped edges, but I kept at it. I had to remember not to lean my knees against the lower cabinet and to keep my wheelchair nearby. At least I was standing in my own kitchen and feeling useful.

I continued using both my parallel bars and the walker, but my left leg refused to totally cooperate. It was harder to move and slower to gain strength than my right leg. When I straightened it, the knee tended to hyperextend, almost bending backward. I didn't feel any pain when this happened but I knew it was hard on the joint and tendons and could potentially cause me to fall. To control this reaction, a fiberglass brace was made for my lower leg and knee. It wrapped under the sole and sides of my foot and up the back of my lower left leg. I needed help to get the Velcro fastened over my knee and to change into extra large shoes. Because I couldn't tell if it was irritating my skin or rubbing red spots, in the beginning I had to take it off and check my leg every 10 minutes. It was a hassle but it did seem to work. I began to use it for all my PT.

I was doing all right with the walker at home but my PT thought forearm crutches might help me get around more easily. I remembered seeing them being used by children with polio. I struggled with them for three weeks before I decided they just weren't for me.

I needed to learn to use my walker in new situations. The courtyard at Sharp had a shallow ramp and a steep one, as well as two different sets of steps. Going up the ramp was easy, but I had to take small mincing steps to descend. I felt as if my walker might run away with me downhill. The stairs were actually easier because my arms had become quite strong. I learned to turn my walker sideways on the steps, using it on one side of me and holding the railing with the other hand. My pace was like a snail but at least I wasn't afraid. I did learn however that 'all handrails are not equal.' Thick, decorative ones are not much use to me. I need to get my hand firmly around the railing, with no slipping and no splinters. I also learned that outdoor metal handrails are not always a good idea. The sun can heat them enough to burn my skin and in the winter they quickly made my bare hands numb.

My physical therapist suggested I try a cane with four little legs at the bottom (called a quad cane). It is a sturdy device that can support a good bit of weight when used on a flat surface. A regular cane seemed too insubstantial and tottering. I started walking between the parallel bars, using only the four-legged cane. When I lost my balance or wobbled, I could lean against the bars to get reoriented. After just a few sessions the physical therapist was able to turn me loose between the bars without a gait belt.

One afternoon, with her holding my lifeline belt, we walked all the way from the gym to the nursing station, using the cane. It was a fierce effort on my part and I had to sit down to rest when I reached the station counter. The nurses and aids who had helped me at the hospital kept asking "But Pam, where's your wheelchair?" They were all so happy for me. Their joy at my accomplishment made me feel I had walked several miles!

Finally the physical therapist said, "You need to work on your strength, Pam, but truthfully I don't know what else I can do for you." Naturally when the insurance company received that message, they discontinued any more physical therapy. It was just eleven months since the accident.

I continued to work at home. I remember spending one day totally out of the wheelchair, using my walker all day. I couldn't carry anything so I draped a cloth carry-bag on the walker to take things from one place to another. Of course that method only worked for 'dry' objects. I could walk from one place to another, but I couldn't do anything unless I was sitting down because I didn't dare let go of the walker.

One day, walking down the hall, I suddenly had to use the bathroom. Cheryl trailed behind me, fortunately. I couldn't stand, balance myself and pull down my pants all at the same time. Rather than let the situation discourage me, I laughed and Cheryl laughed with me.

I knew my efforts were going in the right direction. My body was becoming healthier as I spent more time on my feet. My bones and internal organs worked better and would last longer if I continued doing my version of a walk. Eventually I hoped to be strong enough to balance myself on both feet and free up my hands for other crucial tasks!

I still received occupational therapy, which focused on my hands. I could dress myself except for the pants. I also was working on techniques to take care of the paraphernalia needed for the foley catheter. Over a three-month period, I finally managed to do the foley myself.

One weekend, Franky, my GA friend who'd taken over my yard duties, was working out back. Don was helping him, along with my weekend caregiver.

Rather than sit and watch everyone else working away in my yard, I said, "Let me work on the ferns."

I was handed my red metal pruners. Then one of the 5-gallon containers with tall green ferns was put up on a low wall. I positioned my wheelchair so I was just next to it. I went at it. My arms got tired from holding the clippers in a raised position, my hands got tired from closing the clippers and sometimes I had to use both hands just to get through a small stem, but I was happy. I was outside doing something useful with everyone else. It took me a full two days to clip all eight ferns and I made a terrific mess, which someone else had to cleanup, but my hands were getting stronger and I was getting back into living.

One other old skill brought me great joy. I couldn't imagine that I would ever sew again, but my occupational therapist brought in her portable machine and together we made it happen! I was unsteady and needed a wire threader to get the thread through the needle eye. I found I could sew a straight seam while working the power pedal with my foot. My fingers got tired and I needed special pins, long quilting ones with large round balls on the ends, which I dropped frequently, but I was so excited! I would be able to sew again. I could even do hand sewing though I was slow and had trouble pushing the needle through fabric. I still had my mother's beautiful cherry sewing cabinet with my old machine sitting inside of it. I remembered all the hours I had spent with my mother, picking out fabric and patterns, and then making something wonderful. The thought was a comfort to me.

However, every activity that looked good did not work out. I decided to participate in a wheelchair tennis clinic in Point Loma, near my house. The wheelchair companies brought expensive special tennis wheelchairs for our use. The chairs were light and maneuverable and could be controlled with one hand. Many able-bodied people were there to help. I worked with the tennis racket, sitting in the chair, trying to hit balls for about forty minutes.

It was a disaster. I couldn't hold the tennis racquet in my weak right hand. Someone tried to help by wrapping tape around my hand and the racket handle. It still wobbled and I couldn't change my grip from forehand to backhand. The balls I managed to hit flew through the air erratically. I kept remembering how natural it had been for me to play tennis before the accident, how good it used to feel to run and jump and whack the ball. The contrast to my old athletic self was too difficult to bear. The whole wheelchair tennis experience just disheartened me.

I stayed to watch several very good wheelchair players compete in a match and while I admired their skill, I didn't envy them. Their game was a modified thing, allowing two bounces of the ball. It lacked the hard-hitting excitement I was used to on the tennis courts. I vowed to never play tennis again, unless I could do it on my own two feet, gripping the racket firmly.

Another thing that looked good was the prospect of sleeping in my own bed, in my own bedroom. I could still use the hospital bed in the middle of the house if I wanted to watch TV, or just take a break, but being in my own bedroom would be such a treat and so much more private.

Darlene rearranged some furniture and I quickly fell asleep in my old bed. When I awoke early, my mind went back to its old routine. The light shining in through the glass sliding door told me it was time to get up and go ride Ameego. It was only then that I remembered my condition. I pulled the sheet up over my head and cried. I wanted to be me, to be the Pam I always knew. I didn't want to be this new thing that couldn't even get up out of her own bed without help.

As soon as Darlene came in, I said through my tears, "Get me out of here. I can't stand it. I don't want to be in this room."

My reactions and the flood of emotions were completely unexpected. The experience sent me back to sleeping in the hospital bed in the center of the house.

Still other experiences took me out of myself and made me feel alive in a totally new joyful way.

My new friend Manny and my old friend John urged me to come sailing with them. I had been out on sailboats a few times before my accident but I couldn't imagine what sailing would be like now. How could I get on and off a small boat for starters? We drove to the pier where the boats were moored. My two friends rolled me down the steep marina ramp and along the dock. John produced a climbing harness for me to use. The harness was put around me and attached to the halyard. Then they hoisted me out of my wheelchair and onto the boat deck.

Manny helped me find a secure seat in the stern. He picked up my wheelchair, brought it on board and stashed it below deck. After motoring out past the dock, the sails were unfurled and for me the world went away. There was no wheelchair and no reason for me to do anything except sit back and enjoy the ride. A nice breeze caressed us. We ate tuna sandwiches and homemade cookies while I watched the sea gulls drift over our wake. The water, the sky, the gulls and the occasional barking of the harbor seals was magical. Manny and John saw my reaction and vowed to make sailing a regular activity for all of us. After that first time, each expedition out on the bay made me feel more alive. My wonderful friends saved me again.

I wasn't cured but by the end of August 1997 my official therapy was over and I was on my own. I could use the weights in the Sharp gym two nights a week for a small fee. I liked going there. I could workout and visit with hospital friends and it felt comfortable being with other people like myself. We understood each other. I marveled at one man who was starting up his own business in spite of his disability and another who worked full time as a lawyer. Life wasn't over, but I didn't know how it would unfold for me.

Chapter Ten

My world expands and a huge turning point

IN JUNE 1997, I signed up for a water class for the disabled. It was sponsored by a local junior college and taught by a physical therapist. As I was rolled through the entrance and locker room out onto the pool deck I saw a large mural with several killer whales, some above and some below the level of the sea, diving and splashing amidst great gobs of blue, green and turquoise color. The mural brightened the whole room and I felt less apprehensive about this new activity. Cheryl was with me and her presence gave me confidence as well.

The swimming hall at Mission Beach is immense and imposing. It was opened in 1925 and the "PLUNGE" is the largest indoor swimming pool in Southern California. During World War II it was commandeered to train troops. The pool is 200 feet long and 80 feet wide with an unusually deep end. The shallow water was used for my class.

A special chair lowered me into the water. It rotated 180 degrees and then slowly sank down until I was sitting in water waist high. It was an eerie feeling because I got no sensation of being in the water as the chair lowered. I felt no temperature difference and could barely feel ripples sloshing against my skin. The water seemed like a mirage, an unreal ether surrounding my body.

Someone helped me off the chair and I was standing in four feet of water. As the water rose above my waist, my body sensed the cooler temperature and suddenly my legs spasmed out from under me and I collapsed into the arms of my water helper. After 45 seconds, the spasms ended and I could control my legs. I still have this reaction today and have to be very careful entering a pool.

Once I got used to the new sensations I could stand at the pool edge and do some leg exercises. I tried floating on my back but I could only do this with someone at my side, keeping me safe. I waved my hands and arms under water, moving 10 or 15 feet. After an hour, I was transferred back to my wheelchair, wrapped in towels, the foley was reattached and I found my bladder was feeling overly full.

I had mixed feelings about that pool. On the one hand, it felt wonderful to move my legs so easily in the water. I liked that my legs felt more normal in the water, as if they might actually be able to carry my weight while walking. On the other hand, getting into and out of the pool was an arduous expedition. In addition to the preparations for getting there, afterward I had to be driven home, showered, my hair washed and then I had to be dressed. All in all, from start to finish, I needed four hours for a one-hour PLUNGE session.

In spite of the time and effort required though, I pushed myself to go to the pool. I knew I needed it. I watched an older gentleman who had suffered a stroke as he walked back and forth in three feet of water with an aide. I knew then that I wanted to walk in the water and forgot any thoughts of swimming. The teacher helped me get started, using floats in each hand. These devices, which looked like short barbells, helped me keep my balance as I lurched around in the water. I wanted to be safe but I also wanted to walk alone. A floating line was stretched across the pool in case I needed to lean on something or grab it, if I lost my balance or my legs spasmed. I could walk in the water because my legs didn't need to carry the full weight of my body. My legs got stronger from the resistance of being pushed through the water. I walked forwards, sideways and backwards. I stood alone at the edge and did some exercises, feeling very smug about my watery independence.

I overheated easily on the hottest summer days so the pool felt especially good then. It got so I didn't want to miss a single day of class and was usually in the pool 2 or 3 times a week.

One day in September I stretched my independence. I got my clothes off and into my bathing suit at home. A neighbor drove me to Mission Beach and helped me get up the ramp into the front of the pool building. From there, I wheeled myself down to the class area, plugged the catheter, hiding the bag with my towels and backpack, got some help getting into the water and started my exercises. After 50 minutes, I was lifted out, transferred to my wheelchair and I rolled myself out to meet the special San Diego transportation that had come to get me. Once home, the driver made sure I was able to get in my front door. I showered, dressed myself and then collapsed from exhaustion. Fortunately, Don came after work to fix dinner for me, helped me eat and was sure I got to bed without a problem. I totally conked out about 8 p.m. I was very pleased with my solo expedition and not in the least discouraged at being so tired.

By October, I was counting each time I crossed the pool. The count got up to 33, about 2640 feet. When I had trouble remembering the exact count, I invented elaborate mental games (using prime numbers or historical references or anything) to keep my mind focused on the count. When I was confused, thinking it might be 25 or maybe 26, I made myself take the lower number. Sometimes I didn't care about the number at all. I just pushed my way through the water.

The work in the water began to really help me. Sometimes my eyes filled with tears when I thought 'Who cares if I can walk in the water? I can't walk on dry ground.' Yet by the end of 1997, I could walk a half-mile in the water. It took 50 laborious minutes but I could do it! Walking in the water had become one of the most important things I could do for my body.

I had a nodding acquaintance with some of the older women who came for a water exercise class, taught by the physical therapist while I was walking. Occasionally, one of them would join me for a few laps, which really helped pass the time. Many of them had their own physical problems and had dealt with arthritis, hip replacements and cancer. We became a mutual admiration group. The pool was a place where all of us could contend with our imperfect bodies.

Because of the pool, I walked much better on the ground. With Jeff and Don's help I had taken a few hesitating steps with my quad cane, without using a gait belt. I found I could walk slowly with the cane in my right hand, as long as my left arm was linked to a companion. By December, I was able to walk into the annual horse ladies gathering at Irene's, on Maria's arm. Irene was so impressed she said, "First you come in a wheelchair, then with a cane leaning on an arm! Next you'll be running from the car!"

I was glad she noticed my progress. Maybe one day I would be able to fulfill her prediction.

I wanted to walk, to go places on my feet, so I ventured outside and walked across the street to Eva's house, about 60 feet. I held Don's arm and used my cane, or pushed my walker while he stayed behind me. It was a trip fraught with obstacles – my downhill driveway, a roughly paved street, Eva's uphill driveway and a step up into her house. I was excited to be making the trip under my own power.

Later, I walked in my street, using my walker with a caregiver at my side. I felt safe going uphill, but felt like I would tumble over the front of the walker going downhill. I was afraid wherever the street was not flat. At first, I went past the house next door and then back home. Eventually I went all the way up the hill, around the cul-de-sac and back to my house (approximately 475 feet). The up and down helped me with my balance, my legs grew stronger and I enjoyed the trip. Neighbors came out to talk to me. Other times I simply enjoyed being outside, hearing and seeing the birds, feeling the sun on my face and seeing the green trees.

At first, I imagined that walking would feel like it used to feel. The first times I walked on the parallel bars, and often when I moved with the walker, I had doubts. I didn't trust my legs. They didn't feel like they would support me. Fortunately, I didn't wait for my legs to feel right. Even fifteen years later they still seem wrong, undependable, strange and heavy. But I have learned to use them anyway.

One section of Kate Sessions Park near my house was undeveloped and had several rough dirt trails looping up and down, in and out of small arroyos. I had always loved the park, had run and walked my dogs there. I thought I would never see these dirt trails again. Yet once I could walk with the quad cane and a companion, I went to the park even though sometimes my memories brought unexpected tears to my eyes. I bought a regular cane in the drug store, and used it on the rough terrain where there was no flat surface for my quad cane. I held onto Don, Jeff or Cheryl – anyone who could tolerate my slow steps and halting progress. I walked a hundred feet and returned. I tired quickly and the uneven footing challenged my balance and resolve, but the old me wanted to walk on the dirt, to step around the stones, to see where the rain had worn a gully in the trail. I wanted to watch the desert vegetation green up and bloom. I made it a competition to see if I could go a little farther each time. Eventually I walked the entire dirt trail. It was no more than half a mile but seemed as momentous as getting to the top of Everest and back.

An unexpected benefit came from the trail walks; I gained stability with my feet and legs that I had not previously been able to accomplish. The uneven surface and the up and down strengthened my feet, ankles and legs, making it much easier for me to move around on more level terrain. After several walks on the trail, I could walk around on the grassy part of my own back yard, opening up another mini-world to me.

The sidewalk through the developed section of Kate Sessions Park made a circle .43 miles long. The view of Mission Bay with blue sky, verdant green grass and the changing face of the bay was breathtaking. The park was usually busy with picnickers, dogs and kids. I was self-conscious of my awkward body, but walked there anyway. Many people got used to seeing me and offered words of encouragement.

The first day I went a short way using my walker. Gradually I extended the distance. Eventually I got half way around the loop so there was no turning back. It was an uphill walk to the car in either direction. I walked and rested on the benches along the way, eventually completing the loop. I had to concentrate to keep my legs moving, especially on the uphill, but I was proud when I finished. It took me a year before I could walk non-stop around the park. I needed a long time to finish the loop - 57 minutes the first time. After that I started timing each trip, competing with myself and my previous times!

I was proud of my accomplishments in the pool and the park. I was beginning to feel like a 'real' person and wanted to be useful in the work arena again. I looked to GA but that was a mistake. I found out some funds were available for a special education project that meshed students with science and the fusion experiment. I knew I could do some parts of the project at home, but my inquiries and suggestions were ignored. It seemed I had given my best for 19 years, had left abruptly because of the accident and was never even missed. It hurt me deeply.

Adding insult to injury, GA had decided they didn't even want my name on the employee roster anymore. They offered to amend a rule so I could receive my medical insurance through them as a retiree but it was a hollow gesture. After I became eligible for Medicare (27 months after the accident) the GA insurance no longer applied.

Then I got an encouraging phone call. Some years before the accident, I had hired a woman named Sonia as a consultant at GA for a collaboration contract. In late September, when she called me, we talked about one of her projects. She was putting together an entire issue of a technical magazine. It featured various institutions collaborating on large projects, including operating complex equipment remotely. Four lengthy articles would be featured, including the GA project. These were well under way. She wanted to include some shorter write-ups on other similar projects. She asked if I would search them out and edit the submissions.

I was delighted. My physical limitations were gone when I sat in front of my computer and keyboard. I could only type with 3 or 4 fingers, (usually just two) but I managed. However I was as mobile as anyone else across the World Wide Web and could skip from city to city and country to country at will.

I got busy on the Internet. I searched for relevant projects and scanned publications. I talked with people on the phone. I helped edit the longer papers that were submitted. There was no pay, but that didn't matter to me. My work got good reviews and I was proud to have been part of the project when the magazine came out in May 1998.

I put GA's inability to see me as a valuable contributor to their work force behind me. It was good to know that my mind still functioned, at least when I wasn't tired or distracted. It was a terrific boost for my morale to realize I could still do a professional job in spite of my disability.

I FELT AS if I restricted Don's ability to get around and do things but he'd always say "I'm glad to be able to do anything with you. It doesn't matter that we can't do everything." He was a real treasure.

We talked about giving a dinner party for all my wonderful helpers. Again it was Don who made it possible. We shopped for meat, spices and other ingredients to fix my special version of sauerbraten. He did the preparations according to my instructions and it turned out beautifully. My dining room table (with several added leaves) was barely able to hold all the people who had helped me and to whom I was so grateful.

In October 1997, Don talked me into flying to Albuquerque and driving to his sister's vacation house in Taos. Don had not only visited his sister there over the years, but he'd also done business at Los Alamos National Laboratory (LANL). I had been on many business trips to LANL myself before the accident. Years earlier I had skied Al's Run at Taos and had even cross-country skied at Red River. On my trips to New Mexico, I usually took a day or two extra to visit Santa Fe. I loved the high desert, the juniper and piñon trees, the clean air, and the welcoming atmosphere of the "City Different" with its many museums and art galleries.

I talked to one of the ladies in my support group at Sharp. She had taken many air trips with her wheelchair and she gave me lots of advice: about the chair, about packing things I probably would have forgotten and about notifying the airlines of my special needs. By the time Don and I left, I had a large suitcase, packed full of supplies. It looked like we were going on an expedition.

At the boarding gate, there were three other people in wheelchairs. I was the fourth one on. It was easier for me, since I could stand up inside the plane and walk a few steps to a seat, leaning on the seatbacks. My wheelchair was taken down to the baggage compartment, to be brought up to the door as soon as we landed. I remembered to take everything detachable off the chair, including the seat cushion and arms. I was pretty comfortable with the flight, although I worried about whether my foley bag had enough capacity for the trip, as it was several hours between waiting to board and an accessible restroom on the ground. Everything went smoothly though.

The weather in Albuquerque was lovely, warmish and clear. The drive to Taos took about three hours. We stopped just north of Santa Fe for lunch at Gabriel's. I was excited. It was not only my first post-accident excursion on a plane, but my first very slow entrance into a restaurant, walking on my own two feet (while leaning on my cane and hanging onto Don's arm.) I love Southwestern cuisine and the sopapillas tasted especially sweet that afternoon.

Don's sister's house was a challenge as it forced me to use my cane rather than the wheelchair. There were several steps at the entrance and several steps to the main house level. The bedroom was 12 steps up to a second story. But it all worked out with Don helping me almost constantly. I could walk the small steps and bump up and down to the bedroom on my butt. The last night, I hung onto Don and slowly walked up the steps, with him practically dragging me. Still I was overjoyed to have done it on my own two feet.

The deck at the house was bathed by warm sun, and I could walk along it using the cane in my right hand with my left hand on the railing. I felt like I was doing a 'real' walk as I gazed over the nearby pine trees and distant mountains.

We took a long drive to the Maxwell National Wildlife Refuge. The fall colors were everywhere. I laughed as large numbers of Sandhill cranes passed overhead, honking like clowns in their rosy-brown suits. It was a memorable trip and expanded my limited world.

In spite of many good moments during the trip, I was hard hit by negative thoughts, and how unexpectedly they came on. Memories of how I used to be flooded me. I remembered the ski trips to Taos, the times I had jogged from gallery to gallery in Santa Fe. Tears would begin to roll down my cheeks as my mind and my memories became my enemies. 'I can't get out and into the country, hike and commune with nature, let my soul regenerate. All I can do is sit in this chair and be pushed around by Don. I don't want to be in my wheelchair. My enjoyment of life comes from being mobile, from being on my feet, from running and doing things. The Pam I used to be is dead. I wish I were dead too.'

I didn't want pity. I didn't even want to wallow in these thoughts but they came like dark clouds and took over my mind. Don was very patient and after a short while the moods would pass. Because of these heavy thoughts I was glad to return home, but I was even happier that we had gone traveling together, in spite of my moods. I realized that my world was no longer limited to my house, my street and my special disabled adaptations.

Mid-year 1997 my arm strength and reactions had been tested at Sharp. The amount I could turn my head in each direction was also measured. The vertebra fusion may have limited me, but my movement was only a little shy of normal. The tests were part of a driving evaluation. At the end of the year I decided that I wanted my own vehicle, equipped to take my heavy power wheelchair with me, even if I couldn't drive it.

Jerry, the driving teacher, and the OT who helped with the testing, encouraged me to drive, that day in July 1997.

"You should be able to drive with hand controls, Pam," he said. "Let's go out in the Sharp parking lot and sit in a van that has them."

The three of us went to the van. I stood up from my wheelchair and wiggled my way onto the high driver's seat.

Jerry watched me use my hands and said, "I think this ball attachment should work for you."

A round knob was attached to the steering wheel. I could use my right hand on it for all the steering. My left hand could be used to manipulate a rod that stuck out from the steering column on the left. When this rod was pushed, the brakes were activated. When I pulled down on it, the accelerator was applied. Sitting there in the parking lot I fiddled with the controls.

"Let's just start up the engine and do a few turns around the lot," Jerry said.

I was a little scared. I hadn't expected to actually drive a vehicle just yet. I drove very slowly, getting used to the feel of the controls. Jerry gave directions and before I knew it we were in the neighborhood streets.

"Are you sure you haven't done this before?" Jerry asked. "You make it seem very easy."

"Well I did fly airplanes," I said, gaining confidence. They both laughed.

"Then this must be a breeze," Jerry said.

I did have one problem. I needed to keep one hand on the wheel at all times while the other hand remained on the accelerator/brake control. How would I work the turn signal?

When I talked to my friend Lisa, she suggested I wait a while on the driving until I didn't need hand controls. She had started driving the family car once her legs got stronger and she felt perfectly safe doing it. I liked her idea better. It would solve the turn signal dilemma, give me better control of the vehicle and I would have the flexibility of being able to drive other cars. I didn't want a "hand-controls restriction" on my license. In November, I started a dedicated search for a car and some kind of device to get the powerchair loaded into it.

Despite hoping to drive normally, in the fall of 1997, I started taking driving lessons using hand controls in a large half-ton van. The van I used was equipped with dual controls and I was doing fine, but on the fourth lesson, I suddenly lost my nerve. I was driving on the freeway in moderately heavy traffic, going up a hill. My instructor asked me to move one lane to the left, as traffic permitted. There was no way to put on my turn signal because I couldn't release the gas lever while going up the hill. The adjoining two lanes were empty. As I moved left another car, somewhat behind me, moved right so we began converging into the same lane. Lots of horns blew as cars moved back to their original spots. Nothing happened but I was convinced that I needed a third arm to manage the turn signal. I was also unnerved by the horns. I suddenly felt claustrophobic on a road where K-rails guarded the road's edge. The similarity to the circumstances of my accident loomed up before me. Then, before I knew it, the van was squeezed between a school bus and a large truck as we went up another hill. That did it. It was just too much like reliving the accident.

"Here, you drive," I said to Jerry who could use the other set of controls.

Just before getting back to my house, I asked if I could try driving with my foot, the normal way. I drove up the short block to my house with ease. I asked to try a regular car, rather than the lumbering van, for my next lesson.

In the meantime, Don took me to look at mini-vans. In my heart I wanted a car, not a mini-van, but in my head I knew it was the only solution. I looked at American vehicles and foreign ones. I had decided I must be able to walk from the driver's seat to the back of the van using the walker, open the hatchback tailgate and load or unload the wheelchair. That became the first test I did at the car lot. I quickly eliminated about half the vans on the market because I didn't have the combined strength and balance to open the tailgate. My inability shut-up a lot of new car salesmen pretty quickly. They didn't have a ready comeback for my dilemma.

I had always distrusted the reliability of American cars compared to the Japanese ones, but circumstances were different for me now. I chose a Mercury Villager for two reasons: it was made on the same assembly line as the Nissan in Ohio, with just one minor difference in the brake system and by purchasing an American vehicle, I would receive a $1000 rebate on equipment I installed for my disability. I struck a deal for the Villager. It helped that the van was a lovely Wedgwood blue color.

A few weeks later a Bruno Curb-sider lift, which works like a small crane, was installed in the back of my new van. When loading my wheelchair, the Bruno arm swings out the back, lowers to a special attachment on my heavy power chair, hoists the chair up into the air, and rotates it into the van, all with a simple hand-held control. Unloading is done just as easily in the opposite order. Even with my weak hands and poor dexterity, I could do it all myself.

I had overheard a patient at Sharp saying he had gone to the Department of Motor Vehicles in his wheelchair and gotten his drivers license. I figured I would try, leaning on my Grandmother's sage advice: 'Nothing ventured, nothing gained.' Cheryl drove me to the renewal appointment where I sat in line in my wheelchair. At the call "Next," I pushed myself to the counter and stood up. I handed my old license to the clerk and fumbled with the cash for the renewal fee. After shuffling papers, the clerk handed me a form to sign and then several more papers.

"You OK to drive?" she asked. "Your hands look a little weak."

"Oh no," I said immediately. "My fingers aren't good, but my arms are strong." I waived them all around to demonstrate. "I just can't stand for too long. That's why I'm in a wheelchair."

"OK. Go over there and get your picture taken."

I was amazed that it was so easy.

One day on a weekend when I had lots of energy and was feeling good, Don drove me to an empty parking lot in my new van. Then we switched places. No hand controls, no dual controls, just me. We started off in a circle, figuring if anything strange happened, he could reach over and steer the car, while I did whatever it took to stop the van. After several passes around the parking lot, I ventured onto surface streets. I drove around for about twenty minutes without a problem. I was happy that this old familiar skill was mine again, just the way it had been before the accident.

I stayed off the freeways for several weeks until I was used to the feel of the car. I was glad I listened to Lisa and waited until I could use my legs. A mini-van conversion for full wheelchair access was about $25,000 in addition to the cost of the van. My Bruno lift cost only $2000.

In the beginning I didn't drive alone and I avoided being on the road during rush hour or after dark. By the end of that year I felt very comfortable on my routine trips around town. I could even get on the freeway, when it was not crowded.

AT THE END of 1997, I suddenly decided it was time to get rid of the hospital stuff.. I gave away the potty-chair and had the hospital bed disassembled and moved out. Everything I associated with the accident was gone and my old furniture was back in the spots it had been before the accident.

In spite of the changes, I was having a bad day. I kept thinking 'I can fix the house but I can't fix me. I won't ever be anything like I used to be.'

I began to sob and all I managed to get out was "I can't fix me."

Don watched quietly. I asked to have a Black Russian, which he made for me. I wanted to be numb. I wanted my mind to stop torturing me. I drank it quickly but it didn't even taste good. I had a second drink. Then I felt woozy and crawled into bed. Don stayed the night and we slept together in my old bed. He took care of all the things that needed to be done for me: night bag, clean day bag and regular house chores. He must have made himself dinner too but I don't remember. That night I dreamed I was drunk. In my dream I climbed out of bed and walked down my hallway normally.

I was still upset when I woke up the next morning. My dream just teased me, making me feel even more aware of how much I had lost. It was New Year's Eve but I couldn't even think about another year. I tried numbing my mind by tiring out my body. I went back and forth on the parallel bars fifty times but my mind just kept circling round and round: 'I can fix the house, but I can't fix me.'

Don suggested we go to his condo in La Jolla and stay there overnight, just so I could be in a different environment. We drove to his place. He fixed hamburgers on his grill but I still felt awful. I kept getting hot and cold, and then was suddenly hit by a bought of diarrhea. That did it. I curled up in bed early and totally ignored New Year's Eve and the change from 1997 to 1998.

Despite my bad thoughts, I realized I had gained a measure of independence. I was able to stay alone in my house for a few days using my wheelchair and sometimes my walker. I could fix easy meals and clean up after myself. I had to parcel out my energies, doing only one major activity a day but at least I could do some things myself.

The foley catheter was still my nemesis though. For two weeks in January 1997 I struggled with fevers, leaking bladder, burning pain and uncooperative legs and arms. I took a course of oral antibiotics and got better, even though the bacteria count never receded to an acceptable level.

Low spirits always struck when my body was ill, making my negative feelings worse. I often felt there was no reason to keep fighting. These were isolated periods though and between these moods I struggled, exercised and tried to move on. I tried to purge the bad feelings at my computer, writing down my emotions. I felt no need to apologize for these moods as I considered them a bellwether of my resilience.

Cheryl began to help me out a few hours in the middle of the day. I was happy to have her back in my life as we both missed our friendship. I also felt much safer and more independent because I knew I could count on her help when I needed it.

During a few weeks of physical therapy in February I worked on leg strengthening and maneuvering with the quad cane. I used the left leg brace for four or five months and then switched to just an ace bandage. With no bandage, I began to trust my knee. It still hyperextended when I was very tired, or when I didn't carefully monitor my walking, but I found if I kept my attention focused on my legs, the problem did not occur. I still have to stay aware of that knee and leg today, restricting its range of motion.

I wasn't outright sick, but I knew that I would have to deal bladder infection and resistant bacteria again. I wrote in my journal 'I found out yesterday...that I have 4 organisms in my urine: 2 are e-coli and only intravenous antibiotics will get them all. How do I ever get rid of infection if it doesn't leave my body?' I was scared I would die from these infections. But then my old stubbornness kicked in and I thought 'If I can't arrange my life the way I would like it to be, then I have to deal with what it is.'

I made the rounds of urologists and finally found one I liked.

"Doctor," I said, "I don't want to die because of my bladder. I think it might have a chance to work some on its own and if I still need to cath, I want to be able to do it myself."

He was sympathetic and thought it worth a try. I needed a bunch of equipment from the medical supply company such as gloves, cleanser, lubricant and appropriate catheters. I needed antibiotics for the current infection and I also needed training. He wrote out orders to get me started. I asked for a practical nurse to stay with me for a week, 24 hours a day. If my bladder refused to empty on its own and if I couldn't get a catheter in, I faced possible dysreflectia and another visit to the hospital. I could even have a stroke or die. A nurse would make my experiment safer and I was convinced this new approach was worth a try.

The insurance company dragged its feet, as usual. I gave up on them. I wasn't going to wait around for them to make a decision.

I called Darlene, my first caregiver nurse, and asked if she could stay with me for a week. She needed the money and agreed to help. The necessary supplies arrived and I started on a course of antibiotics, given by a nurse who came once a day. I also started taking Ditropan again, to help lessen bladder spasms.

Two days after starting the antibiotic, we took the foley out. Darlene was as committed to my success in this new venture as I was. We worked well as a team during our week together. I curtailed all other activities away from the house.

"Yeah, come on, more!" she cheered, each time I could urinate on my own.

Then I tried to use the catheter myself, sitting on the toilet, with Darlene giving directions and holding a mirror so I could see what I was doing. It may seem strange, but we were perfectly united in this learning effort, so that everything we did felt very natural. I wanted to be in control of my destiny.

The first two nights, when I sensed a slight urge to pee, I got up and walked toward the bathroom using the walker. Both times, I became lightheaded and sank towards the floor, but Darlene was there to catch me. At first we could not pinpoint a cause for this. I could feel my body struggling with strange uncomfortable sensations. We finally realized my bladder no longer knew how to behave in a conventional way. For the next few nights, I sat on the bedside for several minutes before trying to rise and walk. It worked and after that I didn't have any more fainting spells.

By the sixth day, I could do a self-cath and on Darlene's last day, I was quite confident about my new capabilities. Darlene and I felt like we had gone over Niagara Falls in a barrel together and survived.

Then, twenty days after removing the foley, my body gave out. My bladder leaked uncontrollably and I sagged from a high fever. I had done everything I knew to do but it seemed my body was never going to work properly. Another bad bladder infection had taken over.

I couldn't cope. I sank into the most profound depression I had ever experienced. I rolled my wheelchair into the bathroom, looked at my face in the mirror and collapsed into sobs. My absolute lack of hope paralyzed me. I felt like I was looking up from the bottom of a deep well, with no light shining in from the top. By then I wasn't even afraid to die. I stopped trying to fight anymore. Don stayed with me, doing whatever he could to help make me comfortable. I had him add some clauses to my will, so that everyone would be remembered, especially Cheryl. Later that day, the nurse arrived with a vial of the antibiotic Rocephin and gave me the first shot.

By Sunday afternoon my fever was almost gone and I had enough energy to eat some food. Rocephin turned out to be my miracle drug.

I vowed to never again use any type of catheter in my body. If I couldn't pee on my own, then I would just have to fill up and deal with the consequences. I frequently felt the urge to urinate and my bladder often spasmed and emptied when it felt full but this was an encouraging sign. When wearing the foley, my nerves had never had a chance to work. Now, without the foley, my body was reconnecting with these nerves and giving me more normal signals.

It was two years since the accident and my body was feeling something new. All this was contrary to the usual prognosis. According to the doctors, healing would be complete after a year or 18 months. By that time I would have reached my ultimate post-accident capabilities and not much more would return physically and/or neurologically. Fortunately, I didn't listen to them. I was more connected and in touch with my body than any of them could have imagined.

My urologist switched me from elevil to imiprimine to decrease bladder spasms, but the nerve pain came back in full force. He prescribed a prophylactic to prevent bladder infections. I found out Hyprex turned into formaldehyde in my bladder, discouraging bacteria growth. I was intrigued with the clever chemical reaction going on inside me. I discovered how it all worked from an Internet drug site. I also started taking Cranactin, a concentrated pill form of cranberry juice. This contains a chemical that makes it difficult for e-coli to adhere to bladder walls. Several times in July, my bladder burned uncomfortably and I feared another infection had come to get me but tests never revealed any bacteria. Eventually I started to feel much MUCH BETTER.

At night, I set an alarm to wake me up. I'd get up, go in the bathroom, rinse off and change my wet diaper. During the day I usually could feel the need to go and I had about a minute to get to the bathroom. Although I used lots of pads, I was dry most of the day. My urologist was concerned that my constantly wet state, especially during the night, would provide a way for bacteria to flourish. I brought him notes from a night in August when I'd woken up seven times during the night. Each time I had made it to the bathroom and measured my urine output.

"It's amazing," he said surprised. "I didn't think you would get that kind of feeling back." He was as pleased as I was. Fortunately, I was only half-awake during these nocturnal trips and quickly fell back to sleep.

Once my body was free from bacteria I could concentrate on getting better and stronger. It was a huge turning point in my recovery.

Months later, the insurance company called me, saying they would approve a nurse in my home to teach me self-cathing. I was annoyed at how long it had taken for them to come to this decision and told them I had hired my own nurse and would send them all the information so that they could cover my costs.

"Oh no, she wasn't one of our nurses," the insurance people retorted. "You went outside the system so we won't cover that expense."

I got really mad and decided to fight them. I sent all the documentation on the week Darlene and I had spent together, including progress, problems, a copy of the check paid to Darlene and a copy of her nursing card. The insurance company rejected all this about three weeks later.

Nothing would stop me by then. I handled the whole affair as if it was a business transaction. I decided to overwhelm them with my information. I next had to go to an internal appeal board. I found out how many people would sit on the appeal and assembled a packet of information for each of them. I reviewed all my bladder infections and related hospitalizations. I copied all the orders written up by my urologist and got a statement from him about the success of what I had done. I sent the board every recommendation and order written up by my doctors. I compared costs and showed how reasonable Darlene's fee was. I argued that the insurance company was actually better off cost-wise as I was now more healthy.

The hearing was done as a conference telephone call. Most of the participants were physicians so I didn't need to explain anything. They had all looked through the documentation I had provided. I told them how much better I felt and how much better I was doing. Later that same day they called back, saying they had approved the expense. I felt vindicated. They hoped I would give up and go away but I didn't give them a chance. My business and management skills were still proving invaluable. In the end, I was right and they knew it.

Chapter Eleven

My legal case begins

DAVID DEAN, MY lawyer, agreed to take my case on a percentage basis. A tennis partner had given me his name. Within one month of the accident, he had recovered the $5000 medical benefit from my automobile insurance. It was then that he decided to bring in the firm of Swift and Breen, because of their expertise with accident cases.

In October 1996, all three men came to see me at my home. I was sitting in my wheelchair, not far from my hospital bed, looking out the front window and feeling miserable. Their voices were low keyed and quiet as they asked me questions. It took a few minutes for me to realize that all three of these men were now working on my case. I talked about the accident and what I had been through since that day. I told them how victimized and isolated I felt. Nothing would fix the injury I had received. After an hour, they took their yellow note pads and left.

They came back again in January 1997. I realized that David had done an extremely smart thing by bringing in Craig Swift and Andrew Breen. Not only was the firm very experienced in accident cases, especially those dealing with automobiles, but these men were really fine attorneys. To my surprise, I liked all three of them.

David was slim and efficient. Andrew was the humanitarian, with sandy hair and casual good looks. I always felt I could put my head on his shoulder and cry about the horrible changes that had taken over my life. He would gently comfort me and hand me his clean rumpled handkerchief to wipe my eyes. Craig was handsome, with dark short hair, clean cut features and an intense businesslike manner. He radiated confidence. He somehow made me feel as if I was the most important person in the world. I believed something positive would happen with these three men fighting for me.

The three of them quickly found out that the truck involved was a tow truck, one of several belonging to "Paul's Towing for You," a company located in Los Angeles. Several people saw the truck, for about 15 miles before I encountered it, drifting between and across lane lines. It was so flagrant that they'd noted the license number and phoned it in to the police.

A civil suit, with me as plaintiff, was filed against "Paul's Towing for You" on February 18, 1997. The suit named everyone possibly connected with my accident. This included Paul's Towing for You, Honda Motor Company, the Honda dealer where I had purchased my car, the State of California, and Lasten Corporation who had been doing construction for the State where the accident occurred. Also named were "Does One through Ten." The lawyers told me that names could be deleted from the list, but not added later so Does One through Ten were placeholders in case other people or organizations needed to be added at a later date.

Honda was named in the suit because of the seat belt issue and other possible mechanical aspects. During the accident, my seat belt did not protect me. I didn't remember it locking, and I had slid around on the seat. How did I end up lying across the passenger seat, with my seat belt still fastened? Swift and Breen had my car safely stored in their garage, as evidence and for further testing.

I still have mixed emotions about that car, a 1987 Honda Accord. I loved its deep blue color, the extra space I had with the hatchback and its excellent gas mileage. I routinely got 34 miles per gallon, partly because of the 5 speed manual transmission which I enjoyed using. I had driven the car 128,000 miles, so by the time of the accident, it was starting to need more frequent repairs. I had maintained it regularly though, and it was still running well. I certainly didn't feel pressed to trade it in just yet. I was concerned about safety and knew the car was missing more recent equipment, such as air bags and anti-lock brakes. On one occasion, I had even called a dealer to see if anti-lock brakes could be added but it was not possible.

In photos of the damage caused by the accident there are minor dents in the front bumper and a dent in the left rear bumper. From the outside it looks like the car could have been driven away (except for the leaking radiator.) So why was I so badly injured?

I told myself I wasn't responsible for the accident, that I was just in the wrong place at the wrong time. But to this day I still question what I could have done differently. What would have happened to me in a newer car, especially one with anti-lock brakes? Maybe I wouldn't have lost control of the car. It could have been as simple as leaving skid marks on the pavement, uttering a few profanities at the truck and driving on to PetsMart. I can't keep these thoughts from my mind, even now years after the crash.

Other doubts keep popping up. I should have purchased a new car. I should have gone to work that day rather than abiding by a recent edict in my division to use up vacation days. I should have enjoyed the day a little more. I should have ridden Ameego five minutes longer, or brushed him for one more minute.

My eyes fill with tears when I think about what could-have-been and I still have a fearful vision of that truck coming at me. The terror that overwhelms me is like reliving the collision, as if it is just about to happen again.

The accident took place in an area where the freeway had been under construction. A major bridge and several access ramps were being built to connect Interstate 5 and the new Interstate 56. Cement barriers, narrow lanes and no shoulders were part of the construction process, which is why both California and Lasten were named in the lawsuit. I had always thought 'You can't sue the state. You can never get money from them. They are untouchable.' I was wrong.

By mid 1997, I was getting paperwork from the lawyers. I signed releases so they could get all of my medical records. They gathered information to piece together the actual sequence of events involved in the accident. According to the policeman on the scene, 'injuries didn't seem great enough to warrant a high level investigation.' This same police officer wrote that I had handed him my driver's license. I wished that were true. Since there wasn't any blood, being totally paralyzed was not significant to this officer. Craig told me that the scene should have been investigated more thoroughly at the time of the accident.

The first paperwork came in the form of Interrogatories, (a series of questions) asking for simple information, such as date of accident, my name, address and age, my insurance company, marital status, property damage, loss of work dates.

By May of 1997, the questions began to get more detailed. I had to review each response made by the lawyers and sign the documents. I didn't know about every fact and detail they discovered and I learned much as I read their responses. They tried to keep me informed but I was happy to rely on their expertise. I was interested in all the new procedures; I just wished I wasn't the victim.

Later paperwork stated 'She is unable to care for herself...It is anticipated that plaintiff will continue to require periodic hospitalizations...for the rest of her life...(The accident) has drastically changed her life.' When I read 'injury...rendered her quadriplegic' I cried because I was reading about me. Seeing my condition described in words, in black and white on the pages before me, was torture. It meant it had all really happened. It wasn't a nightmare; it was real.

I had to document all my doctor visits and rehab sessions, with names, addresses and costs. I had to locate all the various doctor bills from Scripps hospital when I barely remembered my time there. I searched through every piece of paper I had received. I made phone calls. Physically going through files was difficult for me, but the worst part was I was documenting my own demise.

By the end of August, accident reconstruction experts had looked at the sketchy information available to them and at my medical records. Even they had difficulty accounting for my severe injury when there was only minor damage to my car. My C5 vertebra was displaced forward from my C6 vertebra, as it might have been if I was hit from behind or from whipping around as the car swerved and bounced. To my surprise, the seat belt mechanism was tested and appeared to be working properly.

As the end of 1997 approached, the news was not good. "Paul's Towing for You" was not carrying much insurance. Since they had contracts with the City of Los Angeles, AAA and the California Highway Patrol, they were required to carry at least four million dollars of insurance, but this had not been done.

"Paul's Towing" needed to verify my medical state. I was hesitant to be poked and prodded by their doctor. Fortunately, one of the staff from the law office drove me to the required appointment and stayed with me during the exam. The neurologist was friendly and had actually consulted on my case when I came into the emergency room right after the accident. The usual things were done to me, starting with pinpricks to see where I could feel pain. Then on to strength tests with me pushing and pulling with my hands and arms against the doctor's resistance. He already knew that I was walking some with a walker and was surprised at how strong my legs were. I told him about all my bladder infections and hospitalizations.

He jokingly said, "I wish all my quadriplegic patients worked as hard as you have."

He also said I should never try to walk with a cane because it was too dangerous, and that I might want to take more anti-spasmodic medicine if I wanted to walk better. I soon after stopped taking that medicine! By the end of the exam, I was tired and had a raging headache. My blood pressure was very high. The doctor saw my body react to this uncomfortable situation with autonomic dysreflexia, that strange body reflex of spinal cord injured people. Once I got home some aspirin and a quiet house helped me settle down.

A week later, his report indicated that I had a considerable return of function, but had substantial hand limitations. He also said the usefulness of my walking was limited. I already knew the things he reported. He certainly didn't have any new solutions for me.

I took standardized tests to document my abilities with my hands. In sterile industrial rooms, I squeezed and pressed various calipers and instruments to measure how well my fingers worked, how strongly I could pinch, and how well I could grip and close my hands. After that, I picked up small pieces and placed them in holes, worked with nuts and bolts, and moved around large objects. After the examiner compiled his results, I asked, "How did I do?"

He answered, "You're in the bottom three to five percent."

I was competitive enough that I didn't want to be in the bottom five percent of anything. I constantly struggled to do things with my hands, but there I was, at the bottom, and that wasn't going to change. I was tired and dejected when the session ended.

Just before Christmas, a woman came to my house to make up a Life Plan for my court case. She had been disabled by polio as a child and she moved heavily on two forearm crutches (the kind with handles and arm cuffs) and sturdy braces on each leg. She looked at my ability to take care of myself, my medical and psychological needs, possible future hospitalizations and everything else that my injured body and mind would need for the rest of my days. She was sympathetic, kind and listened to my answers. She understood many of my problems and physical limitations. She had gotten a medical degree, and now worked as a consultant and expert at assessing future care and associated costs.

We spent almost the whole day going over my situation and by the end of our time I felt as if she was a friend. The costs she estimated would be part of the damages I was seeking and were crucial to the outcome of my court case.

I WOKE UP early on Monday morning, December 29, 1997, too nervous to sleep. I knew this day would affect the rest of my life. One of the first stages of a lawsuit is the deposition (by the people involved and other witnesses) and this was the day of my deposition. I didn't know what to expect. I was anxious about being questioned by opposition lawyers, afraid they would be harsh and ask me to recall disturbing details of the accident.

My lawyers, Craig and Andrew, told me to be honest. If I wasn't sure of an answer, just say I wasn't sure or didn't know. "Don't try to guess," they warned me.

They also told me to answer questions briefly and directly without adding any extra information. I had a habit of giving detailed answers, including thought processes, later consequences and statistical support. I knew I would have to slow down and think before I opened my big mouth.

I needed two hours, with help from my caregiver, to get through breakfast, wash up and dress. A legal staff member picked me up at my house. We arrived at the law office about 9:30 a.m. I was worried and edgy. Craig reminded me to give him a chance to object before answering questions. He kept trying to reassure me everything would be fine.

Craig pushed my wheelchair into the large conference room, lined with law books. A long wood conference table surrounded by chairs filled the center of the room.

I became more apprehensive as people filled the room. It seemed like a much bigger event than I had imagined. Craig again whispered to me that I would do just fine. My wheelchair suddenly felt like a familiar friend in this scary environment. I was positioned near the end of the long table. Across from me sat the four opposition lawyers: one from Texas representing "Paul's Towing for You," one for Lasten Construction, another for the

State of California, and the last one representing Honda Motor Company. They were all somber men in business suits. Craig sat next to me on my right, radiating confidence. A court recorder and a videographer were stationed near the end of the table to document the proceeding.

It began at ten minutes after ten. Slowly and quietly, we introduced ourselves. I swore to tell the truth and then became the center of attention for the rest of the day. I didn't allow myself to focus on the four new male faces as I felt it might divert my attention from each question. Instead, I relied on the secure feelings coming from Craig.

"Paul's" lawyer tried to put me at ease by saying he knew I might need to take frequent breaks during the day; just make my wishes known. I sat stiffly and was not mollified. He made a few more general comments, and then was ready to proceed with the questioning.

He started right in on the accident, asking for details about when and where it happened and how I happened to be on the road at that time. I answered briefly. I hoped it would all be this easy so I wouldn't have to remember the details of that awful day. He digressed to my background, which was easier for me. I was still enthused about my work and my position at GA. I struggled, trying to find the words to describe what I had done each day at work. I talked about my previous jobs in LA and Chicago. They picked up the keyword COMPUTERS but I was frustrated because I couldn't really make these people understand what I did.

Then he jumped back and asked about my activities on the morning of July 8. I told him about riding Ameego and smiled inwardly, remembering how good that part of the day had been. He asked me what kind of a saddle I used. I wondered what that had to do with anything. I even had to clarify that a dressage saddle was a type of English saddle. I thought he was either distracted with the questions or was trying to trick me. I realized that this was not going to be an orderly or even logical series of questions.

After a while, I forgot about the camera. I tried to stay focused and sharp, not missing the slightest nuance of each question. I wanted my answers to be clear and succinct.

He asked me if I had a cup of coffee with me as I left the barn. I could tell he was joking and was thinking of the large award a person had received from McDonald's after spilling hot coffee while driving. I smiled and answered "No."

He continued with questions in areas I had never expected to consider, his voice grating on my ears for most of the day.

He kept jumping around to little bits of information, like selling Ameego back to Michelle for $1, or my relatives in Baltimore, but he always went back to the accident:

Where was I going?

How was the weather?

Was the traffic heavy?

What time did I get on the freeway?

He asked questions about my car and the maintenance done on it. Luckily I had kept meticulous records. He was trying to make me seem responsible for the accident because I'd been driving an old car, possibly poorly maintained.

I could not speak matter-of-factly about the accident. I wanted to yell and scream and sob about all the things that had happened. It was such a horrendous event that going back there in my mind made me relive each moment: seeing the truck, hearing the horns and tires squeal. It was all in a day's work for him while I was forced to relive the nightmare over and over.

"How fast were you going when the accident happened?"

"I was going between 40 and 50 miles per hour."

He pressed more on this point, wanting to know how accurately I could estimate my speed. For the first time, Craig objected to a question. I had been pausing before giving each of my answers, so he didn't have to cut me off. Craig said I wasn't an expert and should not be required to give a more accurate speed when I had already answered the question. I held my breath and waited for the reaction from the other lawyers. But there was no reaction and we sped on as if nothing had happened:

Was the car sliding or skidding?

Did I take my foot off the brake?

When did I take my foot off the brake?

Was I skidding forward?

What angle did I hit the barrier the first time?

What lane was I in?

What did I say as I lay paralyzed in the fast lane and in the ambulance?

In a few minutes, he fired enough questions at me to fill over 20 pages in the deposition transcript. I concentrated on the answers and tried to distance myself from the horrors of that day. I attempted to put my emotions in a little box, where they wouldn't interfere with my answers.

Then there were more questions about my rehabilitation and return home. Finally we took a break at 11:30 a.m. I was glad to get away from the intensity and electric air in the conference room. I had been sitting tensely in my wheelchair all morning and was exhausted. My shoulders were tight and achy. I tried to relax as Craig pushed me towards the back of the office.

"You're doing fine," he said. "Just keep it up. You're probably smarter than any of them anyway so don't worry."

Craig's comments helped me relax and made me feel like I could get through the rest of the day.

We started again at noon.

When did I look left?

How far away was the split between I-5 and I-805?

It just went on and on.

Then the lawyer switched tracks. He asked me what other knowledge I had of the accident. I was surprised, wondering why he would ask me about what others might have seen or said? "I only know what happened from my own experiences," I replied. Craig and Andrew had not filled me in on any of the earlier depositions nor had they shown me the accident report or pictures of my car.

The questions continued to jump around. I found it easier to talk about my day-to-day activities and was able to relax a little during these questions.

But then it was back to questions about the freeway scene. "Prior to seeing the truck in lane three, what did you see?"

The back end of the truck again loomed in my mind's eye, filling my senses.

We finally stopped for lunch at 12:45 p.m. It felt like the questions could go on forever. I was glad to get away from everyone. I ate a cup of yogurt but didn't really want it.

We started again at 1:45 p.m., right back into the midst of the accident. I deliberately blanked my mind of the freeway images and tried to answer questions factually and succinctly, as if I was a newspaper reporter. The questions were worded to make it seem like my reactions caused the accident but I formed my answers carefully so the words couldn't be twisted. My concentration helped me remove myself from the accident and its horrors. I felt detached, like I was watching the conference room proceedings from a light in the ceiling.

No matter where the questions wandered, they always jumped back to the accident. I answered the same questions over and over. It all felt like a mind game. It was a game I needed to win.

After a short break at 3 p.m. the lawyer for the State of California started his questioning. Each lawyer's style was different – one friendly, another sympathetic, another hostile. They all seemed condescending. The State's lawyer's questions were clear and concise. He was rephrasing my answers from the morning about my reactions during the accident. I listened intently to be sure he wasn't putting words in my mouth or misstating what I had said earlier.

I realized the questions were being worded to indicate that the truck really wasn't going to hit my car. I was horrified to think that these men were blaming me for the accident. How could I have done this to myself? I was the innocent victim in the wrong place at the wrong time.

I was tired from concentrating. It was getting harder to recall everything I had said earlier and to repeat those same statements.

The lawyer for Lasten Construction was next. As he began, I readjusted my brain. He asked many of the same questions and I gave the same answers, but I felt myself getting annoyed. I started answering questions before they were completed. Craig reminded me to wait and listen to the entire question. I wanted to be finished and get out of there.

Some of the construction company questions brought out the fact that the barrier on the right was above a hill that dropped off into Sorrento Valley. Later, I realized that this information could be used to prove that the barrier prevented me from crashing over the edge of the hill. It didn't seem to matter that the road should have had a fifth lane and a shoulder, which probably would have allowed me to miss the truck and regain control of my car. He asked me how long it took to enter the freeway, check for traffic and encounter the truck.

I snapped, "I don't want to guess, it was a lifetime," because for me that short instance had obliterated my life.

Lastly, Craig asked me a few questions. I felt like I was being held by warm hands, in a safe place. He emphasized that I had to apply my brake and steer to avoid the tow truck.

At 4:36 p.m. it was over. I was drained and anxious to go home. The opposition lawyers left quickly. Craig thought it had gone very well.

Several weeks later I read the 200-page transcript and made corrections. The accident haunted me, day after day. I knew that until the entire trial process was over, I would not be able to put that horrible moment behind me.

ON FEBRUARY 9, 1998, Craig called to tell me a meeting with Honda, Lasten and the State of California was scheduled for the next day. The meeting was to explore a settlement. A retired judge would be present. Craig wanted me to be available via telephone all of the next day, in case an acceptable offer was made.

Craig didn't call until a little after 6 p.m. but when he did he was in good spirits. Honda had offered a payment so they could be disconnected from the case. Both Lasten and the State of California offered settlement amounts, because of the construction that was under way on the road when the accident happened. The total was much larger than Craig had expected. I was flabbergasted.

I received about 50% of the money. The three lawyers got their share, and I had to pay for court costs and other fees. A significant amount was placed in an escrow account, for future costs and for a $16,000 lien placed by Scripps Hospital.

I was shocked when the lawyers told me that I would have to pay for my hospitalizations out of the settlement costs. I thought 'that's what insurance was for.' But as it turned out, my medical insurance contract had a clause that required me to repay medical costs if a settlement or award was made to me as a result of an accident. This is a common clause in most medical insurance contracts. In my case, this amounted to $200,000.

I didn't understand how Craig and Andrew had negotiated this award from Lasten and the State, but I found out when I read the depositions they had taken. I quickly appreciated the knowledge that Craig and Andrew had brought to my case. They knew exactly how the construction work force was organized and which people to identify and interview, such as construction crew foremen and office clerks. They knew what reports and daily logs were generated and what construction plans and documents were on file. More importantly, they knew how all this meshed together. They uncovered differences between the plan and the actual construction. Interstate 5 should have had a fifth lane and shoulder where the accident occurred.

It nagged at me: if the work had been done correctly, the way it was supposed to be, I might be the old-Pam. I tried to put these thoughts out of my mind and focus instead on how grateful I was for Craig and Andrew.

The trial would be against "Paul's Towing for You." Once again, Craig and Andrew were busy following up on every detail.

I didn't know what to expect during a trial. I had been a big fan of Perry Mason and other TV shows that take place in a courtroom, but I suspected the programs weren't anywhere near the truth. I was curious and interested except for the fact that the trial would revolve around my accident and paralysis.

I became very apprehensive, remembering all the hours of being grilled during the deposition. Craig, Andrew and David gave me the same advice as I had been given before the deposition: be honest, be brief and be sincere.

Craig decided he didn't want me to sit with him at the plaintiff's table during the trial. He thought the jury might be a little more sympathetic if they didn't have to look at me day after day. Craig told the jury right away that my physical condition made it difficult for me to appear in court every day.

Although I wanted to know every detail of the trial, I didn't want to hear the expert testimony about my condition and prognosis. It wasn't until four years later that I actually read the trial transcript. Even then, knowing what I did, it made me feel absolutely miserable about the life and care the experts predicted I would need.

The trial started on March 2, 1998, Pamela A. Henline, plaintiff vs. "Paul's Towing for You, Inc.," d.b.a. "Paul's Towing for You," et al.

The deposition had not seemed so terribly official, even though it was done under oath with all those people present. The trial was a different matter. It was formal, in a courtroom, with a judge, and a jury and although I wanted the trial to happen, I wanted it to be finished quickly. I didn't want to think any more about that terrible day, to keep remembering and reliving the horror of not being able to move.

Proceedings started on Monday, March 2, 1998, when the judge heard some motions and jury selection was started. On Tuesday, the jury selection was completed. The jury was composed of relatively young people, which caused my lawyers some concern. Young people, they reasoned, might not be familiar with long-term suffering or sympathetic to how totally my life had changed. But they also reasoned that the three young men in the computer industry would be able to appreciate my working career.

Craig gave his opening statement, as did the lawyer for Lasten, who stayed on the case to try and get some settlement money back from "Paul's."

Before the start of questioning, the defense stipulated that the "Paul's Towing for You" tow truck had been at the accident scene. The defense lawyer deferred his opening until later. There were no witnesses the first day of the trial.

I was home, waiting nervously. Craig updated me over the phone each evening.

I read over my deposition and it looked like I would be needed in court the next day. I dressed carefully, in navy blue pants, a blouse and jacket. But I still felt disheveled and messy. There was no way to sit in a wheelchair without having my clothes appear rumpled and ill fitting.

Wednesday morning, the day of my first appearance, four accident witnesses testified: one was a woman who had been located only a week before the trial began, but she had a very clear recollection of my accident. All four people reported watching the tow truck as it sped down I-5. They'd seen it drift from its lane into the next right lane and jerk back many times. One couple had even gotten close enough to take down the license number. The couple had then pulled around the tow truck to avoid an accident, which seemed inevitable.

Before court, at the law office, I saw a picture of the actual tow truck. No wonder I thought it was a huge semi! It had a large rounded high cab in front and the back was a very high flat bed, long enough to hold two cars, end-to-end.

Craig pushed my wheelchair the two blocks from his office to the Hall Of Justice after lunch. Even though it was a beautiful sunny day, I felt serious, somber and slightly afraid. My wheelchair jarred me as it rolled over trolley tracks and several curbs along the way.

I waited apprehensively in the hallway outside the courtroom, where I wouldn't be seen, until all the jurors had returned from lunch. When everyone was seated and the proceedings resumed, Craig pushed me through the double doors of the courtroom. The first thing that caught my eye was a three-foot by two-foot x-ray picture of my spine resting on an easel. The bones were sticking out of alignment. I had never seen it before and it gave me the willies.

The courtroom was new and attractive. The walls gleamed with wood paneling. The jury was seated on my right while the judge sat high above it all. I looked toward the jurors and tried to smile. Craig pushed me to the side of the witness stand, which was equipped with a small elevator. The lift raised my wheelchair to the height of the witness box. I thought about how I could place my hands on the ledge in front of me and maybe smooth them out so they'd look close to normal. But I just let them lie on the counter, twisted and misshapen, in their real state. I smiled nervously as I was sworn in. I felt small and insecure, sitting in front of a full courtroom and 12 jurors. I hoped my voice wouldn't crack. I didn't want them to pity me but I did want them to have empathy for what I'd been through.

Craig's questions started around 2:30 p.m. and I became a little less nervous as we progressed.

I was brief about my background - how I had worked my whole life, how I put myself through college with scholarships and loans. I didn't want the jury to think I was some rich girl, with a high paying job, an expensive horse hobby and no ordinary real-world concerns.

I tried to describe my job. I talked about all of my activities and my love of animals and the outdoors. At this point, each juror received a book of pictures of me, smiling and looking happy, running, hiking, sailing, skiing, riding Ameego and playing tennis. It had taken me weeks to go through old photographs for this book and it had been painful having to see all the things I could no longer do and would never do again.

Then I answered questions about the accident and the time immediately after. I knew going to trial meant I would have to relive the accident again in front of these people. Craig made sure we covered everything the defense might ask me in cross-examination. He didn't want the jury to think we were trying to leave anything out. I talked about my hospitalization at Scripps and Sharp Rehab. I talked about how hard it was for me to do even simple tasks. I tried to keep my emotions in check. I didn't want to rant and rave and lose my composure but it wasn't easy. Inside I was shaking.

About 3:00 p.m. the judge declared a break because an expert witnesses had come down from LA. The witness wasn't available to testify at a later date so the rest of my testimony was postponed. I later read that the expert, who had tested my manual dexterity, told the jury it would be impossible for me to find a meaningful job because of my poorly functioning hands.

I left the courtroom in the midst of my testimony, feeling like the most important scene of my life had been put on hold. Although a friend, who was seated in the audience, told me I had come across warm and sincere and Craig and David said everything went well, my mind wasn't relieved. I went home and worried all night about the cross-examination the next day.

The next day I again waited in the law offices until after lunch before I was called. Two experts, a life planner and an accountant, had been on the stand in the morning. I was happy

Craig would still be asking the questions as I knew the cross-examination to come would be hostile.

After being sworn in again, Craig asked me about my pets and what had happened to them. I told him I had sold Ameego to Michelle for $1, because she would give him a good home and love him as much as I did. A picture of Ameego came to my mind: his beautiful head and his nickers for my carrots. Suddenly I was so sad that my eyes started to water and my voice broke. I paused. It was a distressing moment and the jury could feel my pain.

Craig changed to a new area of questioning and said, "Let's talk about what you can do, instead of what you can't do."

I talked about exercising, at home and during rehab, about how hard I worked to make my body get better. I told the jury what I could do around the house. I told them how I used my computer. I tried to impress on everyone how long it took me to do everything. I talked about how hard each little thing is for me compared to everyone else. I wanted the jury to understand that nothing was easy any more and how each day was another trial of endurance.

Craig asked "How do you feel about yourself and what are your goals in life?"

I hadn't answered this question before. I didn't know what to say. I didn't know how I felt about myself or the strange new person living inside a body that didn't work.

I finally answered, "I have three goals - first to get healthier by getting the indwelling catheter out and starting up on an intermittent catheterization program." I knew that the jurors had been told about catheterization, so I could say this quickly and not be embarrassed. "Second, I want to keep working physically, trying to get better and to walk. And I also want to try to work a little, for the people contact, self-esteem and excitement of doing something worthwhile." During this time, I saw some of the jurors watching me closely and smiling at me.

I answered a few questions about my lack of stamina and ability to work. Then Craig asked how I felt about myself. I hesitated since I didn't have an answer.

Finally I said, "You have to figure out who you are, and I haven't done that yet. I don't know when I will. I am not happy with the changes in my life. I feel like I am 'Pam-before' and 'Pam-after.' I'm trying to make the best of my situation, but I have to figure out how to do that. I am not going to say my life is over because I am still learning how to keep going."

Craig's questions made me think about how much my life had changed and how little I knew about my soul or who I really was anymore. It was sobering and scary to inhabit the body of a stranger.

Then Craig had me verify a list of medical expenses that were submitted as evidence. He sat down and the defense began.

Chapter Twelve

A Verdict and a Judge's Ruling

AT FIRST, THE defense lawyer had a nice voice and a quiet manner. He asked me direct questions about the accident and I responded with short answers, keeping in mind what had been said at the deposition. There was confusion about whether I was in lane 3 or lane 4 because some of the witnesses had conflicting statements. I was also slightly confused. Everything had happened so fast on the freeway. My clearest recollection was of sliding across a lane and hitting the right barrier.

Using a model of the road and toy cars, the lawyer moved the cars.

"Isn't it possible that you were in lane 4 and the truck was in lane 2 and you converged on each other in lane 3?" he asked me in an accusatory voice.

Knowing they wanted to make it look like my fault, I said firmly "I was not changing lanes, so that is impossible."

The next thing the lawyer did seemed strange to me. He got out a copy of my deposition and gave it to me. I thought 'do they really want me to handle this thick book with my hands?' The book was one and one-quarter inches thick, with a spiral binding. He turned to a page and line number and asked me to locate the same place in my copy. He read the question and I read my answer but there wasn't anything in the deposition about the accident that hadn't already come out. At one point, he jumped to page 157. I had to fumble with my hands trying to turn the pages to the right place. The pieces of paper kept slipping through my fingers. He started to read while I was still fumbling with the paper. I could feel the jury watching me.

After reading from the deposition there were more questions.

"Did you take up any new hobbies since the accident?" he asked.

I volunteered that I did more with my computer at home, specifically that I surfed the net looking for information about spinal cord injuries.

He asked if I had done any work for pay, in a tone of voice that seemed to indicate that I should be out in the world working and not trying to collect money at a trial.

"No," I said, "but I helped a friend gather and edit articles for an issue of the ACM Insight magazine."

"Do you want to do this kind of work?" he asked in a demanding tone.

"No," I said again. "It was just to get my feet wet and to finish up some stuff about collaboratories that I had done at GA." I couldn't understand why so much was made of this small job. I felt like I was being tricked into losing some new kind of mind game.

Next the lawyer for Lasten asked me a few questions about the terrain and drop-off next to the side of the freeway. Again, I read a little from the December deposition.

Craig asked a few more questions on redirect. I reiterated that I was unsure about being in lane 3 or lane 4. On recross-examination, I was asked only about how much of the truck was in my lane and by how many feet.

I was on the stand for about 45 minutes. It hadn't been as grueling as the deposition but I was worried because I hadn't been able to tell the jury about who I really was and how much of a nightmare my life was because of the accident. Still I was relieved to be done for the moment.

A friend from GA testified next and talked about how we had hiked, cross-country skied and played tennis together. When asked if I kept up with him hiking, he said he had trouble keeping up with me. There was no cross-examination.

Irene, from the horse barn, testified and said I was as close to being a professional athlete as anyone she had ever known. The plaintiff's case was done.

I wanted to hear the rest of the testimony on the following days, but I waited it out at home and got updates from Craig and David each evening.

On Monday, March 9, all the lawyers had a long closed session with the judge about whether the background of the tow truck driver would be allowed. "Paul's" lawyers wanted to limit the questions to his employment and church attendance. But the judge ruled that if some background was brought out, the door was open for more questioning. The judge joked about how damning this would be to the defense, since the crack cocaine and alcoholism in the man's recent past would be exposed.

When court was resumed, the defense lawyer gave his opening statement. He argued that I had overreacted while driving. This had resulted in my loss of control. The tow truck driver and I, according to him, had been converging on an empty lane.

Two police officers testified.

The owner of "Paul's Towing for You" testified that the driver was fired some time after my accident, when he failed to show up for work. Then the driver testified. He didn't even remember the accident until after the lawyers had talked to him. He was asked how he had rehabilitated himself from his use of crack and alcohol. He talked about how he'd gotten the job with "Paul's" through his pastor.

On Tuesday morning, three men, who worked on the construction of the road, testified as to the actual condition of the road at the time of the accident. A small amount of information from a fourth man was read into the record from his deposition. In the afternoon, a vocational expert, speaking for the defense, talked about my ability to work. His expectations were naturally much higher than our expert's.

Wednesday, in closing arguments, Craig talked about all the people who had seen the accident and how my life had changed since then. He talked about how brave I was, how hard I had worked to recover and about how the rest of my life was going to be rough going.

The defense argued that the road was unsafe and I had contributed to the accident.

It took the judge a long time to instruct the jury. Besides the usual admonishments about fairness, doubt and decision-making, he reviewed a six-page document the jury was to complete, which asked which of the parties was actually responsible for the accident.

The case went to the jury about 2 p.m.

Craig was hoping the jury would take some time to deliberate. He was upset because one of the jurors had kept his arms crossed during Craig's closing argument but had taken notes during the defense's closing argument. Then when the defense got to damages, the juror had stopped writing.

On Thursday at noon I went to the law office to wait. At 1:30 p.m. the court called to say there was a verdict. The bailiff seemed to be in a good mood as Craig and I entered the courtroom. Craig thought it was a good sign that the bailiff was smiling and relaxed but still he fidgeted next to me as we waited for all the lawyers to arrive. Craig whispered "bad" to me when none of the jurors looked our way or smiled. The jury foreman gave the 6-page verdict form to the judge who only looked at pages 1 and 2 before giving it to the court clerk to read. Craig made another "this is bad" forecast as the bailiff began to read:

"Was the tow truck company negligent? .. YES."

Both Craig and I were holding our breath; now we both sighed.

"Was Pam Henline negligent?"

I felt numb all over and barely breathed as I waited for the answer.

"NO."

I let out a small gasp of relief.

Craig squeezed my arm and whispered, "Are you all right?"

I nodded, glad to have him at my side.

"What do you find to be the total amount of damages?"

A large amount was listed for economic damages, and a significant amount for non-economic damages. Suddenly, I found myself sobbing quietly. Craig put his arm around me. It was too much to absorb.

The judge thanked the jury and asked the lawyers if there were any questions. The defense lawyer asked for a poll of the jurors. In a civil trial, a vote of 9 to 3 is sufficient for any item. The jury was 12 to 0 on all questions, except non-economic damages, which polled at 10 to 2. As we found out later, the two people who had disagreed on the non-economic damages had actually wanted a larger award for me.

The jury was thanked and began to file out. None of us were sure what to do as the 12 men and women walked past me. Three of the ladies gave me a hug and most of the others shook my hand. Some of the women were weeping along with me.

Later, one of the jurors wrote, "I saw in Pam a heart that accepted her circumstances and that was motivated in spirit to rise above them. I saw no bitterness, self-pity or revenge. That alone was a confirmation to me of her nature as a human being."

I was relieved it was over. It seemed wonderful, sad and almost anti-climatic. I'd spent weeks and months focused on the trial. I was awed with these lawyers who I had reached just by chance. They were wonderful, caring and extremely competent people.

Then came the bad news. There were no monetary funds to collect from "Paul's Towing for You." In fact, "Paul's" had nothing for me. It would be up to the lawyers to see if there was any way to collect my award, which meant more work, and possibly more law suits.

Waiting until the very last day, "Paul's" appealed the ruling against them to the Fourth Appellate District in the Court of Appeals of the State of California. Meanwhile Craig and Andrew continued to investigate "Paul's" insurance company situation. Eventually, they found one carrier who paid out one tenth of the judgment. After court fees, lawyers, etc., I received a portion of that amount. A detailed financial report was gathered of "Paul's" assets. As it turned out, all of the tow trucks were leased and most of the payments were done on a monthly basis. There were no substantial assets. I might have been able to take over their business, but I would have had to run it as well.

More than a year and a half later, on December 29, 1999, "Paul's" filed an appeal stating why the judgment should be overturned. It was 34 pages long and argued two technical points. The first point had to do with the use of expert witnesses by "Paul's" and the timing of their requests and motions to the judge. The second point argued that the information about the driver's prior alcohol and drug addictions should not have been admitted.

Our response, on March 20, 2000, was equally as technical and spanned 31 pages. The arguments countered the points already submitted for "Paul's."

"Paul's" countered our submission on May 11, 2000, with another 23-page brief.

I read each brief and felt that all of the arguments were impressive and believable but couldn't imagine how the appeal judges would decide.

Oral arguments took place before the court in September and on October 2, 2000, the appeals court ruled that the original verdict was valid and the monetary judgment against "Paul's" stood. They would be liable for interest on the money for all the time since the original verdict on March 12, 1998.

Craig made a case against one of the insurance companies based on documents, letters and statements. A day before a judge was to rule on the insurance company's liability, they offered to settle. I received a portion of the jury's award from them. Six years after the accident, the lawsuits were finally over.

With disability insurance and the settlement amounts, I had the financial resources to take care of myself. It would just provide for my care and for my future needs. I knew I was one of the lucky injured ones but the money wouldn't heal me. The tow truck driver went scot-free and the tow truck company suffered very little.

I still have trouble driving near large yellow and white trucks, or next to cement barriers, especially on the freeways and interstates. The vision of that truck bearing down on my car flashes through my mind. Sometimes it blinds me as I sleep and dream.

I'm grateful for my excellent lawyers and for whatever health I have, but it has been a hard and pain-filled road I wish I'd never had to travel.

ANOTHER LEGAL MATTER came up soon after the accident. My medical insurer, PruCare, had been notified of the accident the day it happened. They approved my eight-day stay in the Intensive Care Unit at Scripps Hospital. By August 1996, the Scripps bill of $82,000 had been turned over to a collection agency, MLR. MLR threatened to put a lien of $16,447.82 on any settlement I received. This amount was the difference between what PruCare actually paid and the $82K. My PruCare policy covered 100% of my hospitalization costs, so I assumed some mistake had occurred. I passed the information on to Craig and Andrew.

Craig contacted MLR and they faxed him some boilerplate text which was incomplete. MLR was less than helpful when he contacted them. Normally, lawyers don't try to recover such small amounts, as the costs quickly overrun the award, but MLR had riled the wrong lawyer.

They (Scripps, MLR, and PruCare) ignored requests for information and wouldn't discuss the matter. I felt Scripps was trying to take advantage of me. We had to file a lawsuit against all three on April 9, 1998.

I felt that the lien was adding insult to my injuries. I was paralyzed and struggling with life, and the hospital was illegally trying to extort more money from me. They were morally and practically wrong. I wasn't going to be a victim again.

Craig thought we had a clear-cut case. We were suing for the lien amount and psychological damages. Every time the court ordered MLR, Scripps or PruCare to produce documents, they stalled. They appealed each ruling of the judge, so that more time was needed for a second ruling. Craig and Andrew considered MLR's lawyer to be a bumbling idiot.

The paperwork and investigation went on for months. Anonymous tips were called into Craig's office about people at Scripps and MLR – who was sleeping with whom, or which employees had made sudden large expenditures. My lawyers dug up information about clandestine relationships between employees of MLR and Scripps. They located paperwork indicating one MLR employee had a relatively small income, but in a short amount of time had made large deposits to a checking account, had sent a child to private school, and bought a condominium as well as a car. It was unfolding like an episode of 'General Hospital.'

All of the Scripps records were scrutinized. I had been kept for 8 days in an intensive care unit, and then released to a rehab hospital. Obviously I should have spent some time in a regular hospital room at Scripps. The itemized bill had amazing charges: one Valium pill - $95.00; one latex glove - $5.00. Some of the services or drugs had not even been provided. I had heard about these kinds of charges at hospitals, but I didn't think it really happened, and not to me!

MLR did everything they could to delay and make us give up. They even filed a counter suit against my lawyers and me. The suit was a first for Swift & Breen, and it only spurred them on in their efforts to expose MLR. Later MLR sued Lasten, the State of California, and Honda, trying to get the money I'd received from them. Each action just made MLR seem like an even more sleazy operation.

When the news of my suit became public, many people and lawyers began contacting Swift & Breen. It seemed Scripps had pulled the same dirty deal on them too.

On Monday, October 12, 1998, I appeared at a deposition for MLR. Three lawyers were there, representing MLR, PruCare and Scripps. Craig and I sat next to each other. A court reporter took everything down, but no video taping was done. I wanted everyone to know that these unscrupulous people were cheating me. I knew that MLR would try to make me look like the bad guy. At least I wouldn't have to relive the accident.

I didn't like the lawyer who represented MLR.

"Look at the last page, Ms. Henline. Did you sign this paper?" he kept asking. He spent most of his time pointing to the last page of each Interrogatory.

"Yes I did. I read the interrogatory and I signed it. That is my signature," I said.

"Did you understand everything you read in this document?" he demanded.

"Yes, but only in the sense a lay person can understand all the answers," I responded.

He droned on and on, document after document, his tone always accusatory. His pounding seemed pointless. Even the PruCare and Scripps lawyers did not look happy with the proceeding. Finally I said I felt like he was harassing me. His constant haranguing voice was giving me a headache.

On top of that, the foley catheter had been taken out four months prior to the meeting, which meant I needed to take frequent bathroom breaks. That day I was particularly uncomfortable. I thought I might be getting another infection. I was in no mood to be pleasant to this man.

During lunch, Craig said I was doing fine. He told me the MLR lawyer was a jerk, but not to worry. I had an appointment with my urologist at 4 p.m. so I knew we couldn't go on all afternoon.

Still I was under fire from 10 a.m. until 3:20 p.m. They asked me about psychological damages. I told them about symptoms I had suffered as a result of the lien. I knew that some of my bladder infections were aggravated by the stress and strain of this lien and law suit. I told them this interrogation was getting to me, and that my bladder was acting up. I felt achy and feverish that afternoon when I headed for the urology appointment.

The deposition was continued December 7, 1998. It lasted from 10 a.m. until 2:30 p.m. A different lawyer represented MLR. It wasn't nearly as bad as the earlier confrontation. I sailed through the day without a worry, and was relieved when it was finally over.

On December 2, 1998, MLR dropped their cross-complaint. Craig and Andrew hoped that at this time the judge would let us amend our suit to add false accusations and malicious prosecution, which would make our case even stronger. MLR carried insurance for this type of misdeed.

Paperwork continued to fly back and forth. Contracts between Scripps and PruCare contained a specific clause that said Scripps would not go after the patient for any money since PruCare was solely responsible for payment. On March 18, 1999, the presiding judge ruled that the lien was illegal. Later, the court also ruled that I had the right to sue Scripps and MLR for their negligent and intentional acts.

By now the media had found out not only about my case, but all the other people who'd had similar circumstances with Scripps. A reporter from the Los Angeles Times contacted Swift & Breen. They gave the reporter some information and permission to talk with me. A photographer came to the law office and took several pictures of Craig and me. A long article appeared in the LA Times on April 17, 1999, describing the entire situation of hospital liens.

We were scheduled to go to trial shortly and the reporting struck a positive cord with most people. In fact, because so many people had similar situations with Scripps, another law office filed a class action suit.

In April, a local TV station, KUSI, followed up the on the LA Times Article by interviewing me. I talked for several hours about myself and my feelings of being 'used' and 'abused' by Scripps and MLR. I told the reporters that the accident was enough of a nightmare without unscrupulous companies making it even worse. A photographer filmed me working out on the adapted equipment at Sharp Rehab and shuttling along on my walker. The story was shown on the 10 p.m. news on May 6, 1999.

Yet even in the glare of the public exposure, MLR did not want to settle. Several required meetings for arbitration were useless. Instead MLR delayed and delayed.

Finally in January 2000, MLR began making noises about a settlement but they first wanted the judge to reverse the illegal lien ruling. It couldn't be done. We never would have agreed to such a stipulation. Once again, a trial was on the docket, but was delayed.

Craig and Andrew were busy with other cases and were content to delay a few more months. Strangely, in June 2000, a judge ruled against the class action suit. A different law firm (not Swift & Breen) argued their case before a different judge than the one overseeing my case. This ruling was appealed, but later was not resolved in favor of the accident victims.

The case was taking up time that Craig and Andrew needed for other clients, and as it turned out, MLR did not have sufficient assets to pay a likely court verdict anyway. On June 8, 2000, we arrived at a monetary settlement whose terms are confidential. It could have been better, but it could have been worse. Scripps stopped using the services of MLR, and MLR went bankrupt and closed down. Unfortunately, Scripps is still placing liens and attempting to collect them through an in-house organization. Scripps also changed their contracts with HMOs to allow them to collect from the patient.

The lien practice used by Scripps is fairly common. The Wall Street Journal publication, Smart Money, ran a lengthy article in July 2000 that explored the issues and talked about my case and several other similar cases around the country. I hoped that my suffering and the endless hours spent by Craig and Andrew would help other people in a similar situation.

One other substantial benefit came out of the MLR suit. PruCare had remained largely immune from the actions. They made no effort to defend me under the terms of my contract with them, which was supposed to protect me from the lien. They did agree however that I did not have to repay them for medical treatment from my settlements or other future awards. I no longer had to keep $200,000 in an escrow account.

More than six years after the accident, the legal maneuvering was behind me. I learned a lot about good and decent lawyers, and a lot about charlatans who took advantage of the sick. I learned about the U.S. court system, which did support me when I desperately needed help with my life.

Chapter Thirteen

Horses Help Me Heal, a New City
And Adventures in the Snow

ON APRIL 22, 1997, I sat on the floor of a cubicle in a veterinarian's office, cradling my dog Shadow's head in my lap. Her beautiful black coat was flat and limp and her expressive light brown eyes were glazed over and unseeing. I had rescued my beloved wolf-dog six years earlier at my horse's stable. Now she didn't recognize me and was numb to the world from liver failure. I held her through her last long sigh, after the vet injected the anesthesia overdose.

I felt at that moment like all the important things in my life were being taken away from me. Shadow was a powerful connection to my old life, to freedom, to movement, and particularly to horses. I needed to find something that would bring joy and hope back into my life. To me, this meant horses. I had to ride again.

I knew something about therapeutic riding long before my accident. In 1974, I was riding at Acorn Hill in the Chicago area. There I met John Davies. He had come from England to take over the everyday operation of the barn and to start a therapeutic riding program. I remember being very impressed with his gentle and competent way with horses, as well as his sensitive caring concern for the human race. There was no way for me to know then how important his philosophy would become to me after my accident, but a poem he wrote made a lasting impression on me, as did his book Reins of Life.

I Saw a Child

I saw a child who couldn't walk-
sit on a horse, laugh and talk.

Then ride it through a field of daisies
and yet he could not walk unaided.
I saw a child, no legs below,
sit on a horse and make it go
through woods of green
and places he had never been
to sit and stare,
except from a chair.

I saw a child who could only crawl
mount a horse and sit up tall.
Put it through degrees of paces
and laugh at the wonder in our faces.
I saw a child born into strife
Take up and hold the reins of life
and that same child was heard to say,
Thank God for showing me the way...

Hippo[*] therapy was first introduced in Europe following two epidemics of poliomyelitis after World War II and came to North America in the 1960's. When Liz Hartel of Denmark won the silver medal for dressage at the 1952 Helsinki Olympic Games—despite being paralyzed below the knees from polio--medical and equine professionals began to take active notice.

It was learned that the smooth, gentle, rhythmic movements of the horse help to relax spastic muscles and build muscle strength. Balance, sitting and even breathing improve. A horse's walk is close to a human gait. Moreover, the forward movement with the hip/pelvis moving left to right, back and forth and tilting forward and backward is the same as when a human walks. By sitting passively on the horse, the rider's pelvis moves through all the walking motions, helping the person to regain his/her walking ability.

---

[*] Hippo is Latin for horse

Recently, I watched a partially paralyzed adult start riding. In four sessions, he went from hyperventilating, immobile from fear, to moving around on the horse, raising his arms and twisting and looking in all directions. Riding was clearly bringing a new dimension to his life. When we spoke he told me each session recharged his whole week.

On June 6, 1997, my friend Maria drove me to the therapeutic riding arena at the Helen Woodward Center (HWAC). I had wanted to volunteer at the center before my accident, but I hadn't made time in my busy schedule. Now I was looking at the program from the other side.

On my application to HWAC, I listed my disabilities and physical condition. I said my goals were to get back on a horse and go on an independent trail ride. At the time, I thought my second goal seemed unreachable, but I was going to try. The director explained that I would begin by riding for no more than half an hour. Volunteers would walk on each side of me and someone else would lead the horse.

I was looking forward to my first ride with both anticipation and fear. I knew it would be difficult. How would I get up on a horse? Could I even sit without the back of a chair supporting me? Would I like it in my altered physical state? I think I was more afraid that I might not enjoy the ride than I was of the dangers.

The center was located near the Santa Fe River, in mostly open country. I had ridden Ameego on the riverbed trail before the accident. That first day, everything was still green from the winter rains. The air was fresh and a light breeze blew down the valley from the ocean.

Two large platforms stood near the entrance of a riding ring that was covered over with a roof and open on all sides. Maria pushed my wheelchair to the ring and then rolled me up the ramp onto one of the platforms. The other platform stood several feet away. I smelled the faint odor of horses although I couldn't see any barns or corrals. Then I heard movement and several people came around the corner of a high wooden fence, leading a small pony. I had expected to ride a horse, not a pony. I wanted to simultaneously laugh and cry, because pony or not, I was still afraid.

Yankee was a black and white pinto Chincoteague pony. She wore a bareback pad with reins attached to a halter. When she was led between the platforms she seemed small from my position high above her. I had ridden ponies her size as a child and had even been thrown by one. The memory prompted a worry that I might be injured but I pushed the thought aside.

I didn't know how to get on her as I could barely stand up. The volunteers came to my side to support me. I hoisted myself up on my legs using the wheelchair arms. Another person, on the other platform, lifted my right leg over Yankee's back and then helped me sit down gently. At first I was afraid I would fall off but after a few minutes I began to relax.

Sitting on Yankee was like coming home to a familiar and comforting place. Her coat was raggedy with winter hair and I enjoyed the rough feel of it as I ran my hand along her neck. Loose hair came away on my palm, which reminded me of all the other springtime's I had brushed and curried my horses, Ameego and Salty. The sights, sounds and smells were as good as I had remembered and the thoughts made me feel alive.

There was a person on each side of me, both of them resting a hand on my leg, to keep me securely on the pony's back while another person led Yankee. No one had to hold me on however. I sat up without help as we walked around the arena. I didn't lose my balance as we turned corners and stopped at various places. Then, before I knew it, my first session was over. I had been on Yankee's back for 25 minutes. It had been so easy!

I was overwhelmed with the feeling of freedom I had on Yankee's back. I didn't need a wheelchair. I could go around the ring many times, using her legs, not mine.

On our drive home, Maria and I stopped to visit Ameego. I had not seen him since that awful morning almost a year before.

He recognized me immediately and whinnied. I looked at him, knowing that I would never be able to ride him again. But I wasn't overcome by my thoughts about Ameego. I was still so excited from having been led around on a little pony.

After my first time up on Yankee, horseback riding became the highlight of each week. Nothing was going to stop me. On days when my butt was painful, I tried to ignore it, sometimes taking several strong painkillers just so I could ride. My outlook and mental state improved whenever I thought about my next scheduled ride.

Each time I rode it became easier. I guided Yankee through cones and walked across poles lying on the ground. The pony resented my attempts to turn her with the reins and even nipped at the person leading her. As we headed toward the gate, she would walk faster, clicking her heels, hoping to return to her corral and hay. I made her stop or turn away from the gate. She showed her displeasure by nipping or by rounding her back, but instead of being afraid I enjoyed the challenge of outwitting her. After so many years of thinking like a horse, I knew exactly what to expect from a willful pony. My body took longer to respond than it used to - to change weight and balance, to press with a calf or heel - yet every time I rode, my nerves seemed to recall the old pathways and patterns of movement. My balance, strength and stamina improved steadily and my heart simply soared with happiness.

It wasn't long before I outgrew Yankee. I was introduced to Questa, a well-proportioned dark chestnut half-Arabian horse with a lot of Western training. She was 15 hands tall (60 inches at the withers) and I loved her from the first minute I rode her. Her walk was much smoother than the pony's and I could control her easily, with just a halter. I rode her with no one holding onto a lead rope and no one hovering at my side. On that first day, after we trotted a few steps, I felt invincible.

My second ride was even better. She wore a bridle with a snaffle bit. Each rein was knotted to accommodate my weakened hands. Now I could ride without any help at all. I used my legs lightly on her sides, gently holding the reins. She lowered her head and walked forward. I couldn't resist the temptation to try a leg yield*. I pressed her side with my right leg and after a little hesitation, Questa moved a few steps to the left. I was elated. I still knew exactly what to do. My body sensed Questa's movement and I could communicate my wishes to her clearly.

Over several months I worked on lots of difficult maneuvers including mounting and dismounting by myself from the tall mounting block and riding with a saddle. This all took time and patience - for me and the horse. It wasn't all smooth riding.

The first time I attempted a posting trot was a disaster. Posting to the trot is where a rider stands and sits in time with the horse's steps to prevent bouncing. My mind knew what to do but my body didn't. I felt the exact steps of the horse's gait and when to rise and sit but the messages sent by my head were not getting through to my legs. I had to stop after a few bouncing steps and revert back to a beginner's lesson - posting at the walk. Up, down. Up, down. Up, down. My legs tired quickly. I pushed my hand on the saddle to steady my body and help my legs raise me but soon my legs quit moving and I just bounced around.

The second time I tried to post was totally different. My legs were unsteady, but it seemed as if my body was on automatic, repeating movements I had done for many years. I managed to post down the long side of the ring and around the corner. I remembered the first two times I had used the parallel bars in my backyard, the first afternoon moving 5 feet and the second day 20 feet. Something had happened inside me, to my internal wiring. I was reconnecting on horseback!

My joy at being on a horse was apparent to everyone. I was getting better from the riding. I was having fun and the riding

---

* A simple dressage movement where the horse moves sideways and forward

never felt like 'therapy.' While doing my dressage movements, I was constantly using my legs, asking Questa to bend her body and change directions. I realized again how much I loved dressage, and how much I enjoyed teaching it - to both horses and people. These little leg movements added up to a considerable physical workout for me. My trunk muscles also gained strength as I sat up on her back, reached forward and leaned side to side.

The very best part was that I felt like a different person when up on a horse. I felt joy, freedom and lightness. I escaped from my ill-working body. The good feelings carried over into the other days of my week. Even on days when I got depressed, looking forward to riding again helped me get through.

In September, I rode Questa for a Benefactors tour. I described to the audience how much the HWAC riding program had improved every day of my life, physically and spiritually. I wanted to share my joy of riding and to encourage others with disabilities to try riding. Perhaps I could get more people to volunteer and contribute funds to the many other therapeutic riding programs around the country. With that goal in mind, I wrote a short article that was published in several national horse magazines.

By March of 1998, from the high mounting platform, I managed to get on and off of Questa without help. I wasn't particularly graceful but Questa stood patiently while I coaxed my right leg up onto and off her back. I was trotting more, mostly doing sitting trot. Unfortunately, volunteers were in short supply, and often all I could do was walk around in circles. It was clear I had outgrown the program and was ready to move on to bigger challenges. I needed to find another program where I could ride like I used to, before the accident.

WITH THE DIRECTOR'S encouragement, I located another riding program in Bonita, a suburb of San Diego. At the facilities of the Bonita Equestrian Therapy for the Handicapped (BETH) I met a retired horse that knew some dressage. His name was Mark and he was a tall chestnut warmblood gelding. He looked huge to me. At first I was apprehensive about getting on such a big animal. Mark might be much more than I could safely handle and it was a long way to the ground if I fell off. Still, the opportunity to ride a real dressage horse was irresistible.

A very tall platform with a ramp was located next to the outdoor riding ring. It was tall enough for me to easily reach my leg over Mark's 66-inch high withers. For our first time together, Mark wore a bareback pad and a snaffle bit. A helper walked alongside in case I had trouble. Mark quickly responded to my queues for a leg yield, shoulder-in, haunches-in and half pass at the walk. I tried a few steps of these movements at the trot and was exhilarated when Mark moved correctly beneath me. I remembered the signals to the horse as if I had practiced them only yesterday. Then, once the instructor saw that I could handle Mark, she let me ride independently in the spacious outdoor ring. I was amazed that I could do all this. I felt as if I was riding without any disability, the way I had before the accident.

In the beginning, I used my wheelchair several times at BETH, but it got in my way so I switched to my walker. With it, I could help get Mark ready, as he stood quietly in the grooming area. The first few times, I brushed some of Mark's neck and lifted the light bareback pad onto his tall back. Volunteers did the rest. It felt good to get my hands dirty, to learn the horse's personality and to take care of him.

Each session I did a little more to get Mark ready. I brushed a little further down his front legs, then a little further down his back legs. I brushed all around his hooves. It was hard for me to bend and keep my balance, but I was motivated to do the whole job myself. I stooped over and handled the brush. One day I picked up a front foot and cleaned it out, while a volunteer stood nearby in case I lost my balance. I couldn't grasp the small hoof pick, but eventually found a fat round one that I could grip.

I rubbed my hand over Mark's neck and softly across his shoulder. Mark's spring coat felt smooth and sleek. The coarse hairs of his mane and tail separated into flowing tresses as I brushed through them. I was becoming the old-Pam, who moved around horses in a natural way and I loved every minute of it. I was doing much more than I imagined possible and each new task brought me more confidence and courage.

I worked on simple dressage movements with Mark. The volunteers at BETH clustered at my side, circling the ring with me, as I explained the various dressage movements I was doing.

One afternoon, I coaxed Mark into a few steps of canter but he had bad back legs and the canter felt unsafe to me. Even walking seemed to hurt him as he good-naturedly carried me around the ring. Poor Mark was lame and not ridable a few days. I had to switch to another horse, named Wallstreet.

Wallstreet (where do these names come from? – I love this one) did not have any dressage training, but he was willing to learn. His almost-black coat shone in the sun and was a marked contrast to the white stripe running down his face. He learned quickly to walk on the bit and to respond to my leg pressure. As the volunteers leaned on the fence, watching me ride, I heard remarks like "Wow, he never looks that good when anyone else rides him." These words were a joy to my ears.

I did more of the preliminary tasks and eventually put my saddle up on Wallstreet's back and the bridle on his head. Wallstreet made all this possible by standing still and patiently waiting as I fumbled with buckles and straps. If he had raised up his head, or pushed at me, I would likely have lost my hold or fallen, but he never did. Once the bridle was over his head, he stood immobile while my fingers buckled the noseband and throatlatch.

Wallstreet's trot was very smooth and I soon felt confident enough to try some cantering. I learned that I could not canter for more than a few strides though, because my legs spasmed away from the saddle, loosening my seat and threatening to throw me to the ground.

On the first hot day of 1998, I went for the 'independent trail ride' which had been my goal a year earlier. I rode a small, quiet brown and white pinto pony. It was pleasant walking through some woods and along a path next to a stream. The horses knew the way. Several volunteers walked alongside our group. It was quiet and uneventful, except for one brief instant when my pony attempted to graze. When she stretched her short strong neck to the ground for some grass, I was suddenly pulled down on her neck. I folded at the waist as my arms were nearly pulled off. Once was enough! I resorted to thinking like a horse and began to anticipate any more attempts by the pony to snatch a bite of grass.

A new instructor began running the BETH program in the spring of 1999. Her name was Alice and she soon started making plans for some of the BETH riders to participate in the annual CALNET show. The show was held in Los Angeles and sponsored by the North American Riding for the Handicapped Association (NARHA)(renamed in 2011 to Professional Association of Therapeutic Horsemanship International (PATH Intl.)). Some of the show's classes were done at a walk, with side walkers for the rider, and someone leading the horse. Others classes had horses walk over obstacles or do simple dressage tests. I was asked to help prepare some of the other riders and also to participate in the show as a rider. It was a wonderful opportunity for me to share my love of horses with everyone at BETH.

Under Alice's supervision, I stood in the center of the ring, holding my walker or sometimes leaning on a large barrel while I worked with several of the students who rode independently.

One day I was a few feet from Jon, who had walked his pony next to me and halted. He was a young teenager with bushy red hair. He rarely talked, but quietly followed directions. I asked him to do a round-the-world, where he lifted his legs to sit sideways, then faced backwards, then to the other side, finally ending up facing forward. He had done this maneuver easily other days, so I didn't anticipate any problems. A helper stood nearby and the horse stood quietly. Suddenly, Jon started to dismount and was sliding down toward the ground. I rushed to his side, weakly pushing him back up on the horse.

"No, no," I said. "Just stay on Flicka today."

It was a comedy of errors. I awkwardly moved to help, while Jon, because of his autism, did not want to be touched by anyone, including me. He did manage to stay on Flicka and I didn't ask for another around-the-world. Jon was better off just sitting correctly and walking around the ring.

I particularly enjoyed teaching the volunteers, all of them teenage girls, who were horse-crazy. They reminded me of myself when I was young. They didn't know even the fundamentals of riding: how to hold the reins, post on the correct diagonal or change directions when riding in a ring with other horses and riders. They were hungry for all the knowledge I dished out. They had bodies that worked and I had the know-how. I rode vicariously with them and felt it was I holding the reins as they increased their skills.

I began to ride other horses in the program, including the ones going to the show. New environments and strange sights did not spook these horses. Sometimes I rode twice a week and was mounted for over an hour. I became very confident riding these steady horses. I sensed the individual movement of each horse and figured out how much training they had had in their past. I became physically stronger that summer because of my horse activities and the riding gave me a place to be me. My life had a niche that made everyday better. It was invaluable to be part of a group again and work towards a common goal.

I enjoyed my contacts with the people at BETH and worked very hard, without actually being aware of it. I knew that my life would be miserable without my horse partners. Once I was mounted on a quiet steed, I was on a par with normal people.

The CALNET show was quite a large affair. Many years earlier, I had been at the same show grounds, riding Salty in upper level dressage but I didn't let old memories spoil the event.

Tiny disabled children wandered around the ring on slow moving horses, smiling as if they owned a candy shop. Older children walked and trotted with someone skipping along at their side. An older man riding in a group class really impressed me: he was blind and someone had to call out from each of the corners of the ring to orient him, but he moved around the ring confidently. The whole event filled me with gladness.

In the show I rode a small appaloosa horse named Toby. The first class was a trail class, where we were to maneuver through ten obstacles smoothly and finish up within a prescribed time in front of the judges. My division of this class included turning, backing, trotting over poles lying on the ground and passing over a wooden bridge. As I entered the ring, my mind went back to the old groove, carved out by my many rides on Salty. I concentrated as we went from obstacle to obstacle and was unaware of anything else. We were making good progress until the final bridge. We had practiced over a wooden walkway many times at BETH with no hesitation but for some reason this bridge looked different to Toby. I was surprised when he stopped suddenly. This was a test of my ability to communicate with a horse and for him to trust my direction. I sat very quietly when he stopped, then pressed my legs to his side and gently but firmly urged him on. Toby responded and trotted over the bridge, making the wooden planks clamor and rattle. A comment on my performance sheet said 'Very well ridden, especially at bridge.'

Another class in the show was an elementary walk-trot mini-dressage test. I memorized the movements and Toby was very obedient as we did circles, serpentines, halted and backed. I liked the feeling I got during this ride. I concentrated on each figure, accurately moving through the pattern. All my past experience was right there, at my command. I wasn't the least bit nervous. Strangers clapped for our performance and I stopped next to the judge's stand when I was finished. He remarked that the test was very good but "A little more animated trot would be nice." He really couldn't tell the extent of my disability, and didn't realize that Toby's animated trot would have jounced me off of his back. Instead of explaining my physical condition to the judge, I smiled and thanked him. My riding skill had camouflaged my ill-working body. I was elated.

Late Sunday afternoon we returned to BETH. Everyone from our group had medals, ribbons and certificates. The horses were happy to be back in their own corrals and we riders were tired but contented.

When I was riding, I almost forgot the events of July 8, 1996 because it felt so wonderful to move around on a horse, free and disconnected from my disabilities. I was reclaiming the Pam I remembered, not the Pam who had died in so many ways that awful day.

DON AND I had been engaged for eight months and he had become such a wonderful part of my life that we decided to live together. He sold his home in La Jolla and we consolidated our two households.

I no longer was totally dependent on others for care and daily living assistance. I had not had a bladder infection since mid 1998 and was not using a catheter, which greatly improved my health and my sense of independence.

Don and I decided San Diego had become too large and uncomfortable for us. I hated the terrible traffic, the smoggy days, the long lines at theaters, in the grocery stores and long waits in restaurants. Don was ready to retire from his job and I very much wanted to put the dark memories and constant reminders of my accident away and out of sight. We began to consider New Mexico.

In April 1999 we flew to Albuquerque and spent four days looking at houses in Santa Fe. Our realtor showed us one-story homes with wheelchair accessibility. I wasn't using a wheelchair, except at night, but I knew that my body could change rapidly and I needed to be prepared for future problems if they arose.

I hobbled in and out of the car and a score of dwellings while hanging onto Don's arm. The realtor was amazed at my pluck and endurance.

Finally we found a house we liked. It wasn't perfect; the bathroom and walk-in closet doors were too narrow for my wheelchair and the large step in the garage could not be easily ramped. But we loved the vigas and corbels, the coved ceilings, the pueblo style, the high clerestory windows in a bright kitchen-family room. There was a large yard enclosed by stucco walls, which would work well for the dogs.

There were two dogs now. My niece was relieved to return Whisper, my Lakeland Terrier. I was just as glad to have him with me again along with Jordan, my devoted golden retriever.

Don and I made an offer, which was accepted after some negotiation. The weather turned chilly during our stay and an unexpected storm dropped five inches of snow. It made the place seem even more peaceful to us.

We packed up and moved in August 1999. Although I had lived in the house in San Diego for 22 years, I had no regrets about leaving it. By the time we left it was associated only with my accident and disability.

We were off! I drove my mini-van while Don drove his Audi. We used radios to communicate as we caravaned across the desert.

I was excited and full of energy. I enjoyed driving as long as I could take frequent breaks, often using my port-a-potty in the van. We stayed overnight near the Arizona-New Mexico border and arrived in Santa Fe mid-day on Sunday.

Our new house was wonderful. A gardener had been watering the yard since June and I was amazed at the lush vegetation. Flowers were blooming everywhere. I didn't recognize any of them, but as time went by, I came to know Yarrow, Purple

Coneflower, Mexican Blanket Plant, Lambs Ears, Snow in Summer, and many more. I looked forward to a new life that didn't constantly remind me of my past. I felt that here I could build a new me.

I needed to find a place to swim. I learned that a local community college had a good indoor pool. A lady in disabled services encouraged me to come out and see it. At the fitness center building someone offered to show me around. We moved slowly down the hall, walked around the locker room and then out to the pool. Everything was spacious, light and clean, and looked very inviting. There was a special chair to lower disabled people into and out of the water. I decided to register immediately. But the pool tour had tired me out. I found myself dragging just to get to the front of the administration building. Registration for classes started at the far end of the long building. Clearly I was not going to make it.

"Do I have to go all the way to the back, way down there to register?" I asked a woman.

"Sit here and I'll help you get registered," she said. "I work here. I'll do all the traipsing around and bring the paperwork to you."

Her kindness felt like a wonderful introduction to my new hometown.

I began going to the pool two or three times a week. I'd wear my jogging belt in the water. I started out standing in the water, at the side of the pool, doing exercises. I also floated on my back, waving my hands under water. I tried the backstroke, using just my arms. It was tiring at first but I gradually was able to increase my distance to a full length of the pool. It felt good to pull hard, get out of breath, and feel my blood circulating. The joy of using my body outweighed the minor annoyances of changing clothes, showering and dealing with wet hair.

Swimming made me stronger and increased my endurance. I remembered the recent past, when I could do just one activity per day. Now there were days when I swam, picked up a book at the library, helped fix dinner and stayed awake until bedtime. I was beginning to live like a real person again.

One day as I left the pool, I passed by the Resistance Center. 'I need to get my body in there,' I thought. I approached a staff member at the desk. He smiled and said he'd be glad to help me get started. I told him about my strange body and said I wanted to strengthen my legs. He showed me how to use four weight machines with low weights that would work most of my leg muscles.

Everyone in the gym was smiling as they moved around from one piece of equipment to another. I had to be careful, since I didn't sense pain and I didn't want to over do it and hurt myself. The next day I was stiff but it felt good.

Since there weren't many other activities I could do to add leg strength, I decided the leg machines were perfect for me. Each time the routine became a little easier. I noted with pleasure, that on a few of the machines, I was using more weight than some of the other women who were not disabled!

The exercise helped me walk better. My legs lost their skinny sickly look. I no longer feared seeing my body in the mirror. In some ways my body felt like the old-Pam, where the exercise was a natural activity for me, not a struggle associated with rehabilitation. After a few months, I added three more machines for my legs and later I added arm exercises.

IN FEBRUARY 1999 I had tried skiing. Don and I had traveled to Winter Park Colorado to meet my German friends John and Ella Visser. The National Sports Center for the Disabled (NSCD) was located there. They had been teaching the disabled to ski for about 30 years. I had seen pictures of paraplegics and quadriplegics 'skiing.' They sat on a seat attached to skis while two helpers used tethers to balance the ski-seat on each side and a third skied behind with a tether to control the speed. It reminded me of a little child being pushed in a baby buggy.

Eventually, some individuals learned to balance and turn with no assistance but I didn't want to sit in a seat and call it skiing. I did see it as a new way to get outdoors and use my body so I was willing to try. I was concerned about re-adapting to a sport that I had done well as the real-Pam, the before-Pam.

On the first day, I had signed up for cross-country skiing. Before the accident, I had gradually switched my allegiance from downhill skiing to cross-country skiing. I had thrived on moving all day through the snow and trees, where there were no crowds and the scenery was unspoiled. I had spent wonderful days at Yellowstone, Mt. Hood, and Yosemite, sometimes covering 12 to 15 miles in an afternoon. It had seemed so effortless then, but now everything was complicated by logistics and my undependable legs and unsteady body.

The weather at the Colorado cross-country area had been pleasant, with some sun and not much wind. A volunteer helped fit me with skis and boots, and then supported me as we walked outside the building to a large meadow, with prepared ski-tracks sloping away from us.

I was worried about my balance and slow reactions and I was fearful of falling. For stability, I used a walker that was fastened to two skis rather than regular ski poles. My old assurance was gone. I took a few hesitant steps while holding onto the walker. I didn't want to depend on the two women who stayed by my side, but I needed them. After a few sliding steps, I lost my balance and started to tumble backwards. They were there to catch me. I pushed myself to keep going, carefully leaning forward. Within two or three minutes I was much steadier. It was easy to move my legs and slide a short distance with each step. It felt very much like my memories of cross-country skiing. I was happy to be outside in the crisp air with mountains rising around me.

I wanted to have enough energy to return to the lodge, so I turned around after 25 minutes and headed back on the same ski tracks. The return trip seemed even easier, as I was now going slightly up hill and wasn't so worried about losing control. For the last few steps, my instructor gave me regular cross-country poles. I moved confidently with them and felt much less restricted than with the ski-walker. In my mind's eye I saw myself almost the same as before the accident. I was even wearing the same red ski jacket I had used so many times earlier!

By the time I sat down at the lodge I had gone approximately three-quarters of a mile in 45 minutes. It wasn't much compared to what I used to be able to do but I was very happy with my accomplishment. The idea that I might be able to enjoy cross-country skiing again filled me with anticipation.

My happy feelings were dashed during the next two days. I was scheduled to try the bi-ski and mono-ski units, where I would ride sitting on a molded seat attached to two (or one) skis. From the first moment, the effort was complicated and awkward. I had to pile on clothes, especially warm socks and boots, since I would be sitting still. A long wheelchair ride took me to the main downhill ski slope and three people helped wedge me into the seat. I was strapped down like I was going for a space shuttle ride. Then the apparatus had to be maneuvered to the ski lift, hoisted aboard and transported to the hilltop. On the lift, I felt like Humpty Dumpty, likely to fall off and go splat at any minute. I was totally unable to affect my own destiny. Once off the lift, the three experienced volunteers tried to teach me to maneuver the ski unit. They were patient and precise but it just didn't work for me. The movements I had to make with my body, sitting over the skis, were exactly the opposites of skiing on my legs. I invariably leaned in the wrong direction, and fell on my uphill shoulder. The tethers kept me from getting totally out of control but after 80 minutes of bumps and crashes I was pretty disheartened. The bi-skis were supposed to be fairly easy but they weren't for me. It wasn't until the end of the session, when I saw the two side-tether helpers ski up along side of me, that I knew I had been moving forward with my own balance. I felt little satisfaction and no joy from the accomplishment.

The mono-ski session the next day was even worse. I was never able to balance at all. There were more bumps and crashes. To make matters worse, I was so strapped down that getting in and out of the ski seat took up a lot of my energy. It was so time consuming that I was not able to pause for a bathroom break. Both days my bladder had become painful and spasmed out of control. I was well fortified with absorbent pads but that didn't offset my discomfort or my embarrassment.

I wanted to opt out of the whole skiing scene. I was discouraged because I could not do what I had tried to do. I felt I would never be able to conquer this new endeavor. I liked skiing the old way, the way the old-Pam had skied, swooping down the mountains with grace and ease. Back at our motel room I cried. I didn't go to dinner. My appetite had disappeared along with my dream of skiing.

I still had one more day. The NSCD schedulers found me helpers so I could try to ski on my feet, the real way. In the staging room, I could barely move with the heavy ski boots buckled securely on my feet. My woman instructor was soft spoken and strong and the wheelchair ride followed by a snowmobile ride up to a gentle slope was exhilarating.

I wore short skis and used outrigger poles. These were forearm crutches with ski tips mounted on the bases. To prevent me from crossing my skis at the tip, metal clips held the tips together in a fixed position. I could ski in the basic snowplow position with the front tips together and the back of the skis apart.

It was wonderful. It seemed so easy and so natural. I remembered how to make slow snow plow turns and didn't have to work at it. I just let the skis slide. The shallow grade made it easy to ski to the lift just below our snowmobile. The instructor was amazed at how well I did and I was ecstatic! I loved using my new body in an old familiar way. The bad feelings of the previous two days disappeared. I found the new-Pam could do one of the things the old-Pam loved.

I turned and traversed the short hill several times. There was even time to stop and visit a little restroom just for the NSCD clients. I needed a rest and smiled as sunshine warmed my face while my legs took a break. My instructor then changed my skis. I tried a more advanced toe attachment, dubbed a trombone. The toes were still attached, but one ski-tip had a ring and the other a slide bar. This allowed me to slide each ski about 18 inches while still keeping the ski tips close to one another. This felt even more like the sport I remembered. After one short run, we started down the long beginner road toward the lodge. I was tired but happy. The day was a total success and I had even been able to share my triumph with Don. NSCD had provided him with snowshoes and given him a snowmobile ride up to my ski hill, where he snapped a few pictures of me.

Once we were settled in Santa Fe, I was determined to ski again. There was a top-notch ski area and a disabled ski program in our local mountains. I was going to ski the way 'real' people did this time. The March afternoon was warm and sunny as Don and I drove up the twisting road to the ski basin. It was exciting for us to see the desert plants and dry ground turn into tall spruce trees and aspen groves nestled in the snow.

We found my instructor, Earl, and I was fitted with rental equipment. Earl and I then moved toward the lift at the base of the mountain, as he held my arm tightly. The lower area was in the sun and much of the snow had frozen into slick ice. I was less sure of myself as my skis slid on the ice and threatened to dump me on the wet glaze. Earl steadied me as we boarded the lift. I shrank back when I saw the steep hillock that was part of the lift's disembarkment but there was no time to hesitate. Earl steadied my arm as we plunged off the side of the lift and stopped where the terrain leveled out.

We stayed on that short shallow hill, riding the lift five more times. I did gentle turns and Earl taught me how to control the newer shaped skis. As the runs progressed, I felt more and more comfortable on the skis. It seemed like very little work to let the skis slide, turning and controlling them with my body, legs and weight. As a matter of fact, it was much less work than walking. One time down I was too daring, got out of control and fell on my side. I tried to stand up but couldn't. Earl was there and pulled me to my feet. I wasn't afraid but suddenly realized that my legs were starting to feel like noodles. I decided I'd better quit while they still held me up.

It took a great deal of effort to walk into the ski lodge and exchange the rented equipment for my own shoes. Thank goodness Don was waiting for me as I could barely walk to the car. Even though my legs were totally exhausted I was high from happiness. I could ski like the Pain-before.

Chapter Fourteen

New Heights from the Back of a Horse

I KNEW I wanted to ride but I couldn't find a therapeutic riding program right away. I scoured the Santa Fe newspaper until I found a "Call for Volunteers, Therapeutic Riding Program." I called and said I wanted to participate as a rider and do whatever I could to help.

As it turned out, the program was shut down for the winter and wouldn't begin again until spring. This did not slow me down. I decided to meet with members of the organization and in a short time I became a member of the board. This charity also had other recreation, art and housing programs for disabled adults and children.

I met some of the volunteers who tended the horses during the winter and several times one of them helped me so I could have a short ride. I was anxious to begin riding regularly when the weather warmed up.

In April 2000 I met with other volunteers at the Lion Ranch just west of Santa Fe, for an introductory session. The therapeutic program had a separate area for their specially trained horses. It also had a fenced ring nearby. Many trails surrounded the ranch. I become familiar with the routine and each horse. Although I wanted to help like the regular volunteers, I couldn't do the more physical jobs, such as cleaning corrals. But I was happy to spend an entire day cleaning saddles, bridles and setting aside older equipment for repairs. It felt good to be a valuable contributor to the program.

I began riding regularly in the spring. Usually I went on a trail ride with another participant and several volunteers, including Dee, the ranch owner. Dee kindled my deep interest in all things horsy, inspiring me to subscribe to several horse publications I had let expire after the accident. I felt so much more alive when my mind was engaged by horsy thoughts and I wanted to rekindle my old expertise. I was ready to jump back in with all four feet.

There was a team event at nearby Goose Downs and for several years the therapeutic horse program had sent three riders to the Downs to participate. There were three teams assembled for the event, each with four members: a cross-country course horse and rider, a stadium jumping horse and rider, a pony club member, and a rider from the therapeutic program who would ride a walk-trot dressage test. I helped to organize the therapeutic riders since I was the only person who knew about dressage. I was also chosen to ride.

The Goose Downs facility covered many acres and seemed scary and wide open when we got there. We didn't bring our own horses but the Downs provided us with three dependable mounts and we were able to practice on them several times before show day. The two other riders were led through the dressage pattern on their horses while I rode independently. I was on a tall horse but gained confidence quickly since he was quiet and easy to ride.

Show day was hot and sunny. I waited nervously in the shade, using a squirt bottle to keep cool. Just past noon we mounted up and rode towards the show ring. The earth was parched. Large cumulus clouds filled the sky but never seemed to block the sun. I was worried about overheating without knowing it, so I donned my riding jacket just before entering the ring. I rode through the short dressage pattern confidently. My borrowed horse was a perfect mount and together we had a good ride. The audience even applauded as we finished.

I was smiling as I left the ring. Later the judge told me I had ridden a better test than many of the competitors in the regular classes. Her words were music to my ears.

Before our rides at Goose Downs, the director of the therapeutic program wanted the two other riders to see an actual dressage 'test.' One of her friends, Karen, volunteered to demonstrate. Everyone was impressed by her performance, although none of ours would be so grand.

Karen was still recovering from her own disabling auto accident. She often rode stiffly when the pain bothered her and she was wary of being injured by a fall. I shared the same concerns. We understood each other immediately and became close friends.

"Tell me what happened to you," Karen asked when we were introduced.

I told her about the car accident.

"I had a broken bone in my neck from a car accident, less than six months ago," said Karen. "I can help you ride. I have some nice quiet horses."

We talked about our dressage backgrounds and horse experiences. We realized I could help Karen with her Second Level dressage horse and she could provide safe horses for me to ride. We agreed that I would come and ride early the next week.

We got into a relaxed routine with one another. I arrived in the cool early morning. Karen got the horses ready and boosted me aboard. I rode a large spunky pinto pony. I was delighted as I trotted him around, doing leg yields and shoulder-ins. Riding him reminded me of the movements I had done on my own horses, Salty and Ameego. It was such a good feeling. Karen warmed up her chestnut horse, Keys. When they settled down to work, I rode next to the low rails of the dressage ring, encouraging Karen to sit straight, soften her body, and straighten Keys before asking for a flying change.

She liked my comments on her ride and I was delighted to be back on a dressage horse. It was a perfect arrangement for both of us.

After a few months of getting to know each other, Karen arranged for me to be "the judge" of a faux-show so I could help some of her students overcome their fear of riding in real shows. I had each rider pick a dressage test and ride it before me in a regulation size dressage ring. I scored each movement as the test progressed. I did not give overly generous scores just because they were beginners. I wanted the riders to have realistic pictures of their performances. After each test, I'd spend ten minutes working with each rider, helping them improve. My knowledge was valued and I was glad to help. I loved teaching the kids and the adults. Even though I couldn't ride as well as these novice riders, I experienced their pleasure as we worked together and they improved.

I also kept riding at the therapeutic program. I liked the trail rides where we'd walk through piñon and juniper trees, up and down the banks of dry sandy arroyos. I usually rode Keno, a small bay gelding who was probably over 35 years old! But he was steady and sound and didn't mind a short jog.

There wasn't much shade on these rides and on very hot summer days the heat often kept me from riding. I took to carrying a water bottle and dripping it liberally on my head. I also wore a water-retentive scarf around my neck and a lightweight long sleeved shirt. Still on several occasions the dry heat of the high desert exhausted me. I'd head for my car, run the air-conditioner full blast and sit there until I cooled down.

By September when the days were cooler, I started to ride Keno twice a week. A few rides lasted as long as two hours.

I decided to ride in the upcoming fund-raiser for the therapeutic program, dubbed a Ride-a-thon. About 100 riders were to participate and each of us secured pledges to help the riding program. My friends were generous with their donations on my behalf. It was decided I would ride Keno and stay in the back, doing a nice slow walk. I hoped to ride for three hours but I wasn't really sure I was up to it. I also knew that the excitement of so many horses and unknown rough terrain could be dangerous. But I was going to try it.

Santa Fe weather is famous for being fickle and changing quickly. Initially I was worried about heat, but the day of the Ride-a-thon was overcast, breezy and threatening to rain, as a cold front swept into the state. I dressed in a winter ski coat and warm gloves. I smashed a thin ski cap under my riding helmet. Horses milled around excitedly as everyone arrived at the trailhead in the Santa Fe National Forest near Abiquiu.

I left with the last group of riders. Six of us walked the trail, churned up by the earlier horses. I stayed warm riding at first. The beautiful countryside and pleasant conversation was a distraction from the threatening weather. We crossed several dry streams enclosed by steep banks. Keno was well mannered but lunged up a few of the embankments. I was glad I was riding in a Western saddle, which provided much more support, with its horn in front and its high back cantle. I felt much more secure in it than I did in my flat dressage saddle. It was a full three hours later when we approached a clearing that was set up with straw bales for seats. I could smell barbecued chicken on the grill. My group was the last to arrive.

I found I was chilled through and through. My legs were so numb I could barely move them. I couldn't keep my feet in the stirrups and needed support as I dismounted and tried to walk. I was very proud to have come so far but I was glad I didn't have to go any further.

My ride raised several thousand dollars for the therapeutic program but even more exciting for me was that my ride exceeded every expectation I had when I listed 'a trail ride' as a goal in 1997.

EARLY ONE MORNING in 2001, Karen was riding Keys at a nearby stable. I watched and coached her as she rode. Tracy, the trainer at the facility was also riding. She was a small woman with a quick smile and commanding voice. After introductions and a few horse comments, Tracy suggested I try a lesson on one of her quiet Western Pleasure horses.

I had learned to ride as a kid on a Western saddle but my allegiance had switched to dressage (and a flat English-like dressage saddle.) Since the accident, I wasn't strong enough to canter using my English saddle and I wanted to be able to do everything I had done before. I hoped the added security of a Western saddle might allow me to safely canter more than a few steps. Canter work was usually a part of the training of every horse, and the faster gait was fun.

Tracy led a pretty Appaloosa mare, Tashka, into the indoor riding arena. The horse waited patiently as I tried to get my right leg up and over the high back of the Western saddle. I felt as if I had never ridden before. The signals to direct the horse were different and all of the equipment felt unfamiliar.

The mare was well trained and moved off effortlessly when I used Tracy's signals. I soon found I liked the support of the Western saddle. The jog trot was easy to sit. The mare was attentive and stopped quickly when I said "Whoa." Tracy persuaded me to try a lope. It took me a few minutes to get my cues organized, but the resulting lope was smooth and easy. I held onto the saddle horn and felt like I was on top of the world as I made several circles.

That first ride convinced me to come again. Three weeks later I arranged to take lessons twice a week. Tracy did not normally work with disabled people. After seeing me ride, she agreed to take me on as a student and said she thought I could become a good rider in spite of my disability.

I had watched Tracy do the reining maneuvers, which included running fast large circles, small slow circles, fast runs down straight lines ending with a sliding stop, followed by a quick half-turn (a rollback) and lope in the opposite direction. Horse and rider also did spins in place, going around at least 4 times in each direction. The sliding stops looked spectacular but scary to me, especially since the horse was traveling so fast. It would often slide ten or twelve feet!

I wanted to improve my horsemanship in this new discipline. It was so different from dressage! Tracy brought new exercises to each session to help me improve my strength and coordination. She thought the most difficult aspect of this new riding would be for me to unlearn my earlier dressage experience.

About six weeks after my first ride, I was introduced to Dunnit, an experienced reining horse with major show wins. Reining was becoming very popular, with the first World Championship scheduled to take place in Spain in 2003.

I was a little intimidated by Dunnit at first. I didn't want to ride her poorly and mess up her training. I knew I would ask for maneuvers incorrectly. From the beginning, I wanted to hold the reins tightly, putting pressure on the horse's mouth. Tracy taught me that a reining horse needed to move gracefully and smoothly with little contact, a loose rein and a relaxed head. I was accustomed to keeping my legs gently against both sides of a horse but now I had to work to keep them away from the horse. If I tried to ride without thinking, I instinctively did the wrong thing. The previous 25 years of dressage riding techniques had wired me for a different kind of riding.

As it turned out, Dunnit trained me! If I used an incorrect signal, she wouldn't respond. During my first lesson on her, I couldn't even get her to walk off in a straight line from a stop. I decided to jog her some and get used to feeling her movements and way of going. She was small, with good gaits, and her jog was comfortable, rhythmic and easy for me to sit. After a few days on her I was able to lope in a left circle. I had trouble giving her the exact cues, but was rewarded with a slow lope as smooth as silk when I used the correct ones. I held the saddle horn for security and I loved the freedom of moving around the ring. It was why I wanted to learn reining in the first place. Tracy gave me cues for a spin, but my body was too uncoordinated. Dunnit only gave me an idea of the power and speed she had for this maneuver. I wanted to fly around the ring on Dunnit, effortlessly sliding to stops and spinning like a top except I was afraid to go very fast. But I was determined to learn.

I tried to analyze why reining seemed so difficult when dressage had been comparatively easy for me. I knew my disabled body was a slight problem, but it was not the major one. Dressage is performed with a steady contact on each rein, giving the rider a means to communicate with the horse. I wasn't used to holding the reins loosely in one hand. This changed my balance and the way I sat in the saddle. I felt like I had lost control and the horse could run away with me. It reminded me of driving a car, where the gas pedal could speed up or slow down on its own, and where the steering wheel was off limits.

Practice was the key. Tracy kept telling me to ride with a loose rein. Each time I rode Dunnit my cues got better. When I said the magic word "Whoa" Dunnit immediately lowered her haunches and slid about a foot into a stop. Her movement was smooth and flowing, not abrupt or pogo-stickish. I found it very easy to sit tight in the saddle when she stopped this way. I also liked the extra control that came from my vocal signal. I could say "Whoa" whenever I felt I was in trouble or off balance and Dunnit would respond.

A few more lessons and I was giving better signals for a spin. Dunnit was very happy to keep twirling. During one lesson, we went both right and left many times. I was concentrating on riding correctly and failed to notice I was feeling light-headed. When one of the staff came to help me get off, I was slumped in the saddle, hoping never to move again. I had motion sickness from all the spins! I had to lie down in the office for over an hour before I could stand up and drive home.

I didn't want the motion sickness to reoccur so I bought acupressure bands to wear when I rode. They go on each wrist and a small button presses into the wrist. The pressure point is supposed to block the feeling of motion sickness. I have found this remedy always works. Later when I was traveling they were even effective on a boat in rough seas.

Each reining lesson made me even more addicted to this new type of riding. I had never imagined being able to do this kind of riding or wanting to do it.

My friend Karen came to watch one day and video taped me loping and doing stops on Dunnit. I was amazed when I saw the tape later. I thought I looked pretty tentative, holding the saddle, and going very slowly. But there I was, with a big smile on my face.

Nothing approached the freedom I got during each ride. To have such a special relationship with a large animal was fantastic.

I missed several weeks of riding when Don and I traveled to China but when I returned I found that all the walking and stairs on our trip had made my legs stronger. I could lope one full circle on Dunnit without holding the saddle! Then I'd stop, rest, and try again. It felt as though I had made a giant leap forward.

"You looked like you were having too much fun!" Tracy laughed after watching me ride.

When the weather turned cool again, I rode later in the mornings, after the sun had warmed the air. I became one of the regulars and rode during the group lesson. On cold or windy days we rode inside, but on nice days we stayed outside. Sometimes it was just me but often there were as many as six other riders. I learned a lot from watching the others and listening to Tracy's directions. The atmosphere was positive and encouraging for everyone.

The outdoor arena was in the middle of a large field, with an arroyo leading away, and traffic passing on the farm driveways. There was noise and movement everywhere. When the breeze blew, small tumbleweeds rolled down the road. The ring itself was at least twice as large as the indoor one, and was fenced all around. It took me a few weeks before I could relax during my outdoor rides. Both Tashka and Dunnit were well behaved but I am sure they felt my nervousness. As I became more confident, I began looking forward to being outside. My world expanded to include the far hills and the blue sky. My legs didn't restrict me and my heart soared. The joy of riding surged through me again, just as it had when I was a youngster.

I still needed someone to hold my horse while I maneuvered, but I could now mount and dismount without help. From a mounting block about two feet high, I'd raise my left foot into the stirrup. Then I pulled myself up using a hand on the horn and one on the back of the saddle. The hardest part was persuading my right leg to go over the high back of the saddle. I'd lean forward and drag my right leg across the horse's rump, letting it fall down on the right side. It helped that both Tashka and Dunnit were small and neither horse seemed to mind my bumping them or the unusual movements I made.

Dismounting was much easier. I'd lean forward and again drag my right leg across the horses back with both hands holding onto the horn. I always felt somewhat vulnerable while sliding my leg across the rump, for then I was perched for seconds in a precarious position. I had to rely on my balance and a quiet horse. While my left leg was in the stirrup supporting my weight I'd delicately change balance so my left hand was on the horn, right hand on the cantle. Then I'd lean on my arms, take my left foot out of the stirrup and lower myself slowly to the ground. My arms were strong so this last part was no problem.

I knew how lucky I was to be at this stable, with safe horses, great teaching, caring staff and friendly riders. Everyone encouraged me and a few people even grew teary-eyed when they saw how much riding meant to me.

I helped out before my ride as much as I could. Dunnit's stall was directly across from the crosstie area where the horses were saddled. I could halter her, remove her light sheet and lead her to the crossties. I had trouble fastening the heavy breakaway snaps, but I managed to perfect a method of doing this, using both hands. I could brush her and put on her bridle. I could only watch, however, when the staff bent and tightened protective wraps on her legs and swung the forty-pound saddle onto her back.

I still rode for about 20 minutes each week with Karen, while she rode Keys and a new horse named Wheeler, helping her with dressage movements. As winter settled in, I coached her even though it was too cold for me to ride in her outdoor ring. My body just didn't work well in the cold and the horses were too frisky.

Then Tracy suggested I should show Dunnit the following Spring in a reining competition. I never thought I would be able to compete in an open show, especially reining. It required a fast pace for a good performance. I was still afraid to do more than the slowest lope. Tracy told me most shows included a Green-as-Grass class, for inexperienced riders and I certainly qualified for that! She smiled and assured me Dunnit was solid and reliable. She also knew I would enjoy the challenge. My whole view of riding and reining changed when I thought about entering the show ring and competing against more capable riders.

I STARTED 2002 by riding on New Year's day. I knew I needed lots of work before I could enter a show ring. On January 1st, I was wearing so many layers of clothes that I could barely get on the horse. But cold or not, I had to practice riding Dunnit.

The staff at the barn rode Dunnit three days a week and I often heard comments on what a little witch she had been on the previous day. However, they were able to be more firm and secure than I was. They could push her through her bad moods so that she performed well. I was having problems getting her to walk, much less lope off on the lead I indicated. Some days she was irritated that I was interfering with her stall rest. She'd actually go sideways instead of walking forward. Then she'd twist her body and kick out at the spur when I asked her for a lope.

To make matters even worse, Tracy had planned to breed Dunnit in February or March, which meant the horse had been taken off birth control medication. Everyone noticed Dunnit was much more cantankerous when she was coming into season. Her thoughts were obviously concerned with the studs she was meeting and not us, the riders.

Not being able to do simple maneuvers on Dunnit made me feel very incompetent. I couldn't dependably get any of the movements that would be required in the 10 National Reining Horse Association (NRHA) patterns. I hadn't even attempted to put the elements together into anything resembling a pattern.

I wouldn't give up. I struggled to get Dunnit to do flying lead changes. When I used my stronger right leg there was usually no problem. But left to right, using my weak left leg, was very difficult and usually failed. The problem was compounded by my fear of riding the horse fast enough to make it easy for her to do the change! My mind went back to Salty. I remembered how effortlessly I had done flying changes on him, including the fifteen one-time changes during our last dressage competition together. I was a different person now and much weaker but I vowed to keep trying and to prod my body to become stronger.

Each session with Dunnit, I tried to ride a little faster at the lope. Dunnit's smooth gait made this pretty easy going for everyone else, but for me, having to hold onto the saddle to feel secure, it was a different story. Tracy coached me through each spin and gradually I began to improve. To spin on Dunnit, I learned that less was more. All she needed was a small correct signal. Then I had to sit quietly and let her do her job. My acupressure bands let me spin without getting motion sick again.

The group lessons were long. Much of the time was spent watching (and learning) while each rider did a small portion of a pattern. I was often aboard Dunnit for an hour and 45 minutes at a time. I was gaining endurance but along with it came a new bane: saddle sores. I was trying very hard (too hard!) to use my seat and created several rubbed places on my butt. I tried every kind of Band-Aid and bandage available. Eventually I found waterproof medical tape was the best remedy and preventative.

In March, Tracy gave all of us who planned to ride in the show some videotapes from national horse shows. The riders and horses made it look so easy. They never seemed to make a mistake. At least I learned what I should do, but I had my doubts as to whether I would ever look as good. After watching the tapes, we all started to practice portions of the NRHA patterns. The patterns were simple to memorize. With just one reading the pattern was in my head. That made me feel a bit more in my element. They were not nearly as complicated as the Olympic Level dressage tests I had ridden on Salty. Once a pattern was in my head, I more naturally looked ahead, preparing the horse for the next maneuver. I concentrated so much that I even lost some of my fear of coming off the horse or of going fast.

On Friday April 5, I went to a nearby stable to practice for the show. The show would start at 8 a.m. the following morning in the same indoor arena. The horses had been hauled the short distance in the two large commercial-size horse vans and about 10 of Tracy's students were there to practice.

I got on Dunnit after Lori warmed her up. We wanted to be sure Dunnit was comfortable and calm in the new ring before I got on. Lori had been helping me for several months, getting Dunnit ready before I rode. We had similar philosophies about horse handling and riding and I was confident Dunnit would be well prepared when Lori said she was ready. Still I was nervous about being in a new place. Dunnit was cool as a cucumber and she helped me relax.

We had time to get used to the size and feel of the new arena before the show. Tracy managed to orchestrate us all in that small space, where we practiced circles and run-downs. I stood out from the others. Everyone else wore fancy cowboy hats. I looked decidedly strange in my bulky protective safety helmet. I had worn this helmet during every ride and wasn't about to change for a show.

A letter had even been sent to the NRHA asking if I could ride in my helmet (permission was automatically given). An exemption was also made for me about dropping the bridle at the end of my ride. Usually the rider dismounts and drops the bridle in front of the judge to show that a legal bit is being used. I would stay on horseback and someone else from the ranch would drop the bridle for the judge.

I had trouble sleeping the night before the show. I kept visualizing what I would do during each moment of the ride. I rode Pattern One on Dunnit about a hundred times in my mind. By morning the ride was perfect in my head.

It was show day and waiting was difficult. The Green-as-Grass class was the last of the day. It was not possible to know exactly when the class would start, as it depended on how many horses were entered in the earlier part of the show. I fidgeted around at home until noon and then drove to the show grounds. I wore my freshly washed jeans and a denim cowboy shirt. I needed to arrive early so I could ride Dunnit and get warmed up. Lori had ridden her earlier. It's an art to have a horse ready just when it is time to enter the ring. Fortunately, I came up fourth in the draw and didn't have to wait long once my class started.

Don wasn't a horse person, but he arrived shortly before my ride to encourage me and take pictures.

Pattern One began by loping into the ring through the entrance gates. Tracy reminded me that Dunnit knew all about showing and might want to take off at her usual fast show pace. That day Dunnit was in no hurry but I could feel her attention surge as we got into the ring. She paid attention to me as we slowly loped down the center. Our first stop was not very impressive and the rollback had us heading off-course. I turned her back down the centerline. At that point I clicked into my old horse-show-mode, focusing on each part of the pattern. I could hear Tracy in the background, coaching and yelling words of encouragement (all that noise is part of the fun!) I was determined to stay in the saddle, to not hold on to the horn and to remember the entire pattern. I had missed one lead change, had trotted to get it back and picked up several penalty points. It was over in about five minutes. Most of the maneuvers were too slow and were marked down accordingly[4]. My score of 61 was announced as I left the ring. I knew I'd done my best. I was relieved to be finished and still alive to talk about it.

"And pretty good too for this rider's first show!" I heard on the loud speaker as everyone clapped.

Lori helped me dismount. We hugged each other and patted Dunnit. We both had tears in our eyes. As I stood outside the arena, I remembered all the horses that had helped me recover. My life had changed so much. I still wasn't sure of my own identity. I was constantly changing physically but over the six years since the accident I had gotten more and more active and more mobile and I was so much happier since I could ride again. My life felt good and shortly it would feel even better! I was going to get my own horse.

WHEN TRACY RETURNED from Texas, she invited me to see a video. She'd been looking for horses to buy and sell. On the small TV in her office, I watched as she rode a quiet chestnut gelding around a large ring. She did a slow lope, several easy stops and some flying lead changes. The horse was dead quiet, with good manners. Tracy thought I should buy him.

It would be a big commitment in time and expense. I knew it was the right time for me to consider purchasing a horse. I needed a special animal that would have enough pep to perform but would also be safe. (I also knew no horse would ever be 100%

---

[4] A note on reining scoring. A rider enters the ring with a score of 70. Each of the eight to ten maneuvers is scored separately. A maneuver done correctly receives a 0. If the move is done well, scores of .5, 1 or 1.5 may be given. Similarly, poorly done maneuvers may receive a -.5, -1 or –1.5. Penalty points are assessed for bad behavior or mistakes such as loping off on the wrong lead. These range from -.5 to -5. So a ride with no mistakes and nice maneuvers will score a total of 70, a very desirable score for most riders.

safe.) I mulled it over and five days later told Tracy I was interested in trying the horse. First I wanted to bring him to Tracy's barn and work with him for a month in New Mexico. Tracy thought this would be impossible, but I was determined to at least give it a try.

Knowing I could be persuasive I called the owner in Texas.

A broad accented voice answered the phone. "Yeas, Ma'am, I own that hoarse," said a young man named Paul.

I told him about my special situation. I said it didn't make sense for me to come down to Texas but I promised a good home for the horse. I asked a few questions about the gelding's health and past. Paul was obliging and we quickly arranged a compromise. I would have the horse seen by a vet in Texas. Then, if all was well, the horse could come to New Mexico for a week on trial.

Things got busy quickly. Paul and I worked out a trial and purchase arrangement, with many faxes flying back and forth. I arranged for transportation and insurance for the horse, Smoky. I also arranged for the vet to examine him in Texas. Thanks to cell phones, I soon found myself sitting on Dunnit during a lesson while talking to the vet in Texas. He said Smoky was extremely sound and healthy for a 12-year-old horse. I was excited. I had a horse to try!

Still I was afraid no horse could compete with my special feelings for Salty and my fond memories of Ameego. Then Smoky arrived. I got to the barn about 5 minutes after he had been led off the trailer into a stall. He stood quietly looking at the activity in the aisle. He seemed a little tired and his eyes were running from the dust and wind of the trip. I moistened a rag and went in his stall with a halter. He hung his head as I attached the halter buckle and looked at me curiously. His ears seemed large and pointy as they swiveled at me. His eyes were a dark liquid brown, soft and kind. I rubbed his neck and face, as he sniffed at me, learning my smell. I slowly wiped each eye for him while he stood very still, his head lowered as I tended him. He then wolfed down the carrots I had hidden in my pocket. It was a good start.

I had a week to decide. I would ride him the next day, and every day for the following week.

Early in the morning, Tracy put a saddle and bridle on Smoky and rode him for a few minutes so I could get a good look at him. He was a big quarter horse, tall and long. He was rangy looking and unfit since he had been in pasture for four years. He was a pretty red color, with just one small white spot between his eyes.

His tallness was evident as I tried to get my left foot into the stirrup from the mounting block. He was at least 4 inches taller than Dunnit! He waited patiently as I dragged my right foot across his hindquarters and settled into the saddle. I didn't mind being up higher. In fact I rather liked it! My other horses had been about the same size. His walk and jog were comfortable and easy for me to control. He was easier than Dunnit for me, being not nearly so opinionated.

I was nervous about being on a new horse, especially one I might buy. We didn't know each other and he might be too much for me to handle. I had trouble getting him to be energetic enough to break into a lope. Once he did, however, I had to grab for the saddle horn. Dunnit had an extremely smooth lope so I barely moved around in the saddle. Smoky's long strides seemed to go way up and way down, throwing me all over the saddle. He was perfectly behaved as I did a circle in each direction but I had to grip the saddle with my right hand to stay on.

I thought, 'He's nice, quiet and responsive. But how can I ever stay on him?' I had to be sure I could ride him.

Over the next six days we got to know each other. He never pushed at me with his head. He held up each hoof for me when I asked and he liked to be brushed. When I led him down the aisle, he walked several steps and waited for me to catch up without pulling on the rope. He seemed perfect except for his lope.

Lori rode him several times in the outdoor ring so that he could look around and we could be sure he was quiet outside. On the first morning I rode him outside he seemed taller and a little faster, with his large ears pointing at distant things that caught his attention. I expected him to shy or bolt, but he was just curious and attentive to the environment. Every day I had less trouble riding him. He loped off easily in both directions. He did nice steady spins.

On Friday, I had a revelation. Instead of trying to rock forward and backward with his lope, I tried to sit in the middle of the saddle while he moved around me. Suddenly I was not being thrown all around his back and could let go of the saddle for a few strides. However, when cantering or loping, I always held onto the cantle with my right hand. Otherwise I didn't have enough confidence or good seat to stay on during reining maneuvers.

After a week, Smoky was growing on me. Each day he showed me more personality. He was so sweet on the ground and truly seemed to like me. He enjoyed all my attention and I loved his soft nose nuzzling for treats. The bond between us grew stronger on each encounter. I felt like a real horsewoman again! It was obvious. He was a very good horse for me. He might not be a world-class winner, but he was a capable steady mount that I could ride safely. I was happy when I called Paul and told him I would keep Smoky.

I began riding Smoky three times a week. We worked together naturally. He was much easier to ride than Dunnit. Over the next three weeks I practiced spins, tiny sliding stops, roll backs and circles. Smoky still looked around a lot outside and didn't always seem to be paying attention to me, but he was well behaved. As I gained confidence, my signals to him became more precise and subtle. Just a small pull on the reins toward my shoulder and he was off and spinning – one of his favorite maneuvers. I found myself a bit hesitant, knowing that even the best horse could act up or be frightened, but when those thoughts crossed my mind, I'd sit up straight, square my shoulders and just concentrate on going forward.

A show was scheduled for a Saturday in June, in our outdoor arena. It seemed too soon, but I was persuaded to ride in the Green-as-Grass class. On Thursday, I rode in a lesson and practiced parts of Pattern Number Seven. Then I got nervous. I tried to relax the next day as I visited Karen and watched some of her riders. But that night I dreamed I wasn't ready for the show. I couldn't find all of my clothes and Lori wasn't there to help. I kept looking for Tracy. Smoky had on his saddle but I couldn't find the bridle. I knew I wouldn't be ready to ride when my time came. That's when I woke up. By the time I drifted back to sleep, I had ridden the pattern about 200 times in my mind. Each time was better and finally I knew I would be able to enter the show ring the next day and give it a go.

Saturday was a hot day. I woke before the sun was up and went to the barn early. I watched Tracy ride several of her horses in the Open Classes. Her performances were exciting and accurate, with fast spins and long sliding stops. She was the model we all hoped to emulate, sometime in the distant future.

I spent much of the time in the shade, away from the show ring, checking Smoky's corral. He was now permanently located in another barn, where he had a large stall and an outdoor run. I wanted to be sure the wire lining in the run didn't have any sharp edges or any places where he might get a foot entangled.

Just before lunch, I rode Smoky for about 15 minutes in the indoor arena. Then Lori took him down to the outdoor ring. During this time, all of the show participants could practice in the ring. There were horses milling around everywhere. Advertising banners were tied to the fence. Horse trailers and trucks filled up the empty space adjacent to the ring. I was afraid to ride Smoky in this busy atmosphere. He was used to a quiet outdoor ring. Most horses are afraid of changes in their routines and environments and their instinct is to flee from danger. I didn't want Smoky to bolt out from under me and I didn't know how he would react to all the hubbub. He seemed wide-eyed and jumpy to me. Lori was riding him when he startled as another horse brushed by closely. I was glad he was so good but I was even happier that I hadn't been on him. I was getting more nervous each minute and I knew my nerves would upset Smoky.

My Green-as-Grass class was last and I fidgeted as the afternoon wore on. The breeze grew stronger. This was a double-edged sword for me. I stayed cool but I hated the wind. I associated it with a spill 2 years earlier, and with horses bolting away from wind-driven objects. Don arrived at the show grounds to take pictures and cheer for me. About 4:30 I rode for a few minutes in the indoor ring. Then Lori walked down with me to the show area. Lori stayed by my side in case Smoky spooked. After a few minutes of walking, I loped him in a couple of circles and then waited near the entrance gate. There were 17 horses in the class. Suddenly I wondered what I was doing there – a crippled old woman, trying to ride.

At the call of "Next Rider," I entered the ring and waited at the end. The pattern started with a run up the center. I tried to calm my nerves and then asked Smoky to lope. Smoky knew he was in a show pen.

I felt his attention focus on the end of the ring. He was ready to take off at his usual show speed, which would have left me in the dust. My right hand held the back of the saddle, and I sat quietly, hoping he would listen to me. The scariest part of the pattern was up first: three runs down the center with sliding stops and rollbacks. Smoky stayed calm as I made myself relax. I went slowly past each marker before asking for tiny sliding stops. I was going so slowly that on one rollback Smoky trotted instead of loping. After the third stop, I backed up the required amount.

Smoky stopped squarely in the middle, ready for my next command. On the first spin, which was to the right, he started doing the four turns steadily and evenly, but slowed down a bit before the end when I dropped my hand. To the left, he spun and stopped precisely, looking at the judge.

I couldn't do a fast daring ride so I focused on the pattern and on riding each figure accurately, more like my earlier dressage performances. The first circles were round and in the right place. As we turned to circle in the opposite direction, I urged Smoky to change leads. I was using my stronger right leg and he changed exactly in the center. I felt terrific. It was like riding on a cloud. The second set of circles was also accurate as Smoky allowed me to guide him and rate his speed. The second flying change however was difficult because of my weak left leg, but Smoky knew what to do and responded at just the right time.

I was almost done. Just one more rundown to survive. Smoky calmly loped down the ring and stopped. I dropped the reins and stood still. That's when I finally let out a long sigh and started to breathe again. We turned and quietly walked toward the gate. The few people left in the crowd clapped and yelled "Good job Pam." My slow and accurate ride earned me a 63 and fourth place.

I realized Smoky was a one-in-a-million horse. I had just finished a show ride on a horse I barely knew but we had done it together, two beings communicating and respecting each other. It felt like the most exciting thing I had ever done in my whole life.

Even as an able-bodied person, in my wildest imagination, I never would have ridden a horse (and my own horse to boot!) in a Western saddle, or competed in a reining show. Now, after six years of battling paralysis, I had done both. My horse erased my struggles, disappointments and depression.

My life was no longer a nightmare. It was better than I had ever dreamed. I was filled with hope and buoyed up by my accomplishment on Smoky. I now enjoyed life in ways I never imagined possible. I had never expected so many good things could happen to me as the result of a terrible injury. I had wonderful friends and Don, the love of my life.

Epilog One

Living in My Body

IN THIS SECTION, I have written about many of the ways I have dealt with my Spinal Cord Injury and regained physical abilities. The most important point I want to convey is that most of us who have had a physical setback can make unexpected progress, whether it be from injury, a hip replacement, a stroke or other disease. Two rules apply: be creative in finding solutions and work with competent people and progressive physicians to stay safe. Don't believe everything you read, hear or are told by others, including your doctors. Search for a supportive environment and people. And keep working, as changes can take some time.

If I had let everyone help me all the time while I was in a wheelchair, I might still be in that wheelchair. My friends learned quickly that I needed to try to do things myself and that eventually I would ask for help if I really needed it.

I did several things that could have been risky, but were handled in a safe way. I went to therapeutic riding sessions with an indwelling catheter. Sometimes this caused some irritation and a slight amount of redness in my urine. And I made the risky decision to stop doing any sort of catheterization. I had found a supportive urologist and we closely monitored my bladder to be sure it did not become overly full and cause autonomic dysreflection or other problems. I was fortunate because my bladder preferred to spasm and empty rather than get too full. I later learned that several physicians thought I would die within 10 years from complications of bladder infections. The infections have now disappeared.

I WANTED MORE out of life than I could get confined to a wheelchair. Doctors told me only a fraction of pre-accident capabilities could be regained, and that after 18 to 24 months, improvement would cease. A neurologist even told me I should never walk with just a cane because it was too dangerous to risk a fall. He might have been right, for someone else, but I needed to walk. I let his advice go in one ear and out the other. I wanted to be the way I was and if this wasn't possible, I would work to get as close to that status as I could.

I was determined to use all my energy to understand and regain mastery over my injured body. I knew how to build strength, how to recover from injuries and how to push myself. After all, I had been an athlete. I have used this knowledge to make my paralyzed body function better than anyone had predicted.

I am like an electric toy with a weak battery and a loose connection. I can no longer take my previous dexterity or grace for granted. To counter my condition I decided to treat my life as an athletic event. I've made each day a competition with my own body.

I learned the first time I moved my big toe in that hospital room that it was possible to use mental energy and concentration to forge a link to the unmoving parts of my body. It is connections between my brain and my body that I have since tried to maximize. The connections may be imperfect, and in some instances impossible (i.e. moving my little fingers properly), but I could reconnect my brain and my body and achieve more mobility. Just as world-class athletes rehearse their events in their minds, I rehearse mine. They visualize their gymnastic moves or their downhill ski runs. For me, walking down steps is an athletic event, and I use the same kind of concentration. My conscious mind-body connection has become the most powerful tool in my recovery process.

When I started walking back and forth across the pool for endless hours, I felt as if I was burning the walking motion into my body, my brain and my spinal column. It seemed as if my eyes were swiveled in my sockets, facing inward. My first attempt to walk on my parallel bars was a disappointment and I was exhausted after five feet. Yet, two days later, I easily walked 20 feet. Similarly, the first time I tried to post in my dressage saddle was a muddled mess. I managed a few steps and then had to stop from fatigue. The following week I got half way around the large ring before my legs were tired.

In the intervening periods, I looked inward and thought about how I had walked or posted. I went over the motions internally, without ever actually doing them. Then when I repeated the movements a second time – on the parallel bars or on horseback - the nerve connections were more ready to work, like highways where the construction barriers had been removed. I was reconnecting and my nerves were relearning.

It has only been in the last five to ten years that researchers have begun to recognize the importance of exercise. They have found that people who have been paralyzed for years have regained some leg movement via over-stimulation. Patients are now held over a treadmill in a harness, while someone makes their legs move in a walking motion. When I started to attend formal Feldenkrais classes about two years after the accident, I heard about 'Awareness through Movement.' This therapy teaches a person not only how they move but how they *can* move. (It was developed by Moshe Feldenkrais, a physicist who overcame his own severe knee problems using this method.) When I took the class I realized I had already been using the Feldenkrais techniques and they had helped improve my condition.

I discovered this ability to re-teach my body in the pool. The nerve stimulation I got from pool walking took advantage of the few nerve pathways left in my spine. The longer I kept at it, the more the nerves helped me to walk reliably outside the water.

It's a great thing – to be able to walk. Without it much of the world would be closed off to me. It doesn't matter that I walk very slowly and must think about every move I make, before I move and when I move. It's okay to have to concentrate on what

I'm doing and to carefully watch where each foot goes. I can't walk fast because my legs become uncoordinated and I can fall. I cannot send all the impulses I need to move my leg properly so I must *think* my way through my walks. I say to myself: pick up a leg, put it down, and then do it again with the other leg. (Interestingly enough, when I am tired, I MUST watch my feet. Watching my feet seems to increase the number of nerves being used.) It's okay because it's walking. It gets me there but not like other people. Not only do I have to concentrate but I have to worry about how each leg feels.

If I take large steps, nervy unstable feelings threaten to make my legs collapse. As a result I've learned to take smaller steps and always be ready to lock a joint. Several times the nervy feeling has taken over leaving me stranded and afraid to move. It has happened in parking lots and in stores. When it happens I look for a shopping cart to support me, or I stand and wait, hoping the bad sensation will go away and it usually does.

Another part of my everyday is having to monitor my body all the time, even when it isn't telling me anything. For example, when I wear new shoes I stop and take them off every 15 minutes to see if there are any rub spots or blisters developing. I have to be one step ahead, anticipating potential problems.

Some days (maybe 1 out of 10), I get up and my legs are leaden. Rather than trying to pick them up, I push them around. On those days I worry that my legs are always going to be bad or that maybe I am losing capabilities. Lately, I have had more burning sensations in the front of my legs, under the skin. Perhaps the nerves are giving out and have been used up, consumed. I find I must keep fear pushed to the back of my mind but it never goes completely away.

Some of my discoveries about nerves and how they work have happened accidentally. After a Feldenkrais class, I met some friends at Starbucks. When we put in our order, I forgot to ask for decaf. Later, when I went to my car, I noticed I was walking 2 or 3 times faster than usual. At home that afternoon, I didn't need my cane because my leg reactions were so much faster. My legs almost felt normal, as if more nerves were working and were attuned to me. I was thrilled.

Then came the down side. After four days of having a cup or two of coffee with caffeine each morning, my lower legs and thighs had a strong burning sensation under the skin. The pain became so severe I found myself curled up on the couch, immobile. The coffee did seem to stimulate new nerves to work, but those nerves became supersensitive and then caused pain. A few days later, when the caffeine was out of my system, the nerves went back to their old state. I still have a bit of coffee now and again but I know what to expect. I can get a little more mobility but I have to be willing to live with the consequences.

My other nerve discovery was the effect of alcohol. Don makes a great margarita, which I like very much. If I say I'll have one, I have to ask, "Don, are you prepared to take over making dinner?" If I have a glass of wine, I am fine. But if I have a little tequila, I can barely walk. My legs drag and I feel like I have lost my connection to them. It's not that I've had too much to drink. It's that the nerves to my legs are inebriated and in that state they leave me high and dry.

My body doesn't register pain from my chest down, especially pain from something sharp. Yet just inside my right knee there is one spot about the size of a silver dollar where I can vaguely feel the prick from a dull pin. From time to time, I retest myself with the pin, to see if anything has changed. One evening, I was testing this sensitive area and then pricked a place about 4 inches away on my leg. There was no feeling of pain from the usually numb area so I moved the pinpricks back towards the feeling area, to locate a line between pain/no-pain. Then I pricked several times in the sensitive area, followed by more pricks in the closest no-pain area. After going back and forth three or four times, the no-pain area suddenly could feel pain! With pricks moving back and forth, I moved the pain sensitive area five or six inches up my leg. I focused on my inner connections while doing this. I believe my actions recruited nerves during the process, giving them a chance to react. The newfound pain sensitivity lasted about half an hour. I haven't found a way to sustain this phenomenon yet, but I am still working on it. Maybe I will be able to bring more normal sensations to some parts of my body using this method.

My system has acquired the nasty concept of nerve pain. This occurs in various parts of my body. The pain can be so severe as to dominate my life, but I won't let it stop me from getting better. At one point in my recovery I struggled for three months with burning pain in my bladder, especially at night. (It wasn't another bladder infection, as no bacteria or evidence of infection was found, and my temperature remained normal.) It turned out to be nerve pain.

Many nights over that period the bladder pain was bad enough to wake me up four or five times a night, initiating trips to the bathroom. Then my body gradually adjusted to the new nerve feelings and the pain subsided after 4 months. Since then I only occasionally have these episodes.

Once the bladder pain subsided I thought I was out of the woods. I decided to eliminate the amitriptylin I was taking for nerve pain. I decreased the dosage by tiny amounts every two weeks, until I was taking a quarter of a pill (6 mg) every other day. After two weeks at this level I stopped completely. I felt alright until the fourth day. Then suddenly every dubious nerve in my body screamed out. My legs, my butt and my bladder were on fire. I immediately started back on half a pill (12 mg). I was much more comfortable. I have had to accept that pain is a part of my everyday life and that I need some medications.

Many SCI[5] patients find Neurontin very helpful for pain. I tried it. It did take away my pain, but it also put me in La-La Land. I couldn't think and I couldn't connect to my legs, even when I took very low dosages. Occasionally I'll take 100 or 150 mg

---

[5] Spinal Cord Injury

when I go to bed because it helps me sleep and the nerves in my body feel fresh and relaxed in the morning. I just don't use this medicine during the day because, pain or no, it is more important for me to be able to function.

A big part of my everyday is dealing with spasms of one sort or another (Like the Eskimo who has many words for snow, I have several descriptions for my spasms - Pain, Stretch, Nervy, Restless, and Bladder.) Medication can decrease spasms, but again it leaves me with little strength or control over my body. So I try to deal with spasms in other ways. My greatest weapons against spasms have been exercise, stretching and strengthening my muscles.

I can feel and react to some stimuli with Pain Spasms. A few drops of cold water on my leg or foot will make it jump. On a hot day, when the pool water seems cool by comparison, my foot jumps back out of the water at first. As I enter the water, I don't sense temperature until the water reaches my chest. Then my body spasms and my legs bend and draw up under me. Consequently I've learned to put my feet in the water carefully and hold the pool ladder or side while I lower myself into the pool.

A hard poke or bump will also make my leg or foot jump away. Usually a dull pinprick causes no reaction but not always. I can rub my feet enough to draw blood with no reaction but cold lotion on my feet at bedtime makes them go into spasms.

My hands are the funniest combination of both worlds. They feel pain at about 90% of normal, but if I hit or hurt my hands, they spasm and hurt at the same time.

In some cases, pain spasms are very debilitating. Before the auto accident, I had sciatic nerve pain from running too much. After the accident I re-aggravated the sciatic nerve when I fell off a horse. It was a windy cold day when the small horse I was riding bolted and I fell to the ground. I landed on my left side and was very stiff in my legs, back, arm and shoulder. The next morning I couldn't walk. I didn't feel terribly bad but the sore muscles and ligaments spasmed totally out of control when I moved. I took muscle relaxants and pain pills, and spent two days back in my wheelchair. I very gradually started to move around again. Three very gentle sessions in the pool helped my sciatica heal as I got over the injury.

Since my legs first started moving on their own, (about 4 weeks after the accident,) I've gotten what I call Stretch Spasms. Even now when I straighten my legs from a bent position, they will suddenly stretch out and my toes will point, especially when I am in bed. I've tried to straighten my legs gradually, one at a time, to avoid this reaction, but at a certain point I just lose control. Many times my hands contract with them, even though I haven't moved my hands. Because I've often been through this experience I know what to expect. I try to be calm while my body does its own thing.

When I am tired or have been sitting and I stand up, my legs want to straighten uncontrollably. I can prevent this by keeping them bent and walking a few steps, walking in place or just rocking back and forth on each bent leg. Sometimes I have to do these motions for a minute or more. A few times my legs got away from me and rocked me uncontrollably up onto my toes. Fortunately, I was able to steady myself on a chair, wall or other piece of furniture, until the spasm stopped. I've learned to be ready for these spasms, especially in the evening.

When I stretch to reach something with my hands they will spasm. This can happen when I reach into the mailbox or down to the floor, to pick something up. My hands contract and I can't open them. I've learned to get a little closer to the object I'm after and not to stretch so far. Things out of reach I pull closer with my cane, or I tell my dogs 'get it.' They vie with each other to pick up the pencil or keys. (They know they will get a treat when they bring the object back to me.)

Ultimately the best remedy for my stretch spasms has been exercise. When I have been to the pool, my legs are much less likely to spasm the rest of that day. I always walk better when

I get off my horse, especially when I ride on a bareback pad. The riding has stimulated all the nerves without overtiring them. Moderate walking also helps, but too much walking makes my legs spasm more. I've found everything has its own delicate, ever changing balancing act.

Sometimes it feels like a knee will collapse from the nervy feelings I get. These I call Nervy Spasms. They can happen after I have been on my exercise cycle or my three-wheel bike. I figure my knee is a little sore and what would be pain is being translated into a nervy feeling instead. When this happens I must keep my knees almost straight to keep them from collapsing. There have been a few times when I didn't anticipate or get these feelings, and I have fallen. Ultimately, the nervy feeling is caused by muscles and ligaments which have become tight and pull in the knee capsule. Regular stretching will prevent the nervy knees.

Often the bottom of a foot is supersensitive. Then it jumps away from the floor as I walk and push off. It feels like my foot is floating up off the ground with no effort. I try to take advantage of the motion when I am walking but when the jumps are too large, I can lose my balance. At those times, I must keep my foot flat as I walk until the feeling passes. Although nervy spasms are annoying, they are not like pain. They are unpredictable, however, and therefore can be dangerous.

Another nervy feeling comes across my groin. This makes me feel as if my legs will sink out from under me. The feeling is often caused by my sitting or lying in a funny position. It usually goes away when I straighten out my body and wait. A few times, though it hasn't gone away quickly. I assume then I have aggravated a nerve by over stretching or over exercising. Since it's hard for me to know when I have done too much, I again have to anticipate and pay attention. Even the slightest change in how my body is responding can give me significant feedback. A few times I have had to restrict my activities or worse, resort to using the walker or my wheelchair because the nervy feelings are warning me that I've inadvertently done too much. Those times can be very discouraging and usually make me angry and irritable. I have found that stretching must be part of my daily routine. It seems to keep some of those nervy feelings away.

I also get Restless Spasms, somewhat akin to Restless Leg Syndrome. As an athlete, before the accident, I experienced this when I was learning to ski at age 25. As I fell asleep, just after a ski lesson, my mind would think back about the skiing and my legs began automatically reviewing the new movements, jumping around in the bed, all by themselves. Back then it was funny. Nowadays restless spasms of this sort come at night or in the evening, when I am tired. One leg moves a small amount, stays still, then moves again, about 20 seconds later. It's like a metronome with a steady beat. If I get in bed and fall asleep right away, my legs are still and quiet. But if I happen to lay awake for five or ten minutes, it's a different story. Usually it's just one leg. I've found it helps if I lie on my side with the moving leg underneath. Thank goodness they don't usually both gang up on me at the same time! Most times when the spasms continue, ibuprofen will quiet my leg so that I can sleep. When this doesn't work, lying down with my legs elevated sometimes helps. Other times I just get up and read a book and eventually can sleep.

I have experimented with various ways to make my legs stop having restless spasms. I have concentrated on blocking nerve messages to my legs but so far haven't had any success. I've tried to override the jumping by tensing a muscle and keeping the leg in a particular position. This has also been ineffective. Eventually the movements just stop, although until that happens, my legs keep me awake.

New theory postulates that the signals that cause spasms emanate from the spinal column and not the brain. I am not sure this is true. It was during a half hour of leg spasms in Sharp Rehab Hospital that I connected my brain and my big toe. I concentrated on wiggling the toe while it was moving by itself during a spasm. After the spasms stopped, I was able to move the toe myself. Somehow, I had connected body to brain.

The last spasm in my list is Bladder Spasms. My bladder was my worst enemy immediately after the accident. The spinal cord injury cut off my connection to my bladder and the sphincter muscle was paralyzed shut. I suffered through intermittent catherization or an indwelling catheter. The nerves didn't work at all. After two years of catheters, infections, and hospitalizations, I had had enough. By that time, my bladder had become very small, holding only 100 cc (or about a half cup) of fluid. I believe my bladder started working on its own because I gave it the opportunity to do so. With no catheters, the nerves which were still intact had a chance to feel something. I put up with leaking, spasms, messiness and pads while my bladder tried to adjust to its new situation. (I carefully monitored the few signals I was getting from my body. I knew I was risking autonomic dysreflectia and its complications if my bladder became overly full.) After three months, my bladder settled down to its current state, which is endurable, especially since I no longer get those deadly bladder infections. I still get bladder spasms but one Ditropan XL 5-mg daily makes them less traumatic.

I frequently say to people out of habit, "Just a minute, I have to run to the bathroom." Except I can't run anywhere. My legs barely know how to walk and a bladder spasm makes walking harder and hurrying is not an option. Once my bladder tells me it is full, I don't have long to get to a toilet. At first I had about 30 seconds. Now I might have a few minutes. As a result I make sure I know the location of restrooms wherever I go. Also rather than wait until it's too late, I visit them often. To stimulate urination, I press on a spot on my lower right abdomen which creates the urge to urinate, and then I can release the sphincter muscle and pee. One of my mottoes is 'Never pass up an opportunity to use a restroom.' I manage to be out and around without too much trouble (but I always wear a pad, just in case!)

Even though the principle of stimulating the nerves into feeling and reacting is not new, many therapists and doctors still overlook the ability of the body to relearn through feeling. I told a young woman paraplegic about my bladder problems and how I finally eliminated the need to use a catheter. She listened and later told me joyfully that by following the same course she had also been able to eliminate the catheters from her life. I was glad to have helped someone else out of this daily problem. I believe in giving the body a chance. After all, if it doesn't work, at least nothing has been lost.

It did take patience to work through my bladder problems, and patience was not my long suit before the accident. I have only learned it out of necessity since. If I let myself dwell on what's frustrating about my everyday life, I would have given up trying a long time ago. My motto: *If I try new things, I'll eventually do new things.* My efforts don't always pan out but I keep at it, using what patience I've developed. The little finger on my right hand still doesn't work. It sticks out and won't bend at the first joint. I can't turn it under when I make a fist. Sometimes it spasms, waving back and forth like a lonely flagman. I've tried to make the finger move by my will but so far, I haven't been successful. I haven't given up though. I've made some progress with my hands, just by patiently doing battle with everyday objects. It took me about 15 months to finally manage the tubing and connectors of an indwelling catheter but by the end of that time I could disassemble, clean and re-assemble all the pieces. I was very proud of myself. Still, in spite of my triumph with that complicated device, I struggled to open cereal boxes, pop-top cans, milk cartons and jars. I've finally found a good device for jar lids, which grips and helps me turn the top. I also struggle with my hands just to cut my dogs' toenails. I've gone through several kinds of clippers to find the easiest one, but the job is still difficult. Fortunately, my dogs have learned a little patience as well. While I maneuver and strain they stand still and wait. (The nearby treat container convinces them that patience has its rewards.)

My own nails are still a problem. I can't hold and maneuver nail clippers. I use a clipper I was given in rehab that is screwed to a piece of wood with suction-cup feet. I don't have to hold the clippers with this device, only press down on the lever. It's almost impossible for me to use an emery board, especially on my right hand little finger, which moves around aimlessly. I can use small scissors for toenails. (Discovering this only took me about 6 months of experiments!) Another lesson in patience.

My fingers have little dexterity when it comes to small things such as jewelry clasps, bobby pins or hair rollers. All my necklaces now are long enough to fit over my head. I wanted to go back to my short pageboy hairstyle but I couldn't without some way to curl my hair. I gave up on bobby pins. It took me over a year to figure out that I could handle self-fastening rollers. Since that discovery, perusing the various implements at cosmetic and drug counters has taken on new meaning. I am always on the lookout for new inventions that come along and may help my cause. I also can handle a curling iron.

There are companies and catalogs which specialize in useful things for Activities of Daily Living (ADLs). The internet can help one find many types of adaptive devices.

I was able to solve some of my hand problems myself. I am particularly proud of figuring out how to tighten the English saddle on my horse. I could get the girth strap under the horse's belly and slip the buckle onto the lowest hole, but my hands were too weak to grip and tighten the short strap. The secret I discovered was to get the buckle fastened to the second hole and then attach another strap to the first hole. The second strap had a knot in it which I could pull against using my arm strength. Then I could tighten the girth by myself.

I think perhaps the hardest thing I had to learn was waiting. If something was impossibly hard I had no choice but to wait until someone was around to help me. Waiting is very difficult for someone like me. Learning that I needed help and asking for it was a bigger challenge than I ever could have imagined. It meant dealing with other people about my physical limitations. It seems to be very difficult for my friends or helpers to watch me struggle, without rushing in to assist. I had to learn how to ask for help, when to wait for it and when to say no help needed, thanks.

In one particular situation, unwanted help can really be dangerous. If I am struggling with a door, standing and leaning on it or pushing against it, I am most likely balanced, however awkwardly, against that door. If someone whisks the door open, I could easily fall.

I do know people want to try and make life easier for me, but being offered help when I need to work things out for myself is very frustrating. If I can do something alone, even after a long struggle, I want to try and do it! I've had to train the people around me to help only when I ask for it. I appreciate their offers as long as they wait for my answer and then listen to me. I do a lot of struggling but if I didn't I'd still be sitting in a wheelchair.

I ran up against another situation which I somewhat expected but which took patience and understanding on my part to accept: being treated like an alien in normal society. Clearly there is something amiss with my body. I don't walk right and my hands are stuck in strange positions but I'm still an ordinary person inside and I respond to how I am being received by other people. It was a shock to find how often I was being ignored during conversations when I was in a wheelchair. Because I was seated and therefore below eye level it seemed as if I wasn't there. Even after I was out of the wheelchair and walking awkwardly with my cane I was (and frequently still am) treated as if I am unapproachable. Like any disabled person I am sensitive to glances my way and how "normal" people are receiving me. My best defense against this sense of being shunned is to look everyone straight in the eye, smile and say "Hi."

It seems to be the idea of permanent disability which triggers this shunning reaction in normal people. Recently my knee was acting strangely (occasionally collapsing on me), so I began wearing a brace over the outside of my pants leg, to keep the knee straight. Once people saw the brace they assumed I was walking slowly and awkwardly because of knee surgery. Their attitudes were entirely different. Assistance was offered lightly. No one looked away. People felt free to joke about injuries they'd had. I was looked at as a "normal" person with an injury, not one of the permanently disabled. I've considered wearing a knee brace from now on, just to defuse the atmosphere!

My newly learned patience has led to many changes in my attitude about life. I'm never in a hurry anymore about anything. I don't set goals or expectations that I can't possibly meet. Rather than bound up tall mountains, I take tiny steps. This has not stopped me from having new and exciting experiences. Don and I have managed to travel extensively together, seeing unique places and making new friends. He constantly helps me and stays at my side. In the last few years we've been on a safari in Africa, up the Great Wall of China, to the top of Machu Picchu, walked St. Marks Square in Venice and whale watched in Alaska.

After moving to Santa Fe, I decided to become involved in community projects and volunteer activities. For three years, I was a board member of a charity that served people with disabilities. I also helped at therapeutic riding programs. I participated in community planning, from review of architectural plans to street signs to cohesive neighborhoods. I liked working with young people and so I tutored math and science at middle school, trying to pass on my love of math and science.

I keep abreast of medical research. I don't know what will happen with my body over time, but neither does anyone else. Some day soon there probably will be a way to regenerate spinal cord nerve cells. Stem cell research seems the most promising avenue right now, but who knows what may come next? There are also some new medications undergoing clinical trial that may be of help.

I avoid talking about my problems, sometimes even with my doctors, primarily because I don't think there is much they can do. Mainly I keep working out and pushing myself because it is my best option. I never get away from my body. It is always there to remind me that the injury happened and will never heal completely. I can no longer work at anything approximating my former level of performance. I still must spend many hours everyday doing some level of physical therapy just to maintain my mobility. I need the three hours it takes for each swimming session, three times a week. Riding my horse, which keeps me walking and sane, is time intensive, each session taking about 4 hours. Then there are the days when I am sore, overly tired or in pain. Then I must stop everything and give my body a chance to rest.

Even though I know I will not get back my former capabilities, I keep trying because there's no sense letting life just drift by. I intend to enjoy my life and keep moving forward, trying to improve what capabilities I do have. At some point, I might not have any more improvement. But staying active will help me maintain the abilities I have. My greatest discovery about myself, in this long process of struggle and recovery, is that it's simply not in my nature to quit.

Made in the USA
San Bernardino, CA
26 December 2016